THE SINKING
OF THE EASTLAND

"Powerful."
—*Publishers Weekly*

"Dramatic."
—*Seattle Times*

"Chilling."
—*Chicago Sun-Times*

"Riveting."
—*Forest Park Review*

"Vivid."
—*Eastland Disaster Historical Society*

"Gripping."
—*Milwaukee Journal Sentinel*

"Devastating."
—Stewart O'Nan

"Tragic."
—Vincent Bugliosi

"Bone-shaking."
—James Dalessandro

"Shocking."
—*Fox Valley News*

"Solid."
—*Chicago Reader*

"Compelling."
—*Pioneer Press*

"Filmic."
—*Chicago Maritime Society News*

Steamer Eastland.

THE
SINKING
OF THE
EASTLAND

*

America's Forgotten Tragedy

Jay Bonansinga

CITADEL PRESS
Kensington Publishing Corp.
www.kensingtonbooks.com

CITADEL PRESS BOOKS are published by

Kensington Publishing Corp.
850 Third Avenue
New York, NY 10022

"Lost" by Carl Sandburg, © 1916, Henry Holt and Company; from *Chicago Poems*, Dover Edition, © 1994; used by permission.

All Kensington titles, imprints, and distributed lines are available at special quantity discounts for bulk purchases for sales promotions, premiums, fund-raising, educational, or institutional use. Special book excerpts or customized printings can also be created to fit specific needs. For details, write or phone the office of the Kensington special sales manager: Kensington Publishing Corp., 850 Third Avenue, New York, NY 10022, attn: Special Sales Department; phone 1-800-221-2647.

CITADEL PRESS and the Citadel logo are Reg. U.S. Pat. & TM Off.

Jacket photo credit: DN-0064949, *Chicago Daily News* (Chicago Historical Society)

First printing: October 2004
First paperback printing: July 2005

10   9   8   7   6   5   4   3   2   1

Printed in the United States of America

Library of Congress Control Number: 2004106011

ISBN 0-8065-2648-3

Dedicated to the 844

Author's Note

THIS IS A WORK of narrative nonfiction. As most of the individuals who experienced the *Eastland* disaster are no longer alive, I have endeavored to create portraits based on the public record, oral histories, and the remembrances of descendants. Some dialogue is recreated for the purpose of narrative flow, based on the above sources. However, all the names, places, and organizations are factual.

It has been said that history is written not on the page, but around the kitchen table. This certainly applies to the events of July 24, 1915. The capsizing of the SS *Eastland* while still partially moored at the Chicago River's edge was so sudden, so tragic, so profound, that a sort of void was punched into the passage of time. The entire city of Chicago seemed to suffer from post-traumatic stress disorder. Over the years, the *Eastland* tragedy has become, collectively, a repressed memory.

The reasons why the fate of the *Eastland* has been largely forgotten are every bit as American as the event itself. They have to do with our national preference for celebrity over substance, our willingness to replace our awareness of one day's tragedy with the next day's concerns, and the media's frantic haste—even nearly a century ago—to shape our perceptions of what is important, and what is not.

Nevertheless, the history of the incident continues to resonate. It surfaces in family mythologies. At Thanksgiving meals. On porch swings late at night when the lonely sound of Chicago's "elevated" clatters in the distance. It's not too late to assemble the pieces of this powerfully haunting puzzle into a narrative that can serve as a tribute to the *Eastland* victims and survivors, as well as a legacy for those who choose to remember.

This is a Chicago story. The story of a river. The story of human behavior—heroic and cowardly—in an unthinkable crisis. But mostly, it is a book about the heavy burden of memory.

Evanston, Illinois

Please visit www.jaybonansinga.com.

*

PART 1

Low Sky at Dawn

Desolate and lone
All night long on the lake
Where fog trails and mist creeps
The whistle of a boat
Calls and cries unendingly
Like some lost child
In tears and trouble
Hunting the harbor's breast
And the harbor's eyes.

—Carl Sandburg, "Lost"

*

CHAPTER ONE

A Jungle of Iron
and Smoke

July 24, 1915
Chicago, Illinois

BORGHILD AANSTAD awoke early that morning, an effervescent thirteen-year-old with no idea that it would turn out to be a day unlike any other.

It was still dark outside as she freshened herself at the bathroom sink. July had been unseasonably cold so far, and the floorboards of the two flat (a Chicago term for a two-unit apartment building) must have been cool on the soles of her feet. Gathering up the perfect ensemble for the day's activities, she chose a lovely white dress that her mother had given her the previous Easter. She set it off with a wide-brimmed hat trimmed in paper flowers.

She was a petite, delicate-featured Scandinavian girl with shimmering auburn hair, a narrow, handsome face, with high cheekbones and tulip-shaped lips, and eyes that belied any potentially coquettish impression by way of a deep-set, penetrating gaze. The way she held a stare or a perfunctory smile—while being photographed, for instance—suggested a deeper reserve, perhaps a strength, that most girls her age did not possess. The neighborhood kids called her "Bobbie," and probably the name irritated the side of her that relished Easter dresses. But her intense eyes suggested that this boyish moniker just might have pleased her, too.

The rest of the family was most likely waking up, and preparing for the day with equal fervor. Mother Marianne was preparing breakfast in the kitchen, maybe already starting to pack the picnic basket. Younger sister Solveig was most certainly primping, as she loved to do. Uncle Olaf was decking himself out in high style; his Arrow collar was so stiff and sharp you could cut herring with it. A smart suit and a straw boater completed the picture. Did Uncle Olaf also spend an inordinate moment at the mirror, checking the cant of his summer hat? Probably. After all, he and his kin were about to attend the biggest company outing of the year: the Western Electric picnic.

Olaf Ness worked at the company's Hawthorne plant, a mammoth 200-acre facility a few miles southwest of the family's home. Western Electric was the country's foremost supplier of parts for the new luxury known as the telephone, and Olaf was fully immersed in the factory's burgeoning industrial-age culture. All employees, from upper management to assembly-line workers, wore formal attire throughout their nine-hour work days. That meant suits and ties for the gents, and dresses for the ladies . . . dresses that occasionally got caught in the cogs of cable winders, with tragic results. The coffee break had not yet been invented. Unionization was unheard-of. But you could bet your salary that when the work force was offered an occasion as festive as a summer picnic, the rank and file dressed to the nines.

The Aanstad kitchen was undoubtedly abuzz that morning with talk of the impending trip, and redolent with the odor of egg coffee. The Scandinavians brew their java like no other people. In the base of magnificently ornate, wide-brimmed pots, they stew ground coffee beans with an egg-water mixture. The result is an almost transparent drink that is both rich and nutty.

No doubt, Bobbie participated in the expectant chatter in the kitchen that morning. She probably kept a close watch on the clock. The family had a streetcar to catch, and Bobbie Aanstad would not allow herself to miss the departure of that great, shining steamship, the *Eastland*, which she had heard so much about but never seen. The thought of that magnificent boat sent tremors of excitement through her.

"Time to go, girls," Uncle Olaf said in his heavily accented baritone, pushing himself away from the table.

At last, Bobbie thought, as she reached across the counter to help her mother with the lunch basket.

THE CLOUDS hung low, giving the sky the color of old pewter. The forecast for Chicago and vicinity predicted "unsettled weather" for the day, with intermittent early showers and thunderstorms, then partly cloudy and cooler in the afternoon. "Don't get excited," urged *Chicago Daily Tribune* forecaster Henry Cox, addressing disgruntled readers who were hoping for pleasanter temperatures. "Chicago's weather is just equalizing itself." Citizens remained unconvinced. "The wettest year I ever saw," a man said, hopping across a puddle. Cox went on to predict that the sun might come out later but, alas, "a storm is headed in the direction of Chicago from the Rocky Mountain region."

It was not a genial start for a cruise across Lake Michigan; nor was it a promising outlook for a picnic at one of the lake's shoreline garden spots. But the forecast did nothing to dampen the spirits of thousands of Western Electric employees, nor those of their spouses, children, friends, and neighbors.

5

They came in streetcars, horse-drawn wagons, broughams, carriages, omnibuses, elevated trains, and motorized public cabs known as "hacks." A hacker's fare into the city was twenty cents per mile, if you were lucky enough to find one. In 1915, Chicago was approaching two and a half million souls. The downtown area was a great, teeming jungle of iron and smoke perched on the lake, with tendrils spreading westward across the prairie, through Oak Park and into the developments west of the Des Plaines River. Chicago throbbed with stockyards, steelworks, and shipbuilders, the railroad among the largest of its employers. In 1910, more than a quarter of a million immigrant workers were engaged in the expansion of Chicago's rail system.

Public transportation played a critical role in this sprawling activity. Since the turn of the century, and throughout the construction boom that followed the Great Fire of 1871, Chicago's mass transit system had set the standard for the rest of the world. Streetcar routes fanned out like a vast spider web from the downtown business district known as the "Loop," so named because of the circular route most trolleys followed as they reached the center of town. Throughout the early 'teens, the residents of neighborhoods west of the Loop grew skilled at hopping the iron running boards of massive Pullman cars, then riding in style to department stores like Fair's and Marshall Field's.

On that dreary July morning, scores of Western Electric picnickers made the trip down to the Chicago River on foot, in clusters of four, five, six, or ten. Entire families. Entire departments— the mold makers over there, the cable gang over here—walked together in the gray light. Full of festive good cheer, they were intent on enjoying their big day, weather be damned.

They came mostly from the west, from the scabrous, working-class neighborhoods of the so-called "Parks"—Garfield Park, Humboldt Park, Douglas Park, Marquette Park, Hyde Park, and Jackson Park—each invocation of the word "park" reflecting the

city's self-image as a place of sculpted gardens in the afterglow of
the 1893 World's Columbian Exposition. From the blue-collar
tenements and shotgun bungalows of Oak Park, and from the
maze of streets around Western Electric's Hawthorne works in
Cicero, these were the teeming masses of Chicago's stockyard-
perfumed melting pot, the immigrant backbone of the city:
Czechs, Poles, Germans, Swedes, Norwegians, Italians, Irish.

They carried baskets filled with Anola sugar wafers, Uneeda
biscuits, Zu Zu crackers, cold Smithfield luncheon meats, home-
pickled cucumbers, Allegretti chocolates, honey rice salad, and
mason jars full of sweet tea. They carried cases packed with
rolled-up blankets, swimsuits, toys, and costumes for the planned
parade in Michigan City, Indiana. Most of the men wore vested
suits and straw hats or Homburgs, a pack of Lord Salisburies or
Turkish Trophies in their pockets (at twenty cents a pack). Many
of the women carried parasols that complemented their layers of
taffeta, white silk, linen, or crepe.

It was not uncommon for the ladies of the Hawthorne works,
even those of modest means, to wear several pounds of finery to
a function like the annual picnic. Against their talced and
lotioned skin clung girdles, corsets, chemisettes, slips, black stockings and petticoats. Next came the bodices, blouses, tuckers,
pinafores, flounces, smocks and overskirts. Then the heirloom
jewelry—their finest brooches, corsages, or pins. Add to this
ensemble a pair of high-heeled Colonials or calf-high, eyelet-laced
boots, and you have an impressive display of fabric and shoe
leather, which, if wet, would be as heavy as an anchor.

The revelers made their way toward the heart of the city, a
tranquil sea of white, bobbing with straw boaters, umbrellas,
and wide-brimmed hats. But the serenity of the scene was decep-
tive. The party-goers lived in an age of shifting fortunes, political
upheaval, and social flux. The Great War was already consuming
Europe. Only seventy-nine days earlier a German U-boat had

attacked and sunk the *Lusitania* off the coast of Ireland, enraging President Wilson. War drums were disturbing the air. Airplanes were being used in military combat for the first time, and catastrophic technical failures riddled the news of the day. Shipwrecks were almost commonplace. It had been only three short years since the *Titanic*, touted as the ship that couldn't be sunk, had struck an iceberg and gone down off the coast of Nova Scotia, claiming 1,523 lives. The world was at a nervous crossroads. The pastoral life of the nineteenth century was yielding to the brutal industrial urbanism of the twentieth.

Tumult was also infusing popular culture. Thomas Edison's grand invention, the moving picture, brought flickering escapist melodrama to theaters across Chicago. Mary Pickford was starring in *The Dawn of Tomorrow* at the Vista on Cottage Grove for twenty-five cents a ticket. Charlie Chaplin's *Work* was showing at the Bryn Mawr. And D. W. Griffith's three-hour masterpiece *The Birth of a Nation*, unspooling at the Illinois, was considered by many a landmark technical achievement, despite its favorable depiction of the Ku Klux Klan and its use of white actors in blackface. On the book racks, the fantasies of M. R. James and H. G. Wells were fueling imaginations with bold visions of moon travel, invisibility, and wars between human and alien cultures. But perhaps more than any other popular medium, music was beginning to define Chicago as a mecca of change.

New Orleans had given birth to jazz, but its days of musical dominance were coming to a close. The Crescent City's famed Storyville section was being boarded up, and Jim Crow laws that forced segregation of public facilities, were driving Negro musicians north. Chicago, with its more open atmosphere, was an attractive destination. There wasn't a brothel or saloon in town that didn't employ at least one house musician, or "professor," to tickle the ivories, while rowdy customers let off steam. Sometimes referred to as "coon shouters," these balladeers were young black men who usually received a percentage of the take on liquor sold. Their songs were often lascivious parodies of popular tunes of the day, accompanied by wild improvisations.

By 1915, the city was vibrating with Dixieland bands, boogie-woogie piano players, hollerers, stompers, delta bluesmen, ragtime groups, and street-corner crooners. The high lonesome reels and jigs of the Appalachians had pushed in from the east, joining African chants and slave spirituals at Chicago's sweaty, rollicking rent parties. Scott Joplin was a fixture in town, and Jelly Roll Morton had recently arrived from New Orleans. Soon the bland, safe, languid songs of the day, like "The Old Grey Mare" and "Pack Up Your Troubles in Your Old Kit Bag," were giving way to such richer, spicier fare as "Jelly Roll Blues," "Ragging the Scale," and "Maple Leaf Rag." The popular marchlike rhythms and oom-pah bass of nineteenth-century popular music were evolving into the busy, shuffling, driving styles evocative of the twentieth-century city. The music of the industrial age was the clank of railroad spikes, the hiss of the steam engine, and the chug of manifest destiny. For the first time in American history, thanks in large part to Chicago's burgeoning recording industry, slave culture had begun to influence the mainstream. It was a pattern that would repeat itself throughout the ensuing century: the bourgeois corporate complex assimilating the soul of the working class.

The morning of July 24, 1915, promised to be like many others. The Western Electric employees, on their way to the river, clutching their picnic baskets, riding in trolleys and horse cars, represented the waves of European immigration that defined much of America. File clerks, machinists, mill wrights, platers, dye makers, office boys, wire twisters, switchboard assemblers, toolshed keepers, relay builders, alloy rollers, cable winders, and muscular Bohemians smelling of the Bakelite resin that formed primitive telephone housings—on their shoulders was Chicago supported.

Entire families crammed into motorcars. Earnest, expectant faces pressed against the grime-covered window glass. Mothers bounced along in the back, hugging infants to their floral bodices. Children fidgeted on the vibrating seats.

Today was their day off, and essentially they were all in search of the same thing: their own little piece of the American dream.

THE SINDELARS were typical immigrant dreamers.

Blue-collar Americans whose recent ancestors hailed from Bohemia, honest and hard-working, they had embarked on their journey as early as a family of seven, with a couple of tykes under the age of ten, was able. They left their westside home at 4735 W. Jackson Boulevard locked and secure. The residence was nothing fancy, of course, but it was tidy, and held its own alongside the rows of identical facades lining the boulevard.

Most likely, the Sindelars caught the Chicago Surface Line streetcar at Madison Street some time around six a.m. The excursion was scheduled to begin at around seven-thirty, which gave George and Josephine Sindelar plenty of time to corral the children, usher them downtown, get them to the wharf, shepherd them aboard the ship, and somehow find seven available chairs, or at least enough deck space for the whole family to stand together.

At that time, the 2700-model streetcar ran from West Chicago, down Madison to the Loop, with a change-over at Clark Street in order to get to the north branch of the Chicago River. The interior of the 2700 was not as lavish as the Pullman, but it was comfortable. Upholstered benches lined the sides, with leather straps hanging from the ceiling every twelve inches or so for the safety of those standing. Windows could be opened, or closed and shaded. The corrugated metal floor rattled pleasantly as the car clicked along the flush-mounted iron rails.

Chances are that George Sindelar had to stand for most of the trip that morning, steadying himself with the leather strap. He was a sturdy, square-jawed thirty-eight-year-old Czech, with a thick shock of brown hair. In photographs in which he cocked his head and eyeballed the lens, he appeared to have an air of wistful confidence, an easy, direct manner that must have served him well as an assistant foreman at the Hawthorne works. Western Electric had been expanding at an incredible rate—its initial work force of thirteen cable winders in 1905 had grown to a staggering 14,000 employees by 1914—and the handling of the rank and file had become a top priority.

The Sindelars must have huddled closely on that crowded streetcar. They were naturally a close-knit bunch, marshalled by Mama Josephine, who perched next to George on a bench seat, holding five-year-old William on her lap. Ever attentive, Josephine scanned the circle of Sindelar kids with her dark eyes for any signs of trouble, occasionally glancing out the window at the gray dawn and canyons of tenements. She was wearing her finest that day, including a lovely watch and chain that she brought out only on special occasions.

No ordinary timepiece, this was a golden, filigreed talisman, an heirloom handed down from one generation to another in an unspoken tribute to a woman's beauty and grace. Sometimes called a turnip watch, it was an American Waltham, its face ornately monogrammed and engraved, its works meticulously crafted. As it dangled from Josephine's slender neck, her dainty hands occasionally brushed its polished surface as a cleric might caress an icon.

Clustered around Josephine that morning were the rest of her cherished brood, scrubbed and garbed in their Sunday best:

fifteen-year-old Adella with her wavy hair and cherubic face; thirteen-year-old Sylvia with her tomboy looks and her dad's jaunty air; and the little guys, ten-year-old George, Jr., and eight-year-old Albert, with their identical close-shorn hair and wicked grins. Wriggling and babbling on Josephine's lap, perhaps also fingering the alluring watch, was five-year-old William with his page-boy hair cut and his mother's soft features, dressed in a sailor suit, a miniature gold crucifix around his neck.

The Sindelar family happened to be riding on one of the nation's original electric-powered, electric-controlled mass transit trains. But the electricity generated by the motors was not the only energy running through that car. A current of excitement coursed through the Sindelars, too, the kind of anticipation that sets a five-year-old boy to fidgeting.

The same restless thrill animated all the other families venturing east to the river that day. The Hawthorne employees had worked hard for their chance to celebrate.

Surely, they felt they deserved a reward.

CHAPTER TWO

Weird Dreams
and Strange Presentiments

IN THE MID-NINETEENTH CENTURY no one could have dreamed that a calamity of the scope of the *Eastland* disaster might occur in Chicago. Enormous firms such as Western Electric and company towns like Cicero, Illinois, did not yet exist. But tumultuous change lay ahead.

The Chicago/Galena railroad routinely sliced through a territory west of Chicago known as the oak ridge, a stretch of wild grasslands as rugged as a sow's back. This region, at one time a portage route for the Potowatami tribe, boasted a total of fourteen squatter families hunkered down in log cabins and cottages. In 1857 these sturdy souls decided to make their township official. Village founder Augustus Porter named the town Cicero after his previous home of Cicero, New York, and lumber barons like James McKenny began hauling in timber for new developments.

That same year, hundreds of miles away in Ohio, a brilliant young eccentric named Elisha Gray began his formal education at Oberlin College. Born in 1835, Gray had tinkered throughout his childhood with gadgets of his own invention. The new field of telegraphy fascinated him, and while still a teenager, Gray built his own Morse telegraph. "I read whatever I could find relating to this subject," Gray recalled years later, "with the same interest most boys would read *Robinson Crusoe* or *The Arabian Nights.*"

Upon graduation Gray managed to earn a living as an inventor, and many of his patents for telegraph equipment coincided with identical applications being made by Alexander Graham Bell, the future father of the telephone. In 1869 Gray joined Enos Barton, a former rising star at Western Union, and founded a company called Gray and Barton.

In 1872, less than a year after the Great Fire, Gray and Barton moved to Chicago, consolidating their operations and becoming the Western Electric Manufacturing Company. As their shop on Kinzie Street churned out mile after mile of telegraph wire and related components, Gray continued experimenting with "vibratory currents"—experiments that led ultimately to the transmission of music, messages, and the human voice. In 1876, the year Bell made his momentous short-distance call to his associate Thomas Watson, Western Electric stood at the vanguard of a revolution: the birth of the telephone.

Western Electric became the principal supplier of equipment to the network of companies that would become known as the Bell System. The firm grew at a stunning rate. A new four-story building went up at the corner of Clinton and Van Buren Streets, and hundreds of additional shop workers arrived to occupy it. By this time Western Electric also manufactured incandescent lighting equipment, as well as machinery for generating electrical power. But demand outpaced supply. Although "the company's plants are being run night and day," the Boston News Bureau reported, "it has been unable to meet the demand for telephone apparatus." More and more employees joined Western Electric's ranks, and Chicago struggled to accommodate this explosive growth in its labor force.

In 1886, a riot erupted at Haymarket Square (a few blocks from Western Electric's Clinton Street plant), involving workers from the McCormick reaper works. This violent confrontation resulted in several deaths and many injuries. McCormick employees wanted to reduce the ten-hour day to the new, progressive eight-hour day. Authorities blamed German anarchists for the riot, but no one could deny that change was in the air.

The Haymarket affair grabbed the attention of Western Electric leaders. At the turn of the century, Chicago was making 75,000 phone calls daily, an average of eighteen calls per telephone. The Western Electric Company needed to find a new home to accommodate demand—a safe, private, independent facility away from the troubling atmosphere of the city. Cicero and its affordable prairie land seemed a logical candidate. On March 9, 1904, C. W. Houger, one of Western Electric's top managers, traveled the ten miles west, took one look at the desolate, leprous acreage, and mused, "How could the Western Electric Company use a big piece of prairie land?"

The Hawthorne works answered Houger's question in grand style, a massive facility designed to house one of the largest single manufacturing concerns in U.S. history. "We have been having a part in Great Events," Enos Barton observed around the time of the relocation. "The labor question has come right up against us."

The finished plant resembled a medieval fortress planted on the corner of 22nd Street and 48th Avenue, in the heart of Cicero's Hawthorne district. It spanned 203 acres, and over the next decade developed into a town within a town, featuring its own railroad station, athletic fields, company stores, gymnasia, ice cream parlors, laundries, and even a large bandshell. By 1915, more than 2,500,000 square feet of factory space churned with sparks and humming motors, in a facility so huge it would take a person nine hours of nonstop walking to merely pass through each floor of the thirty-six building sections.

* * *

ON THAT DAMP, raw Saturday morning, the great central stone building of the Hawthorne works stood impassive and stoic, while its employees, along with friends and neighbors, headed eastward in cable cars and public broughams.

Carriage wheels and steel horseshoes pounded the streets leading into the city. A tremendous din filled the morning air as vehicles roared over the wooden planking, herringbone brick, cobblestone, and that strange wooden composite from which many roadways were hewn in the early part of the twentieth century. Wooden blocks, measuring ten by ten inches, and cemented together with tar, formed many of the streets, and often they fissured and buckled under the strain of Chicago winters. Horse manure collected in the seams, where all manner of weeds and vermin thrived. The odors of methane and rot clung to the roads, and that unmistakable, coppery stench of the stockyards, only a few miles to the southeast, wafted across the thoroughfares: the smell of blood.

The hubbub only intensified as the Western Electric picnickers approached the heart of the loop.

"This is Clark Street! Clark Street stop!" the conductor bellowed from the rear, urging the passengers out of their seats as the streetcar slowed with a groan. In an era before amplified public-address systems, many service personnel learned to project their voices with the volume of a temple cantor in order to be heard above the steam and clamor of machines.

Bobbie Aanstad slipped off the shopworn leather bench in the rear of the trolley, then staggered after her mother and sister in awkward fits and starts toward the front exit. Uncle Olaf walked ahead of them, grasping straps for purchase. As the car shuddered to a stop it was filled with the cheerful yammer of expectant voices and shuffling shoe leather. Dozens of ebullient

Western Electric employees crowded the exit, giddy with anticipation. Standing in line, Bobbie smelled whiffs of body odors, laundry starch, sun-dried linen, and traces of rosewater on the ladies.

Bobbie took her sister's tiny, pale hand, and followed her mother down the iron footrail.

Light from the overcast sky stabbed at the thirteen-year-old's eyes as she emerged from the sultry closeness of the streetcar. The ceiling of clouds looked threatening, but not excessively so. Maybe the Aanstads would get lucky. Maybe Bobbie's lovely white Easter dress with its big buttons and flouncy collar would manage to remain dry for the duration. Wouldn't that be nice?

The air north of the river reeked of coal dust, rotting fish, and moldering grain, a sharp contrast to the cozy front porches and perfumed azalea gardens further north in Logan Square. And the noise! The scream of elevated trains, the rumble of trucks and pedestrians across the cobbles, thrumming and droning. Nineteenth-century tunnels honeycombed the Loop, allowing wagons and pedestrians to travel under the river. During the Great Fire, citizens used these tunnels to escape the maelstrom.

Looking around the street corner, Bobbie surveyed the teeming throngs funneling into the mouth of the Clark Street bridge, where pedestrian sidewalks flanked the motorway. The elevated express train thundered and clattered overhead. Horses' hooves clopped in syncopation against the planking. Voices rose in exuberance.

The Aanstad girls huddled together as Uncle Olaf ushered them across the rickety span. They had plenty of time. It was only a quarter of seven, but Olaf wanted to board as early as possible in order to get a decent spot on the big boat.

Bobbie followed along, hand-in-hand with her nine-year-old sister. Her heart quickening with excitement, Bobbie strained her neck to see over the tops of heads and horsecars as she crossed the bridge. The span shivered and bucked. Dizziness washed over the girl. To her left she caught glimpses of massive, scorched chimneys rising up over the river—the smokestacks of the *Theodore Roosevelt*, one of the five ships contracted for the Hawthorne picnickers that day—but Bobbie had trouble making out much to the west where the *Eastland* was moored.

The Aanstads followed the crowd until they reached the south end of the Clark Street bridge. There, company officials corralled the picnickers like slow-moving cattle down the wide wooden steps that emptied onto the weathered planks of the wharf—a languid procession of straw hats bobbing in the air and long skirts scraping the timbers. Weathered gray treads, slimy with mildew, creaked beneath Bobbie's feet as she descended.

A narrow walkway ran along the water, leading past shipping firms, baggage rooms, and produce warehouses. The sounds of gurgling engines, frenzied voices, and water lapping noisily at the pilings and breakfronts added to Bobbie's anticipation. Huge awnings shaded the area in long shadows. From somewhere beyond the racket of the crowd, the roar of water pouring into the river caught Bobbie's attention. Where was it coming from?

"There she is!" Uncle Olaf's voice called out, causing Bobbie to jump.

The teenager glanced to her right, over the picnickers' heads, and her gaze rose. And rose. She got her first glimpse of the S.S. *Eastland*.

The *Eastland* sat very high in the water, and it was incredibly huge, far larger than Bobbie had imagined it would be. A gigantic Zephyr of white-washed steel, spanning nearly the entire length of a city block (from Clark to LaSalle Street) the ship teemed with people, milling like ants on its upper decks thirty feet above the wharf.

Bobbie remembered hearing about the *Titanic* disaster only three years earlier, and had marveled that a boat that big could actually float. But this boat! Floating so high out of the water, crowned by enormous twin smoke stacks. Maybe five stories high. *Five stories.* The massive hull dwarfed the imposing, charred-brick facades of the Chicago-South Haven buildings along the south pier. The attendant tug boat, the *Kenosha,* moored immediately to the east, beneath the ship's bow, looked to Bobbie like a child's toy boat in some giant, dirty bathtub. But the most amazing aspect, was the way the washed-out morning light gleamed off the painted iron. The white bulwark positively glowed.

"Come, girls," Marianne Aanstad softly urged in her faint Norwegian accent, steering the girls into the boarding line.

Bobbie hesitated, no longer certain she wanted to board such a behemoth.

"IT DOES NOT care at all," Theodore Dreiser once wrote of Chicago. "It is not conscious. The passing of so small an organism as that of a man or woman is nothing to it."

In 1915, Chicago offered visitors a virtual smorgasbord of depravity, vice, corruption, fraud, thievery, murder, and anarchy. A single city block on the south side might sport no less than twenty-five bordellos, with names such as Bucket of Blood, The Why Not, Black May's, Old 92, and Bedbug Row. Neighborhood druggists sold cheap cocaine and morphine sulfate to prostitutes in the area. Cops called them "air walkers," due to their dazed, drug-induced stroll. White slavery thrived. Naive immigrant girls stumbled into relationships with pimps who would promise devotion, sometimes even marriage, and then lure the young women to "breaking-in" houses where they would be imprisoned, and then repeatedly raped and drugged. "A man can't hold a job in the south-side levee unless he is willing to go out and get girls," an area bartender once testified.

The reformers fought a losing battle. Local kingpins such as

Big Jim Colosimo ruled their little empires with a vengeance. A turn-of-the-century precursor to the gangsters who would one day terrorize the city, Colosimo kept the aldermen and cops in his pockets as neatly as the garish jewelry and watch fobs tucked into his bulging vest.

By the 1910s, wickedness touched every corner of the city. "Only two out of sixty-eight aldermen were not on the take," marveled one journalist who covered the local scene. "Most policemen were for sale, and the pillars of the community—Marshall Field, George Pullman, Carter Harrison and others—were tax cheats." An atmosphere of uncertainty spread a pall over everything. For many Chicagoans, life had lost its inherent value.

The immigrant population often fell victim to this graft and abuse. Activists such as Grace Abbott of the League for the Protection of Immigrants struggled to promote new laws regulating employment agencies who preyed on "innocent immigrant and rural women." Fear and paranoia colored the decisions of most immigrant families. Many foreigners relied on neighbors and local agencies—many speaking their native language—for jobs, education, medical services, and other daily necessities. Even in death, the immigrants kept to themselves, preferring their neighborhood funeral parlors.

Old World superstitions lingered among transplanted foreigners, who clung to old beliefs, perhaps as defense mechanisms in this terrifying age of transition and change. In 1915 spiritualism saw a surge in popularity. Parties and social functions routinely featured seances. Fortune tellers dotted the cityscapes, and clairvoyance seemed, for many, a credible human trait, as plausible as double-jointedness. Overseas, the famous author Arthur Conan Doyle, joined by such luminaries as British Prime Minister Arthur Balfour and American philosopher William James, regularly held seances and launched serious studies of unexplained phenomena. But perhaps the most famous proponent of spiritualism and occult science was the escape artist Harry Houdini, who was at the height of his celebrity in 1915, and deeply committed to the study and exploration of psychic phenomena. Two years earlier, in July 1913, Houdini had lost his beloved mother Cecelia and, racked with grief, begun to believe he could communicate with her, an obsession that consumed the escape artist for the rest of his life.

IN CHICAGO, employees of the Hawthorne works experienced their own versions of these metaphysical torments.

On the morning of the *Eastland* excursion, one such employee, Paul Jahnke, arose with a terrible feeling. A faithful worker at the Western plant for years, Jahnke wasn't the type to abide by superstition. But something odd happened to his wife the night before that preyed on Jahnke's mind.

While standing in the kitchen of their little flat at 4817 West 22nd Street, happily preparing a picnic lunch for the next day, Paul's young bride, Louise, suddenly had a horrible feeling: "Something would happen to the boat." Later that evening, sleep came hard. Weird dreams kept the newlyweds restless. The next morning brought little relief from the foreboding. The young couple decided to go ahead with the trip, but not before making certain arrangements.

Around dawn on Saturday, the building's landlady, Mrs. Altman, heard a knock at her door. She opened it to find an ashen-faced Paul Jahnke standing on her threshold. "Here's our key," he said. "And fifty dollars for my mother if we don't come back from the trip."

Mrs. Altman stood there, dumbfounded. She could hardly muster a reply.

Later, after the disaster, the landlady learned that the Jahnkes had also left a poignant letter on their bedroom dresser, neatly attached to their will. In the letter Louise expressed a wish to leave her bracelet and rings to her beloved mother. "They were married just six weeks," Mrs. Altman opined later. "They were so happy."

Three weeks earlier, a Mrs. J. B. Burroughs of 3547 Indiana Avenue had visited a friend staying at the Palmer House. The friend, a tourist from Texas, told of awakening in the middle of the night to a gruesome apparition. In the hallway outside her room, she saw "a ship turned over on its side, and hundreds of corpses lying in a row."

"At the time we laughed at her," Mrs. Burroughs recalled. "But it was a warning from God."

Another girl, Josie Markowski, an eighteen-year-old Western Electric employee with doe eyes and voluminous braids, who was also an amateur fortune teller, suffered flashes of dread throughout the week preceding the excursion. On the morning of the outing, as her mother ironed the new dress she would wear, Josephine had a premonition that she would never wear that dress again. "Josie told my mother she felt something awful was going to happen and that she did not want to go to the picnic," recalled a neighborhood friend, Helen Glinka. "My mother laughingly told her to go on and have a good time and warned her not to think of disaster, else she might bring it on the boat."

CHAPTER THREE

The Darkening Sky

THE RIVERFRONT, for better or for worse, shaped Chicago's destiny.

As far back as the early 1800's, America's travel routes converged on this low, rugged, and flat land at the southern tip of Lake Michigan, with its swampy bogs, thick groves of hardwoods, and untamed waterways. In 1803, near the mouth of the natural channel that cut through the region, an important stronghold rose up against the frontier sky.

This outpost, known as Fort Dearborn, became the country's first line of western defense, and a critical albeit difficult portage for fur traders and explorers. Sinkholes and hideous mosquitoes plagued the territory. "Those who waded through the mud frequently sank to their waist," reported an early fur trader, "and at times were forced to cling to the side of the boat to prevent going over their heads; and after reaching the end and camping for the night came the task of ridding themselves of the bloodsuckers."

In 1836, settlers carved the Illinois-Michigan canal through this unforgiving bog, connecting the Great Lakes with the fertile Mississippi River Valley to the west, making the portage no longer necessary. Mules dragged barges along the canal, and the

U.S. Army Corps of Engineers blasted through sand bars in order to open up the channel for the bigger schooners. One year later, in 1837, the settlement that had grown up around Fort Dearborn became the city of Chicago, a name which is derived from the Potowatomi word "Checagou," meaning onion, in reference to the smell of wild onion that filled the air in those days.

Almost immediately, Chicago garnered a reputation as a bustling commercial port. By 1871, the year of the Great Fire, more ships entered the Chicago River annually than the ports of New York, Baltimore, Philadelphia, San Francisco and Charleston combined. Enormous warehouses, grain elevators, and stockyards sprouted up along the riverfront, keeping pace with Chicago's status as the leading distributor of lumber, grain, and livestock. Theodore Dreiser called it "the busiest river in the world."

Fueled by this tremendous activity, Chicago flourished. Within forty years—between 1830 and 1870—the town went from a population of 150 to nearly 300,000. Half of these new citizens came from abroad, and often they got their first glimpses of the great city from the mouth of the Chicago River. Along with this prominence, however, came tremendous problems.

In the 1880s, with population exploding, the Chicago River became a repository of waste, which was carried east into Lake Michigan and poisoned the city's water supply, causing serious outbreaks of disease. In 1890, an epidemic of cholera killed more than 2,000 people. City officials realized that something had to be done.

In a cooperative venture the likes of which were never before attempted, the Corps of Engineers literally *reversed* the river's flow. Digging an enormous canal at the end of one channel, gravity diverted the water westward, drawing it away from the lake, and in the process moving more earth than in the construction of the Panama Canal. The entire project took eight years to complete.

By 1900, the river flowed in its new direction, and the new riverfront bustled with markets, iron trusses, crows-nest towers and terra cotta warehouses. South Water Street wound along the main branch, and both foot and motor traffic added to the commotion.

For some, all this activity signaled the death of a more graceful era. The majestic windjammers with their trademark sails became objects of the past, and the harbor developed into a hotbed of commerce, aided by the advent of the steel hull. "There used to be lots of damn good sailors," remembered one of the last schooner captains. "Now it's all steamboats and they take harbor rats aboard and leave the real sailors without a job."

By 1915, noise along the river reached unprecedented levels. Bulk-lumber carriers slammed into the harbor at all hours, their deck hands off-loading timbers as quickly as possible. The sound resembled the atonal beat of drums. "Lumber-shovers," as they were known, often accompanied the banging with the cranking of huge windlasses, which creaked and moaned like banshees. Grain ships brought their own brand of clamor. The roar of corn and wheat and rye constantly tumbling out of giant elevators competed with the blast of steam hoists, the chatter of dockwallopers, the wailing autumnal winds filled with yellow grain-dust, and the omnipresent flow of traffic over aging bridges.

Accidents, including drowning deaths, severed appendages, explosions, and fires, were commonplace. At least once every summer the river water self-ignited—the industrial waste and run-off of horse dung from streets spontaneously combusting—turning the river into a hellish maelstrom. Capsizings became practically routine events. Carl Sandburg surely had this riverfront in mind when he described the "stormy, husky, brawling" city.

INTO SUCH an environment, the Sindelars arrived at approximately seven a.m., reaching the LaSalle Street steps alongside throngs of other early birds. The family of seven descended the stairs hand-in-hand, then approached the 269-foot-long *Eastland* from the stern and waited in line on the weathered planks with the other passengers. Because of the darkening sky, George wanted to get his clan aboard this long, narrow vessel as quickly as possible.

The ship bore the legend EASTLAND across its prow, and just below that, on the bow, a placard proclaimed THE ST. JOSEPH–CHICAGO STEAMSHIP COMPANY. Massive twin chimney stacks belched noxious black smoke. Rows of lifeboats hung off stanchions up along the hurricane deck, and down below, five huge gangway doors gaped open near the level of the dock.

To George Sindelar, those doors probably looked dangerously close to the river; a slight list could send water gushing into the boat. Next to him, his children stared. The hullabaloo of disembodied voices floated down from the ship's upper decks. Arching their little necks in awe, the Sindelar kids saw the giant, black, cast-iron anchor clinging to the bow, and the rows of round windows, faces moving in the shadows behind them. The boat jerked slightly against the pier, squeaking every time a pair of new passengers walked across the little wooden bridges which deckhands had laid between the dock and the gangways.

The Sindelar children noticed something else that morning. They probably didn't mention it to one another, nor did George talk about it with Josephine, but the water pouring out of the ship seemed strange to them. Most people waiting in line to board noticed it, and some remarked on it. "When I started down the stairs to go onto the boat," R. J. Moore later recalled during the Coroner's inquest, "there was a long line, five or six abreast, and I was going along the side of the boat. I saw water coming out of there. I saw it by the ton. Six or seven holes in the side of the boat. Anyway, I remarked to a gentleman they were taking out a lot of ballast."

Finally the Sindelars boarded, and not a moment too soon. A light mist had started falling, and the sky promised heavier rains. Pausing at the foot of the wooden gangplank, George got his tickets ready, while Josephine herded the kids together.

A pair of sullen gentlemen in suits flanked the bottom of the gangplank, scanning the crowd, waiting for George to show his tickets. Vigilant eyes partially shaded by derbies, these men worked for the U.S. Customs Department. They kept track of the head count and maintained order during the boarding. One of the men held a "hand-counter" on which he clicked off a running tally.

The capacity of the *Eastland*—a number scrutinized profusely in the aftermath of the tragedy—officially stood at 2,570, including 70 crew members. The Sindelars had no inkling that the passenger count was already nearing 1,700 . . . and it was only a few minutes past seven. George saw the other line of picnickers trundling up the second gangplank thirty feet away, but he had no idea that passengers were boarding at a rate of fifty per minute.

At last, the Sindelars boarded, using the thick rope handholds to brace themselves as they ushered their children up the narrow gangplank and into the *Eastland*'s hold. First came fifteen-year-old Adella; then thirteen-year-old Sylvia; then the two boys, Albert and George; and last but certainly not least, five-year-old William.

The family stepped onto the main deck, bracing themselves against each other as the ship pitched slightly, then shuffling toward the purser's window just inside the gangway door. Josephine's watch caught the attention of more than a few ladies standing nearby. The ship's low-wattage incandescent lights reflected off the turnip watch's golden housing.

George handed over his tickets. He had purchased them at the plant; 75 cents for adults, 50 cents for children under twelve, no charge for children under five. Then the Sindelars set out across the main deck.

Negotiating the crowds with five children in tow, on a vessel that was softly yawing, was not easy. One can imagine George carrying little William in his arms while Josephine struggled against the crush of passengers with her kids clutching at the hem of her dress. Expectant murmurs surrounded them, bouncing off painted steel walls and varnished, quarter-sawed oak floors. George recognized some of the faces from the factory floor. Josephine exchanged a few cheerful greetings. Every now and then, the gentle listing nudged Mrs. Sindelar against a fellow picnicker.

"Excuse me, I'm sorry," she muttered softly as she shepherded her brood toward the port side wall.

The main deck teemed with people, a unique melange of smells, sights, and sounds. The air reeked of colognes, machine oil, cigar smoke, and faint traces of mildew. The muffled jangle of ragtime filtered down from one of the upper decks. Josephine had heard rumors that there was a dance floor up there somewhere. She might just take a whirl with George later. Maybe after the kids had settled. Maybe leave Adella with them for a few minutes.

Josephine scanned the crowd for a space. Very few passengers seemed to mind the pitching of the ship, and if they did, it was all in good fun. Josephine heard the first playful whooping sounds from above. According to historical records, some time after seven, passengers on the *Eastland*'s promenade deck, on the outer walkway that rimmed the ship, began teasingly to cheer the tilting of the boat. As the Sindelars finally found a small available area of dry space—most likely on the port, or river, side of the main deck—they clearly heard a chorus of voices coming from overhead.

"Wwwwwwoooooooooooo!" Playful shouts pierced the air

every time the boat leaned. Carefree voices. Childlike. As though it were a game.

GAMES, as it turned out, played an important part in Western Electric's corporate culture. Bowling, checkers, billiard tournaments, chess matches, wrestling contests, track races, interdepartmental boxing, and even beauty pageants, were featured from the earliest days of the factory. Also popular were employees' clubs—guns, drama, science, fishing, sewing, radios, motion pictures, orchestra and choral singing—all of which served to keep the rank and file stimulated and happy. And thanks to an employee-run organization known as the Hawthorne Club, the relentless grind and churn of the Hawthorne factory completely ceased for one blessed Saturday each summer.

Founded in 1911 by the factory's entertainment committee, the Hawthorne Club established itself "to bring the employees of the various departments into closer association with each other." The club had no official affiliation with the company, although senior Western Electric management, recognizing its stabilizing effect, wholeheartedly supported it. Initially a men-only club, women soon joined the group in this era of suffragettes and progressive politics.

The Club sponsored lectures, classes, outings, banquets, concerts, and social functions of all types. But the annual picnic soon became the jewel in the Club's crown.

The Hawthorne Club transformed the annual picnic—previously a modest occasion, since 1881 sparsely attended—into an extravaganza. In 1912, for the first time in the company's history, the picnic was held out of town. A total of 3,500 workers cruised across the lake for a gala gathering at a popular shoreline resort in Michigan City, Indiana. The event—complete with sack races, baseball games, tugs-o'-war, swimming, and dancing—had proved a raging success and, according to the Western Electric newsletter, even heavy rains "could not dampen the ardor of the crowd."

"Had the weather been propitious," the newsletter went on, marveling at the turnout, "it is probable that the Transportation Committee would have been compelled to make requisition on the Aero Club for additional transportation."

Michigan City's Washington Park became the annual destination for the Hawthorne Club picnic, offering ideal facilities: charming little gazebos, a bandshell, a bathing beach, amusement park rides, various athletic fields, and even a sophisticated ballroom for those inclined to do the new dance crazes such as the black bottom, the fox trot, and that scandalous new step, the tango.

Local merchants in and around the little lakeside village welcomed the tradition, especially considering the influx of tourist dollars. "The excursionists are composed of a fine lot of people," wrote the *Michigan City Evening News* with greedy delight, "orderly, good looking . . . just the kind of people whom it is a pleasure to have visit us."

Over the next three years, the annual excursion to Michigan City became legendary. In 1913 the number of picnickers almost doubled. A thousand more participated in 1914. Organizers contracted additional boats to the growing armada crossing the lake, and the picnic became an institution. Parades extended the reach of the celebration into the streets of the neighboring town, offering onlookers a marching band, floats, costumes, and suffragettes. Picnickers enjoyed rapid-fire photographic galleries, a roller coaster, a stunt-driving demonstration, a greased-pole-climbing contest, and even a game in which contestants in small boats compete by forcing each other to capsize.

Anticipation for the 1915 excursion swelled to an all-time high. Earlier that year, the factory had reduced many of its employees' hours due to changing economics, and morale needed a boost. The committee staged parades on company grounds in order to promote the picnic. "Wow! Whoop 'er up and get busy," crowed the *July Jubilator*, the new Club newsletter. "We can all make this the biggest, finest picnic and the most successful affair that the Hawthorne Club ever pulled off!"

READERS OF THE JUBILATOR, BE JUBILANT.

Last Time It Was a Submarine
A Long Time Ago Jonah Took a Trip in a
Submarine.

THERE IS NO JONAH ABOUT THIS, BUT IT WILL BE A WHALE OF A BIG SUCCESS

Get Your Tickets Early — 75c.
Children Under 5 Years Free.

In the days prior to the trip, the Hawthorne works percolated with ticket sales, but not all of those transactions seemed completely pure of heart.

Rumors spread of coercion, gossip was whispered that workers were *expected* to attend the picnic and *expected* to buy multiple tickets. Allegations surfaced later, after the disaster, of punitive acts carried out against recalcitrant employees. "I was working for the Western Electric company last year, and did not go on the excursion," Frank Baubles told the *Tribune*. "Shortly afterward I was laid off, and was never able to learn why." Another employee confirmed the unspoken pressure: "We got the impression that our jobs were no good unless we went along. Some of us didn't want to go but we finally decided to because we didn't want to be fired."

The problem seemed systemic. In many cases, foremen distributed the tickets out on the floor, and some of them were a bit overzealous in their promotional efforts. "They forced them to go!" one man complained after the accident, referring to his wife and daughter, who worked side-by-side at the telephone factory. "I begged them to stay at home but Anna told me she would lose her job if she didn't go. She said the foreman of her department, a Mr. Heterson, had warned her that unless she and Agnes went, their names would be scratched off the payroll." Another man, a relative of an *Eastland* passenger, explained that his niece's "fear of the water had become conquered by her fear of losing her job."

Western Electric vehemently denied any coercion. "The foreman, department heads or other officials have nothing to do with the sale of tickets," company superintendent W. F. Henry told the *Tribune*. "All arrangements are in the hands of employees themselves. There is no excuse for anyone saying employees had gone on the boat fearing they would lose their positions otherwise."

Throughout the aftermath of the tragedy, Hawthorne officials remained steadfast in their claims of innocence, repeatedly asserting that company management prohibited any company supervisor or foreman from selling tickets—in order to avoid even the *appearance* of coercion. Nevertheless, many employees sensed, at the very least, a *perceived* pressure to attend. In the coroner's inquest after the disaster, one member of the picnic committee, Daniel Gee, revealed the names of representatives in each department who "were given a number of tickets they thought they could sell." Some of these "representatives" likely saw the opportunity to impress their own superiors by drumming up the largest possible turnout.

Regardless of the reasons, however, on that July morning, early arrivals flooded the *Eastland* at an alarming rate.

* * *

AROUND SEVEN-TEN A.M., the gray drizzle started billowing down on the riverfront.

As the passenger count on the *Eastland* approached its maximum capacity, umbrellas began sprouting on the exposed upper deck. Before long, surfaces glistened with slimy moisture. Passengers scrambled for chairs. Nobody wanted to have their picnic blankets soaked before the ship even left the dock. People jockeyed for space, the frenzy of voices rising up into the misty wind. Stiff-soled dress shoes scudded and slipped on the deck.

Some of the passengers pressed against the starboard railings, waving to their friends down on the docks. Others shuffled back toward the stairs in order to get out of the rain. Onlookers on the wharf began to wonder uneasily if the ship was already overcrowded, perhaps even grounded on the river bottom, which was only about eighteen–twenty feet deep at the Clark Street bridge.

Among these onlookers stood Adam Weckler, Chicago's Harbormaster.

A heavily jowled man in his forties with meticulously groomed hair and an air of buttoned-down professionalism, Weckler took very seriously his responsibilities for moving vessels, bridges, and traffic in and around the riverfront area. He often sat in his crow's-nest office above one corner of the Clark Street bridge, surveying the vast, snaking expanse of polluted waters like a benevolent king in some medieval fiefdom. Weckler employed a staff of assistants, and rarely had to deal personally with things like ballast problems and listing ships. But he took a personal interest in such large-scale maritime movements as the Western Electric excursion, and had come down to the river early that morning to keep an eye on things. What he saw at ten minutes after seven that morning made him nervous.

In fact, Weckler was nervous enough to put on his rain slicker and make his way down the ladder to street level where literally thousands of people, picnickers and passers-by, pushed up against Clark and Water Streets in a phalanx of black umbrellas, carriages, and bonnets. In 1915, Saturday was still a workday. The streets thronged with noise and activity, stevedores yelling, delivery trucks honking at the crowds.

Weckler couldn't take his eyes off the *Eastland* as he descended the damp steps to the dock, pushing his way through the excursionists. On the hurricane deck it appeared to be standing-room-only, people shoulder-to-shoulder. The ship was leaning to the port side—five to six degrees at that point, Weckler guessed later.

"Cap! Cap!" Weckler called out as he stood on the dock near the *Eastland*'s bow, waving up at the ship's bridge thirty feet away.

A stocky man in a uniform emerged from the round, glass-encased pilot house.

Captain Harry Pedersen stood there for a moment, squinting through the drizzle. A paunchy, ruddy-complected Norwegian in his mid-fifties, Pedersen wore a bushy mustache under a prominent nose that jutted impudently over a double-chin. He carried himself with the rough swagger of a tradesman or a lumberjack, and he was fond of chewing on cigars while he worked.

"Mornin', sir!" Pedersen gave the harbormaster a wave with his massive, gnarled hand.

"Put in your ballast, Captain!" Weckler yelled at him. "Trim her up!"

"We're trimming her all the time!" Pedersen shouted back over the noise.

Weckler said something else at that point—probably cautioning the officer to not even *think* about casting off before the vessel had been righted—but it's unclear whether Pedersen heard him. The noise of the throngs probably drowned that part of the exchange.

Of course, Captain Harry Pedersen had no reason to worry. He had been a master of steamships for more than fifteen years, and nothing rattled him. There was absolutely no reason for alarm. There was certainly no reason for the Captain to think that his craft was in trouble. It was ludicrous even to suggest that a boat as neat as the *Eastland* would be doomed.

Ludicrous!

CHAPTER FOUR

Too Many People
on This Boat

IN THE EARLY DAYS of the 20th century, one particular commodity made pleasure boating on the Great Lakes wildly profitable: fresh produce.

All along the riverfront, elaborate produce stands and farmers' markets sprang up to serve local grocers and consumers. Huge awnings shrouded row after row of weathered wooden bins brimming with Wisconsin apples, Mississippi peanuts, Michigan blueberries, Florida lemons, and sweet potatoes from the lowlands of Louisiana. The high keening sounds of vendors' voices carried over the river, barking out the specials of the day: *Michigan apples—19 cents a peck! A pint of bing cherries—today only—one thin dime!*

Independent shipping companies such as the Dunkley-Williams Transportation Company and the Michigan Steamship Company set up permanent routes for hauling fruit along the west Michigan coastline on a daily basis, ensuring freshness and maximum profits for all involved. Since most of the port towns were burgeoning vacation spots, these enterprising shipping companies saw a way to double their money. They fitted their vessels with seats, windows, and amenities such as snack bars, smoking rooms, and calliopes. And they virtually invented a new industry.

A dollar fare purchased a round trip across the lake, including an afternoon in a relaxing resort town (while the vessel was being loaded with fruit), then a dinnertime cruise back to Chicago. The most popular routes included the seventy-seven-mile journey to South Haven, the sixty-mile trek to Benton Harbor, and the thirty-eight-mile jaunt to Michigan City. In this new era of gracious living—of cultured gentlemen in homburgs, and elegant ladies in high-button boots—the excursion business provided the perfect tonic.

Tickets sold briskly. In 1902, the Michigan Steamship Company saw a need for a bigger, faster boat in order to accommodate both the growing produce trade as well as the excursion business, which had now added services for Michiganders commuting to and from Chicago. In October of that year, the company contracted the services of the Jenks Ship Building Company to construct a speedy new vessel.

The new ship had twin-screw propulsion with high steel sides and an iron hull. Engineered for maximum speed and comfort, and a steadier profile in the rolling currents of the big lake, this fleet new craft could better negotiate the narrow channels of South Haven and the Chicago River. Most important, it rode tall and sleek, its thoroughly modern design shaming the clunkier nineteenth-century steamers with their old-fashioned wooden superstructures.

Jenks took eight months to build the vessel that came to be known as the *Eastland*.

Four decks rose above the water. The main deck, which was closest to the surface, featured five gangway doors on each side for loading and unloading passengers, baggage, and freight. These gangways rode relatively low for a ship of this size, only inches from the water when fully loaded. This feature gave the vessel a very small range of lateral stability. A lean of only fifteen degrees brought water into the main deck.

Several amenities, some of them unusual for a lake boat, graced the ship: a bar on the main deck with a refrigerator for bottled beer; a luxurious galley and dining room appointed with oak paneling and ornamental clusters of fruit; and an ornate staircase leading up to the cabin deck. A pair of parlor rooms, finished in mahogany, with ceilings and trim painted a rich cream color, featured private baths. The boat also offered passengers a nursery and eighty-six regular cabins.

Another ornate staircase led up to the promenade deck where a grand saloon, with carved glass and hardwood furnishings, greeted passengers. On the opposite end of the promenade deck, a smoking room provided gentlemen of means a place to relax, savor their tobacco, and discuss the politics of the day. At the aft of the smoking room sat a massive keyboard for a steam calliope.

The *Eastland* featured two "open" decks designed for sight-seeing and sunning. The promenade deck, directly above the cabin level, sported twenty-four deluxe staterooms down its center, surrounded by an eight-foot wide, railed walkway, allowing passengers to traverse the entire length of the vessel. Chaises and folding chairs allowed passengers to take full advantage of the fresh lake air. Above the promenade deck, the hurricane level, also equipped with lounge chairs, presented a breathtaking observation platform, rising thirty feet over the water and crowded by lifeboats, davits, air intakes and exhaust stacks.

The *Eastland* was launched on May 6, 1903, into the Black River at Port Huron, Michigan.

The Jenks Ship Building Company made sure the occasion was festive and well promoted, especially since the *Eastland* was the first passenger ship the firm had ever built. A band played lively marches, and bunting was strung along the docks. School children enjoyed a day off in order to attend the ceremonies, and nearly 6,000 people attended the event. Sidney Jenks, president of the company and designer of the *Eastland*, was present that day, as well as the first captain's wife, Frances Pereue, who christened the bow with a flourish.

The boat slid sideways about three feet, then rolled to a 45-degree angle, as though it were about to fall over. Some of the onlookers held their breath for fear the new ship would capsize. But soon the *Eastland* righted herself, as Jenks would later report in criminal proceedings, "just as nice and steady as a church."

The shipbuilder had big plans for the future. Jenks saw the new century as a boom time for the construction of passenger vessels, and the *Eastland* represented the beginning of this new product line.

The *Eastland* would be not only the Jenks Company's first passenger boat, it would also be its last.

"I DON'T like the feel of it."

The sound of Marianne Aanstad's voice, barely audible above the rumble of other voices, made Bobbie pause as she stood near the starboard wall of the cabin deck. *She doesn't like the what? The feel?* Bobbie had to struggle to hear her mother's voice over the commotion of babies crying, people competing for seats, and more passengers coming up the grand staircase, looking for a place to rest.

"What did you say, Mama?" Bobbie asked, glancing over her shoulder.

"I don't like the feel of this boat," Marianne Aanstad said, gazing at all the people squeezed into that first deck above the main level. Again the ship leaned slightly toward the river side, and the round-faced woman clutched her youngest daughter's hand. Marianne's face looked ashen in the dim light of the hold, her eyes burning with alarm.

For ten minutes the Aanstads had wandered the decks, squeezing their way through the crowds, trying to find a space on which to set down their picnic basket and huddle. Women's coats draped many of the folding deck chairs. The muffled heartbeat of ragtime music filtered down from the promenade deck above them, which made Bobbie restless. She loved to dance, but that would have to wait. There were more pressing problems occupying her young mind.

"What's the matter with it, Mama?" Bobbie asked, raising her voice above the noise.

"There are too many people on this boat!" Marianne pulled little Solveig against her skirt as the ship slowly righted itself back toward the dock. The sounds of playful whoops and hollers pierced the din. "I don't like it," Marianne added in a lower tone. The sound of her voice raised gooseflesh on Bobbie's arms. "I don't like the feel of it at all."

Bobbie glanced over at her Uncle Olaf, who stood behind the girls, holding the picnic basket, scanning the area for potential space. The cabin deck, or "'Tween" deck, as it was sometimes called, was situated in the exact middle of the boat. To a simple, immigrant, working-class girl from Logan Square, the cabin deck looked like a grand hotel. With its mahogany balustrades and great saloon ceiling at one end, it reminded Bobbie of a glorious, bustling lobby, busy with exotic visitors, foreign dignitaries, maybe even royalty. The only clues that they were still on a boat were the iron-riveted portholes along each wall, glowing with diffuse light—and, of course, the leaning motions.

Uncle Olaf's eyes met Bobbie's. They were probably thinking the same thing: Marianne Aanstad knew what she was talking about when she talked about boats.

Born in 1878 in Norway, Marianne grew up in the small fishing village of Neshaugen. Her father, Salomon Martinius Clausen, was a commercial fisherman who occasionally took his daughter out across the glistening fjords of the North Sea and the Baltic. The little girl learned the sailor's trade through osmosis, and after moving away from home in her early twenties and marrying Akim Aanstad, Marianne continued to feel as though she had saltwater in her blood, and the odor of herring in her hair. Amid the tribulations of the torturous two-week passage to America in 1903—huddling in the dirty steerage area with her two-year-old, who was very sick at the time—Marianne still felt at home on the open water.

It was second nature to her. Which was precisely why her uneasy assessment of the *Eastland* bothered Bobbie and Olaf so much.

"Hey! There's a couple of empty chairs!" Olaf pointed at the dockside wall a few feet away. The Aanstads hurried over to the deck chairs at the precise moment the ship began to rock once again toward the river.

"GOT TO STEADY her up again, boys!"

At exactly seven-sixteen a.m., the chief engineer, Joseph Erickson, shouted the order, his voice ringing out across the grimy confines of the engine room, way down belowdecks, in the dark innards of the *Eastland*.

Situated in the bottom center of the ship, directly behind the massive boilers where 125 tons of coal lay in gigantic bunkers, the engine room was not exactly first-class accommodations. Barely large enough to facilitate the chief engineer and his trusty crewmen—oiler Peter Erickson (no relation to Chief Engineer Erickson), assistant engineer Fred Snow, and second assistant Charlie Silvernail—the room formed a greasy cubbyhole of filthy conduits, the air thick with oil and coal dust.

Ballast technology, used to keep ships stabilized, or "trimmed," had not changed much since the nineteenth century. Giant tanks lay along the ship's double-bottom. When the boat started listing to one side, water either emptied from compartments on *that* side, or was pumped into compartments on the *opposing* side in order to bring the boat back into balance. No gauges existed to measure the exact amount of ballast—levels were judged by eye—and the emptying and filling could not be done simultaneously.

When the order to trim the boat had come from the bridge, Erickson acted as quickly as possible, given the limitations of the equipment. The bridge communicated with the engine room via several different methods. A Chadburn telegraph transmitted standard Great Lakes engine commands such as All-ahead-full or Stand-by. More obscure messages were sent by closed circuit telephone. These devices sizzled and crackled with static, and Erickson had to strain his ear against the greasy black handset in order to hear the ghostly voice of first mate Adelbert Fisher bellowing his orders from the bridge.

At seven-sixteen that morning, according to his post-disaster testimony, Chief Engineer Erickson ordered his assistant to open the intake manifold to the number 2 and 3 starboard (dockside) ballast tanks. Erickson estimated that the lean had reached approximately 10 to 15 degrees toward the river. The fastest way to shove it back in line was to add weight to the opposite side— an agonizingly slow process. The oil and sweat beaded on Erickson's forehead as he waited for the physics of the ballast system to do the job.

A wiry man with chiseled, leathery features, Joe Erickson looked like a man accustomed to sweat and nerves, not to mention little sleep and inadequate pay. His deep-set eyes had a forlorn quality, and his shoulders were perpetually slumped as though stooped and rusted by all the time at sea, stoking complex equipment.

He'd certainly logged his requisite share of sea hours. Born in 1883 in Christiania, Norway, he'd been a sailor since the age of fifteen. He came to the States in 1905, and got his engineer's license in 1909. He served as second assistant engineer on the railroad car ferry *Ashtabula*, and by 1913 had moved up the ranks to chief engineer on the freighter *C.W. Watson*. Then he made a decision that caused him not only great problems after the disaster, but altered the course of his life.

He married the daughter of Robert Reid, a federal inspector of Great Lakes steamers. For Chief Engineer Erickson, the family connection proved fortunate, leading to the job as chief on the *Eastland*, secured at the behest of Erickson's bride so that he could be closer to their new home. This new job suited him well—until the morning of July 24, 1915.

UP ON THE promenade deck, the air smelled of pipe tobacco and cigars. Mandolins twanged and voices thrummed. If a passenger on this deck craned his neck, he might be able to see, just barely, over the tops of heads to the smoking room at the end of the cabin—gentlemen only, their dark forms visible through the door's engraved glass window, milling about like ghosts in the blue fog of cigar smoke. The massive pipes of the circus calliope penetrated the haze. Once played to call attention to the *Eastland* as it appeared in the mouth of the harbor, the calliope sat silent. Chicago had grown tired of all the clamor, and had outlawed the playing of calliopes within three miles of the city.

At the other end of the promenade deck, more than a hundred feet away, the dance floor crawled with people. Bradfield's Orchestra—mandolins, fiddles, and a piano—warbled and pounded out a sprightly little martial rhythm on a small stage, trying to keep people's minds off the pitching of the ship. It was the kind of *rat-a-tat-tat* to which folks loved to box-step. Scores of passengers now danced to it despite the boat's rocking motions.

On the cabin deck one level down, the gentle yet constant

pitching back and forth made movement somewhat difficult. Ladies clad in their fancy dresses were growing weary of being elbowed. Some of the children were taking tumbles. Against the starboard wall, the Aanstads watched it all with quiet trepidation.

"This boat feels top-heavy to me," Marianne said again, almost to herself as she held her youngest on her lap.

No one answered her.

Olaf, sitting a few feet away, looked as though he could use a sip of aquavit. He had shoved the picnic basket under his chair, and now steadied himself against the bulwarks with the side of his leg each time the floor leaned.

Bobbie, who was sitting between her uncle and mother, could think of nothing to say. What *could* she say? The ship's crew knew what they were doing. If the boat rocked a little bit, that's what boats did. The Western Electric people had gone on this same journey just last year. On this same boat. There was no reason for Bobbie to worry.

No reason at all.

Moments later, the floor tilted again toward the river. The sound of clanking bottles drifted up from the deck below them, and there was something else—a thudding sound. The Aanstads felt their chairs scoot toward port a little bit. The picnic basket slid out from under Olaf's chair. Olaf grabbed it before it got away, and braced himself.

"Oh my," someone murmured.

The ship slowly rocked back toward the dock, and everybody let out a sigh of relief. Bobbie's stomach remained clenched.

Maybe that was as bad as it was going to get, Bobbie thought. Maybe the crew had finally gotten things under control. Maybe the Aanstads could relax now and enjoy themselves. Bobbie took a deep breath and tried to swallow the butterflies fluttering up from her tummy. *Relax, there is nothing to worry about.*

* * *

THE *EASTLAND* did have stability problems, and when a survey was later taken of the years prior to that fateful morning, a stunning procession of misadventures was revealed.

In July 1903, as she was putting about in the Chicago River just west of the Wells Street bridge, her stern struck the tug *George W. Gardner*, swamping the smaller boat and causing the dismissal of the *Eastland*'s original captain, John Pereue.

Complaints of seasickness became common occurrences on cross-lake runs. A subsequent captain, Frank Hamilton, stated in his notes that the *Eastland* had difficulty in northerly and easterly winds on outbound journeys, on both Lake Michigan and Lake Erie. It was not a passenger-friendly craft. Experts believed that such boats were ill-suited for excursions. "The owners and inspectors of these boats are careful, that is, careful to comply with loading, equipment, et cetera," a marine engineer once told the *Tribune*. "The trouble is, we have no laws properly directed. A boat like the *Eastland* should not be used for excursion purposes. It should carry freight in its hold."

In a post-disaster article the *Tribune* noted: "The government regulations for lake steamers cover 102 pages. 53 pages minutely prescribe the construction of boilers down to the smallest bolt. There is not a single reference to stability. There is not a single specified requirement to prevent a vessel from turning over. Even ballast is not mentioned."

In the summer of 1904, a few miles off the shore of South Haven, Michigan, running at full speed, the ship, for no apparent reason began to list toward the port side. The lean reached 15 degrees, and the captain ordered ballasts filled to correct the list. A few minutes later, the ship pitched back to starboard, much more severely—as much as 30 to 40 degrees—and the captain started ordering passengers to move away from the starboard side of the upper deck. The problem eventually corrected itself, but not before putting the fear of God into many of the passengers and crew members.

In the aftermath of the incident, the maximum capacity allowed by law for the *Eastland* was reduced from 3,300 passengers to 2,800.

Problems developed during or immediately after loading or unloading. Like a bicycle which is unstable when it's standing still, the *Eastland* reached stability only while under way. None of these issues fazed the owners, who proceeded with major renovations in order to increase her capacity. They removed the cabins from the promenade deck, replacing them with an expanded "social" room that would better serve day-trippers. They added a few toilets, as well as a second staircase connecting the main deck with the cabin deck above. More lifeboats went in. And applications were made to raise the capacity.

The maximum number was increased to 2,907.

That September, while in dry dock at the southern tip of Goose Island, the ship was repainted. The new *Eastland*, now clad all in white, appeared almost ghostly on its foggy morning jaunts across the lake.

THE SUMMER of 1906 saw another unexplained incident. On a return trip from South Haven, cruising down the Chicago River with full capacity (over 2900 passengers), the ship began to lean toward starboard. Eventually the ship righted herself, but the event drew several official complaints. The U.S. government sent an investigator to Chicago to look into the incident, and the agent advised that the ship's maximum passenger capacity should be reduced. Thus, the number was officially lowered by more than 500, from 2,907 to 2,400.

The capacity began to seesaw, reflecting the greed and ambition of not only the owners but the excursion industry as a whole.

In 1909, a consortium of investors that became known as the Eastland Navigation Company purchased the boat from the Michigan Steamship Company. One of the principals in the new company voted against the acquisition of the *Eastland* on the basis of gossip whispered among Great Lakes operators.

The ship had gained a reputation among many insiders as a "cranky" boat. Others called her "tender," referring to her instability during loading. In addition to this, public sentiment had turned against the excursion industry. "Many women and children will someday pay the tragic penalty of overcrowded boats," wrote Chicago's superintendent of schools in 1909. "It is only a question of time when there will be a disaster on one of these excursion boats that will stagger Chicago."

The remaining staterooms on the *Eastland*'s cabin level were torn out in 1910 in favor of "public" areas for excursionists. In a desperate attempt to counteract some of the vessel's bad publicity, the *Eastland*'s owners placed the following notice in the *Cleveland Plain Dealer*:

$5,000 REWARD

The Steamer Eastland is built entirely of steel and is ocean type in construction. Her water compartments when filled carry 800 tons of ballast. She is 269 feet long, has a beam of 36 feet and draws 14 feet of water. She has twin screws, driven by two powerful triple expansion engines, supplied with steam from four Scotch boilers.

The material she is built of, the type of her construction, together with the power in her hold, makes her the staunchest, fastest and safest boat devoted to pleasure on the Great Lakes.

All this is well known to people acquainted with marine matters. But there are thousands of people who know absolutely nothing about boats, the rules and regulations for their running, and inspection and licensing of the same by the US government.

In the hope of influencing this class of people, there have been put into circulation stories to the effect that the Steamer Eastland is not safe.

Therefore, in justice to ourselves and in fairness to the 40,000 people that have enjoyed themselves during the past four seasons on this palatial craft (and that without a single mishap), we offer the above reward to any person that will bring forth a naval engineer, a marine engineer, a shipbuilder, or anyone qualified to pass on the merits of a ship who will say that the Steamer Eastland is not a seaworthy ship, or that she would not ride out any storm or weather any condition that can arise on either lake or ocean.

CHAPTER FIVE

Sladkey's Leap

ON HER MAIDEN VOYAGE from Southhampton, England, to New York City, the British White Star Lines luxury liner RMS *Titanic* struck an iceberg, rupturing five of its watertight compartments and causing irreparable damage to its hull. The ship sank in less than three hours, killing nearly 1,500 of the 2,224 people on board, many wealthy celebrities and socialites among the dead.

Countless inquests, articles, books, films, plays, and documentaries followed the *Titanic* disaster, keeping the subject alive throughout the twentieth century and well into the twenty-first. But as early as 1912, the aftermath of this tragedy proved to be a critical factor in the events leading up to the *Eastland* incident.

In December 1913, in London, civic leaders held the first annual meeting of the International Conference on Safety of Life at Sea. Attendees included politicians, scientists, educators, naval engineers, and representatives of seamen's unions. One of the most urgent issues of the day, in light of the *Titanic* disaster, concerned the minimum number of lifeboats required by international maritime law.

Until then, naval architects had recommended that ships be equipped with a certain number of lifeboats allowing for optimum weight and stability. A ship filled to its maximum passenger capacity might not be equipped with a lifeboat space for *every* passenger. In the event of catastrophic failure, however, alternative life-saving methods such as belts and vests served those unable to find space on a lifeboat.

On its sole voyage, the RMS *Titanic* carried forty-eight lifebuoys, fourteen lifeboats, two emergency cutters and four collapsible rafts. As historian George Hilton has noted, this exceeded the minimum requirements of the day, but clearly it did not provide a space on a lifeboat for each passenger and crewmember. And because the *Titanic*'s impact with the iceberg did not immediately kill anyone, this shortage of lifeboat space became a dramatic and tragic element of the sinking.

The Conference on Safety of Life at Sea set about to remedy this deficiency. Around the world, a hue and cry was raised in newspaper editorials, on floors of senates, in houses of parliament, and among the general populace. The resulting fervor became known as the "Boats-for-All" movement, an early example of misguided political correctness run amuck. From then on, vessels began to take on more lifeboats than they could handle.

One of the more reluctant participants of the London conference foresaw tragic consequences. Dr. Herbert Sadler, a professor of naval architecture and marine engineering at the University of Michigan, believed that the extra lifeboats would make ships top-heavy. In 1916, a year after the *Eastland* disaster, Dr. Sadler testified in the criminal proceedings surrounding the incident, and speculated that stacking the upper decks of the *Eastland* with too many lifeboats contributed to the tragedy.

AT PRECISELY seven-seventeen on that July morning in 1915, the Sindelar family, and many like them, knew nothing of the dangers connected to the *Titanic*.

In the *Eastland*'s main deck area—the deck closest to the water, where the largest group of passengers was assembled—the Sindelars chatted idly with each other, commenting amiably on the rocking of the ship. Albert and George, Jr., scurried through the clustered passengers while Josephine chased down little William. Passengers were still boarding at a profuse rate, despite the fact that the ship was nearing capacity. The gangplanks kept creaking noisily as picnickers shuffled across the weathered timbers and onto the rocking boat.

At the forward end of the main deck, a huge lunch counter bustled with activity, churning out meals and snacks for hungry passengers. Candy sellers staggered along with portable displays, hawking assorted taffies in various fruit and spice flavors—19 cents for a one-pound box—as well as milk chocolates and peanut butter crisps. In the aft area of the deck, near the stairs, a cash bar sold bottles of pop and beer out of a massive refrigerator. Chicago was a beer-drinking town: 7 million bottles were consumed each year, and the *Eastland*'s bar was one of the most popular areas on board the boat.

Ed Bartlett and Le Roy Bennet, a pair of burly, jovial fellows who had been friends for twenty-plus years, tended the bar. Semi-professional boxers in their youth, the men still bore the scars of pugilism on their chiseled faces and big, calloused hands. The bartenders' affection for each other was apparent as they poured drinks or pinched toddlers' cheeks. The two men had been inseparable since 1895, when they faced off in the ring at George Kerwin's Saloon. Bartlett and Bennet had battled to exhaustion that night, until the fight was called as a draw, neither man ever besting the other. An ironclad friendship forged itself that night, and the two bartenders worked side by side ever since.

The job on the *Eastland* was a plum assignment for the fighters. They loved kids, they loved their work, and it's very likely that they took notice of the sweet-faced Sindelar children that July morning. But as the minutes ticked away, and the bottles started shifting, the bartenders lost their grins. The refrigerator began to groan with each rocking motion as though it might start sliding across the hardwood.

UNBEKNOWN TO the bartenders or the majority of the passengers, an independent maritime engineer based in Chicago named John Devereux York had written a letter in 1913 to U.S. government inspectors, reaching the steamship inspection agency at a time when the world was still reeling from the *Titanic* tragedy, and the International Conference on Safety of Life at Sea was trying to put things right overseas.

York had inspected the *Eastland* on several occasions and, due to a lack of keel, which caused instability when overloaded, found it to be unsafe. York very simply stated: "You are aware of the condition of the S.S. *Eastland*, and unless structural defects are remedied to prevent listing, there may be a serious accident."

Such rumblings did nothing to deter the ambition of the St. Joseph–Chicago Steamship Company.

After the *Titanic* disaster, most ships sailing American waterways saw their capacities reduced substantially. The *Eastland*'s was slashed to 2,000, but there were easy methods of regaining capacity. In the spring of 1915, Captain Pedersen paid a visit to the boat's owner, William Hull, general manager of St. Joseph–Chicago Steamship Company.

"Mr. Hull," Pedersen announced with his trademark brusqueness, "if we get three rafts of twenty-five-person capacity, and one of fifty, we can get a license for 2,570 people."

Hull thought it over for a few days. Lifeboats required a major expenditure, but he decided to spend the money. The company purchased the additional lifeboats, then consulted the government inspector in order to get official approval for increased capacity. Since the inspector, Robert Reid, was related by marriage to the *Eastland*'s chief engineer, the press made a great deal after the disaster of Reid's alleged conflicts of interest. But the problems with the *Eastland* were far more institutional than nepotism involving two individuals.

"She was not very profitable," Walter Steele, the steamship company treasurer, explained to the coroner's jury after the tragedy. Steele went on to explain that issues of safety and seaworthiness played minor roles in company decisions. When asked if the company had considered safety matters when they acquired the *Eastland*, Steele simply replied: "No, only the matter of profit."

An elaborate renovation of the forward dining room on the cabin level in 1914 added to the boat's increasingly dangerous profile. Years of spilled drinks during rocky journeys across the lakes had started to rot away the floorboards under the linoleum. In preparation for the upcoming season, the owners ripped up all the old warped hardwood and replaced it with two inches of concrete. They also laid a new layer of cement near the aft gangway. Accordingly, the ship took on an extra fifteen to twenty tons of weight.

In addition to the added weight of the concrete floors, eleven lifeboats and thirty-seven rafts now occupied the topmost deck, as well as 2,500 life preservers, each weighing up to six pounds, stored throughout the upper levels. To make matters worse on that July morning, these life preservers lay in huge wooden containers—sealed and securely locked.

AT EXACTLY nineteen minutes after seven, down in the engine room, Joe Erickson called out to his assistants, Fred Snow and Charlie Silvernail: "Boys, I believe we're getting her!"

Erickson felt the ship righting herself as the water rushed into the huge starboard ballast tanks beneath his boots, the manifold making a strangling, gurgling noise.

The *Eastland* slowly returned to zero degrees, which is where she belonged, and Erickson breathed a sigh of relief, wiping oily sweat from his brow. He glanced at the Chadburn, expecting to see the Stand-by order coming down from the bridge any second now.

At that precise moment, Harbormaster Adam Weckler was standing on the dock in the steel grey drizzle, watching the ship straighten up. The heavy-jowled man kept wringing his hands. Weckler was a perfectionist who did not like anomalies like listing boats. He looked up at the *Eastland*'s hurricane deck, and saw hundreds of people up there, huddling under parasols and umbrellas, laughing and carrying on as though nothing were wrong. Glancing up at the bridge, Weckler saw the stout Norwegian captain standing in the mist, chewing his cigar, waiting for the signal.

"Cap!" Weckler called out, his voice barely concealing his reluctance. "When you're ready! You can have the bridge any time you want it!"

Thirty feet to the east, where the tugboat *Kenosha* sat idling near the dock, Captain John O'Meara turned on his heel and went inside his pilot house. The baritone sound of an engine burbling filled the air suddenly as the *Kenosha* prepared to take the slack out of its massive tow line connected to the *Eastland*'s bow.

Up on the *Eastland*'s bridge, Pedersen turned to his first mate, Del Fisher, and gave the Stand-by order (meaning, in Great Lakes protocol, to prepare to cast off). Fisher wheeled around, went inside the cluttered pilot house and gripped the handle of the Chadburn. WHAM! Fisher slammed the indicator down to Stand-by. The signal was telegraphed down through the snaking network of cable (very possibly cable manufactured by Western Electric) into the dark bowels of the engine room.

CLANG!

The chief engineer saw the order click behind the filthy glass of his Chadburn, and made preparations for departure, hollering orders at Peter Erickson. Ash and sparks jumped as the oiler prepped the boilers.

A few feet away, crumpled on the floor of the engine room, covered in so much grease it was practically illegible, lay an old forgotten placard. It said SAFETY FIRST, UNITED STATES STEAMBOAT INSPECTION SERVICE, and beneath that, in equally large letters, TAKE NO CHANCES.

THE SHIP had ten minutes to live.

Bobbie Aanstad, perched on a chair in the cabin area, and swaying slightly to the muffled rhythms coming through the ceiling, wished she were up there dancing with one of the cute Western Electric office boys. She had no idea that the boat was about to careen. . . .

Nor did George Sindelar, who was keeping watch on his kids down in the main deck, chasing little William through the forest of taffeta dresses and woolen slacks. . . .

Nor did any of the other picnickers lined up at the other ships. . . .

Nor did any of the passers-by on Clark Street or South Water Street in their delivery trucks, broughams and horsecars. . . .

To all of them, it was just another Saturday morning.

AT SEVEN-TWENTY the customs agents snapped a chain across the loading threshold at the stern of the *Eastland*, near the huge gangway doors, halting any more passengers from boarding. The ship had reached its passenger-carrying capacity: 2,500 souls.

Inside the gangway, muscular deckhands appeared in the shadows. Biceps flexed. Gnarled hands clutched at the edges of the gangplanks and pulled the timber inside the ship.

On the dock, a flood of straw hats and parasols shifted toward the east, moving all as one toward the S.S. *Roosevelt*, moored on the other side of the Clark Street bridge. A total of four other steamships were scheduled to follow the *Eastland* that morning at half-hour intervals, with a fifth as a stand-by. Eyewitness accounts describe the picnickers moving in a fairly orderly, albeit noisy, fashion. A slight confusion ran through the crowds due to the sheer numbers involved, but people generally behaved well and did as they were directed.

There were exceptions.

One picnicker reached the *Eastland*'s stern gangway just as the planks were drawn in. E. W. Sladkey, a foreman in Western Electric's printing department, stood there, feeling dejected for a moment, staring sadly at the giant steel ship. Then he looked up at the aft promenade walkway, and saw a group of friends waving down to him, urging him to hop on board. With a running start, Sladkey vaulted across the water onto the gangway and stumbled aboard. Eluding angry deckhands, he made his way up to his party.

Sladkey raised the passenger count to 2,501.

ALMOST ON CUE with Sladkey's leap, the *Eastland* again began slowly to lean toward the river as though the one additional passenger had irrevocably thrown the boat off balance.

Taking his place at the aft railing on the promenade level, Sladkey noticed something odd. The majority of passengers up there had gathered on the starboard side of the boat. Many were still outside in the rain, leaning over the railing, calling down to their friends. But the boat was starting to lean toward the *river* side, which made no sense to Sladkey. Shouldn't the ship be canting toward the dock, that is, leaning toward the side which currently bore the most weight?

Down on the dock Harbormaster Weckler turned away from the *Eastland* and started back toward Clark Street. All at once he saw out of the corner of his eye the ship resuming its lean. He spun around and squinted for a better view. What the hell was going on? He wiped moisture from his face and stood and watched, his gut tightening.

The boat looked overloaded to Weckler, and seemed also to be having ballast problems. Weckler was not the sort of man to make such judgments lightly. He had worked for more than six years for the U.S. Navy shipyard at Cavite, building boats, and later had owned his own shipbuilding business, Weckler Boat Company.

He knew a cranky vessel when he saw one.

Somebody hollered something.

Weckler glanced across the crowded wharf and saw a dock-hand in dungarees pushing his way through the crowd, moving toward the *Eastland*'s stern. It was Charles Lasser, a baggage handler for the Chicago and South Haven Line. Lasser reached the piling and fiddled with the mooring line, slipping it off the cleat.

"Wait a moment!" Weckler cried out, shoving his way toward Lasser.

Lasser had already removed the mooring line and was tossing it across the water to a deckhand stationed inside the *Eastland*'s aft gangway. The deckhand caught the rope and drew it into the ship's hold. Lasser looked up. A confused frown crossed his face. He turned, then strode along the dock until he saw Weckler coming toward him. "Mornin' sir! Which one shall I cast off next?"

"No lines!" Weckler barked. "Leave that line fast!"

Lasser froze.

Weckler turned and made his way back toward the *Eastland*'s bow, his fists clenched, until he was within earshot of the bridge. He looked up into the drizzling sky and saw Pedersen pacing across the slanted deck in front of the pilot house. The boat gently leaned to port. Maybe 10 degrees, perhaps a little more.

Cupping his hands around his mouth, Weckler yelled up at the ship's master: "I told you to trim her up!"

Pedersen looked down at the harbormaster and made a gesture with his hands. Later, during testimony, Weckler described the gesture to mean *I'm trimming her as fast as I can.* Judging from the captain's reputation, as well as his behavior over the next few hours, the gesture probably was delivered with some degree of irritation. Weckler had scolded Pedersen before. The previous year, the harbormaster had warned the captain that it was better to trim his boat before casting off, not only for the passengers, but because the *Eastland* had a bad reputation.

"Cap, I will not allow you to cast off," Weckler finally shouted above the noise and the mists, "until you have this boat trimmed!"

The captain assured him he was doing just that.

THE LEAN WORSENED.

Down in the engine room, the sweaty crew members started gripping the edges of bulwark in order to steady themselves—innate behavior for seasoned sailors. A cup of coffee slipped off a shelf. Joe Erickson heard the sound and glanced across the grease-spackled room. Liquid ran across the slatted floor. Troubling noises came from above. Sounds of glass breaking, and worse: the dwindling of voices, the hushing of passengers. For some reason, those diminishing voices worried the chief engineer.

Erickson rushed over to the port side of the room and looked up. He could see water coming into the main deck through a scupper. He whirled toward his men. "Stop the engines! ALL STOP NOW!"

Outside the ship, few onlookers noticed the cessation of black smoke plumes. Few heard the halting of the giant steam turbines. Many of those present were far more interested in the leaning. Bridge tenders, warehouse men, people on their way to work, they all paused to see how far the ship would lean.

Many of these onlookers tried to offer opinions to the captain, who was clearly visible up on the forward promenade deck, standing on the starboard side by his pilot house, hand casually on the rail.

He ignored most of the unsolicited advice.

INSIDE THE CROWDED main deck, as the angle of the floor reached roughly 20 degrees, the aft refrigerator suddenly tipped over.

The massive crash rang out across the crowd, accompanied by the crunch of hundreds of brown bottles shattering against the floor. Mothers instinctively shielded their babies, fathers lunged for their errant children. The two bartenders, Bartlett and Bennet, both possessing speed and strength, managed to keep passengers clear of broken glass.

Amazingly, the fallen refrigerator did not create a panic. Most passengers figured that they were on a ship, after all, and these things must happen once in a while. George and Josephine Sindelar struggled to keep their kids away from the open hatches, but it wasn't easy. Gravity tugged at the crowd. Some of the women had to hold up the hems of their skirts in order to avoid getting wet.

Charlie Silvernail, the assistant engineer, appeared in the forward area of the ship, near the baggage room, alarming a few of the more tender spirits. Unlike the formal uniformed personnel—the wait staff, the purser, the stewards—Charlie Silvernail bore the grime of the ship's bowels on his clothes and his face. He made an effort to appear composed and unruffled as he executed his orders, which had come only moments earlier from Chief Erickson.

"Ladies and gents!" he called out. "If you would please move to the starboard side of the boat!"

The passengers complied without panic. The inexplicable lean continued.

CHAPTER SIX

The Water Is Coming In!

ON THE OTHER SIDE of the Clark Street bridge, while the *Eastland* continued its languid rocking, the band on the upper deck of the S.S. *Theodore Roosevelt*, sensing the need to calm nerves, launched into one of the more popular songs of the day. Many of the picnickers present that morning, especially those of Irish descent, recognized the cheerful, bouncy melody of "I'm On My Way to Dear Old Dublin Bay."

Written in the nineteenth century, the song tells the story of a soldier on furlough, on his way home to marry his sweetheart. On a deeper level, to an Irishman, the song will always be about coming home to one's destiny:

> *Goodbye! I'm on my way*
> *To dear old Dublin Bay*
> *That's why I'm feelin' gay*
> *For oh! I know sweet Molly-O*
> *My colleen, fair to see,*
> *Is waitin' there for me!*
>
> *Her heart with love a-bubblin'*
> *On Dublin Bay!*

The song played on, over the frenzied minutes, as confusion reigned along the wharf, and laughter turned to silence 200 feet away on the decks of the *Eastland*.

"WATER IS COMING IN!"

The sound of a young girl's voice rang out through the pungent air of the *Eastland*'s main deck as the ship continued to lean. The crowd surged backward, away from the open gangways. People stepped on each other's fine polished footwear. Women clutched at their babies. The Sindelars were forced against the port-side wall as the water rippled over their shoes.

Down in the engine room, water streamed into the works, fizzing and hissing across white-hot housing. Fred Snow acted on instinct. He turned and grasped a rusty lever, shoving it back until a whistle started sounding. A high-pitched alarm that normally would have straightened the spines of most veteran crewmembers, the "Modoc" whistle was a standard warning alarm for Great Lakes vessels. The warning went unheeded by most of the *Eastland*'s crew.

The lean halted.

At exactly seven-twenty-five, according to Erickson's post-disaster testimony, the lean reversed its direction. Up on the decks, chairs scooted back to their original positions. Water flowed back out the gangways. Muscles relaxed as the boat pitched back to starboard, until she sat at a fairly even keel. The temporary trim gave all those present a false sense of security. Sighs of collective relief passed through the passengers on all decks.

On the cabin deck, Bobbie Aanstad's heart would not stop thumping. Glances passed among Bobbie, Uncle Olaf, and Marianne. Even Solveig sensed the uneasiness of the calm. Across the crowded cabin deck women straightened their dresses, adjusted their bonnets, and settled back in their chairs. The playful vigor had gone out of the crowd.

61

The musicians on the promenade deck picked up fallen music stands, replaced scattered pages of music, and the pianist kicked off a soothing ragtime instrumental, as dancers made half-hearted attempts at continuing their box steps. Out on the walkway, those hearty picnickers who were braving the drizzle kept their white-knuckle grips on the rail.

The 500 or so who were on the hurricane deck watched as Captain Pedersen strode confidently along the starboard walkway, his stout, paunchy physique clad in a rain slicker, his huge hands clenched. He looked as though he wanted to will the ship out of that infernal harbor with his own neck muscles. He had given the Stand-by, the ship had been trimmed, and by the grace of God he was going to get that temperamental steel lady moving if it killed him. And no fey little harbormaster was going to keep him from his appointed departure.

Somewhere three levels down, on the slickened floorboards of the main deck, George and Josephine Sindelar huddled against the port wall with their children. At that point, they simply waited and prayed that the ship would put out into the lake without further ado. The casual, devil-may-care nature of some of the other passengers probably did much to ease the Bohemian family's nerves. Mrs. Sindelar held on tightly to her five-year-old. The beautiful turnip watch dangled from Josephine's neck, the minute hand reaching twenty-seven past seven—the exact moment, according to the ship's logs, that the *Eastland* began its final deadly pitch toward the river.

MOTION PICTURE audiences in 1915 first witnessed the effect of "slow motion" in *The Birth of a Nation*. An effect achieved by running film through a camera at a faster-than-normal rate, then projecting it at normal speed, slow motion gives the impression of a dream, the feeling that events are suspended in time. The people in and around the *Eastland* that morning experienced something akin to slow motion. Various eyewitness accounts describe that last, fatal lean as a slow yet inexorable list toward the river, slow enough to allow the panic to build gradually.

The first minute or so aroused only irritated groans from the crowd. Men held onto their straw hats. Families reached for their picnic baskets. Some of the women on the main deck started sliding across the hardwood, their high-heeled Colonials offering haphazard purchase. Many laughed in spite of their nervous tension. It all still seemed like a game. Even Bobbie Aanstad, on the starboard side of the cabin deck, found it all a little ridiculous.

On the promenade deck, members of the orchestra literally dug in their heels in order to brace themselves and keep playing. "The crowd had so encroached on the *Eastland*'s dance floor," wrote historian George Hilton, "that dancing had become impossible." Bottles and cups slid back and forth across most of the unoccupied floor, especially on the lower decks where the food services were based.

Lower still, among the sparks and cinders and ash, the denizens of the engine room tried desperately to get enough water in the starboard tanks to return the boat to an even keel. Drenched in sweat and grime, Erickson knew that the Stand-by order had been given, and that meant that Pedersen wanted to cast off. But the ship acted as though she had a mind of her own. And that was bad for Erickson. The ship's stability was solely the responsibility of the engineering department. There was no one else to blame. Erickson knew this. Pedersen knew this. But the vessel was being extra-cranky that day. Erickson thought, *The number 4 and 5 tanks are not filling!* The question must have shrieked in the Chief Engineer's brain: *What is the problem with number 4 and 5?!*

JOSEPH LYNN, an assistant to the harbormaster, had formulated one possible answer to the ballast tank problem. Standing near the base of the LaSalle Street steps, he gazed with alarm at the surface of the water near the *Eastland*'s stern. "I noticed bubbling in the river," he reported later. "Which would indicate the bottom of the river was being disturbed by something."

The intake valve that fed the ballast tanks on the *Eastland* was located eight feet below water level. Many believe that the valve was clogged with silt that morning, preventing the ballast tanks from filling. The valve had a history of trouble. It had frozen during the winter of 1914, and was vulnerable to shallow-water maneuvers. This could well explain Erickson's inability to trim the ship.

Lynn looked up and saw the *Eastland*'s tilt exceed 20 degrees, and suddenly felt adrenaline jolt through his veins. He turned and hurried across the dock, shoving people aside, frantically searching for his boss.

He found Captain Adam "Ad" Weckler near the Clark Street stairway. "Ad! Ad!" Lynn shouted breathlessly. "The boat is going over! We gotta get off the dock! If she goes, we're going with her!"

Weckler ordered Lynn to get to a telephone and call the Coast Guard immediately.

Lynn obliged at a running clip.

THE LEAN REACHED 25 degrees to port. On the main deck water roared into the ship through the gangways. Josephine Sindelar gasped and clutched at William. The crowd surged backward once again, away from the open doors. But still, nobody panicked. There were nervous giggles. Crying babies. A few yelps. People stepped on each other's heels. Baskets and umbrellas slid toward the hatchways, then splashed into the filthy river. Still, nobody was truly panicking.

Water was rippling over the seams of the floor, coursing down the bulwarks, pouring into the boiler rooms and coal bunkers below.

The pitch slowly worsened.

In the engine room, Fred Snow grabbed a moldering conduit to steady himself as gravity tugged the room to port. Wrenches and gaskets slipped off shelves. Dirty steam wafted through the air from the rapid evaporation. Snow heard the shouts of oilers and stokers in the forward boiler room, yelling something about the ship being doomed, and it was time to abandon her.

Something cold and oily snaked around Snow's ankle, and he looked down. The river was inside the engine room. The list had crossed over into catastrophic failure. The ship could not correct herself. At that moment, seven-twenty-nine, Fred Snow made a snap decision.

It was time to get off the boat.

Up on the hurricane deck, the mist blew across hundreds of hapless passengers who were pressed against the port railing as the lean reached 30 degrees. A steady stream of shouts spewed up from onlookers positioned on the docks and the bridges nearby, pouring out also from those staring out of windows and truck cabs.

Out of the chaos: "Folks! Please move to the starboard rail!"

First mate, Del Fisher, stood on a companionway near the bridge, holding onto the rail. He motioned wildly with his free arm at the dockside rail, which was rising up into the sky. "FOLKS, PLEASE MOVE TO THE STARBOARD RAIL!!"

It was impossible to comply. The angle of the list had reached 33 degrees, and the deck was slick from the build-up of moisture. A few desperate souls tried to scuttle up the inclining floor but it was futile. Straw hats flipped up into the wind. Umbrellas sprang inside-out.

Most of the panic seemed now to be coming from the dock, and across the river, and along the neighboring storefronts. "I began to get kind of uneasy," explained Captain O'Meara, who was waiting on the tug *Kenosha* directly in front of the *Eastland*.

"The signal wasn't coming; the captain hadn't worked his stern out."

Another onlooker, a wizened Italian street-vendor named Mike Javanco, saw disaster coming. The old man pulled his vegetable truck over to the side of the Clark Street bridge at the moment the *Eastland*'s lean reached 35 degrees. Maybe it was Javanco's old-world fatalism or Catholic-fueled superstition, but whatever the reason, Javanco lurched out of his truck-cab and rushed to the edge of the bridge overlooking the listing ship, waving his arthritic hands. "Get off!" he bellowed in his thick accent. "Da boat's turnin' over!"

Some of the passengers on the *Eastland*'s hurricane deck heard the warning. "Go on, dago!" one of them yelled with a smirk. "You're crazy!"

A SLIGHT PAUSE at that point: at about 35 degrees. It was as though suddenly the ship had balked. As though she had abruptly changed her mind about going over.

On the promenade deck, straining against the severe tilt, Bradfield's Orchestra continued playing cheerful ragtime music. The sound entranced many, like the droning of a snake charmer.

The passengers remained amazingly tranquil, their voices chattering nervously over the music. One of the picnickers, a slender young man named Willie Guenther, crouched behind the piano, holding onto a balustrade, listening intently to the orchestra. Willie was an avid mandolin player and, transported by the music, danger of capsizing was the last thing on his mind.

The passengers were not the only ones oblivious to the imminent catastrophe. Despite the mass exodus of the engine room personnel, most of the seasoned steamship men present still felt confident that the boat would right herself, especially in light of the sudden hesitation. "I was really of the opinion that she would recover," O'Meara admitted later, when asked about that strange moment of hesitation in the *Eastland*'s lean. "Boats will do that. They will go over a certain distance and find a buoyancy."

In the *Eastland*'s case, it was the last chance to get off the boat.

Nobody took advantage of it.

CHAPTER SEVEN

On the Death Stairs

ACCORDING TO Chief Engineer Erickson's engine room log, the *Eastland* resumed its final rolling motion at some point before seven-thirty. In post-disaster testimony, chronologies differed wildly, but most witnesses agreed on one thing: when the momentary pause ended, the mood on board shifted dramatically.

At 45 degrees, Bradfield's Orchestra stopped playing in the middle of a note. Chairs slid out from under the musicians. Music stands tumbled across the deck. Voices halted as though a switch had been flipped. The silence had an uncanny quality, like a collective inhalation before a scream. Passengers held onto the nearest stationary object, or each other, as the floor plunged. Those who had nothing to hold onto went sliding.

On the main deck, dishes slipped off pantry shelves, crashing to the floor. Tumblers and bottles shattered like mortar fire. The noise struck many passengers dumb as they struggled to stay upright on the tilting floor. The stewards and pantry men all made mad dashes for the companionway.

This pattern of behavior repeated itself numerous times over the next horrible moments: the crew, knowing exactly how to get off the doomed vessel, left the stricken, helpless passengers to fend for themselves.

ON THE DOCKS the silence stretched, an eerie, horrifying lack of noise as the massive ship leaned farther. "There was a sudden hush," reported one onlooker. "All sounds of merriment had ceased. Even as the boat keeled well over, and it was seen that the catastrophe could not be averted, the stillness remained intense."

Aboard the *Eastland*, horror-stricken passengers remained mute as the listing reached 50 degrees. On the promenade level, where only seconds earlier the orchestra had been playing "Maple Leaf Rag," the piano began to slide. Tangles of people surged to get out of the way. Still crouched against the balustrade, young Willie Guenther, music enthusiast, had no time to move. The piano plowed into the starboard wall, crushing the young man, killing him instantly, an event that happened so quickly, very few even noticed it.

On the crowded cabin level, Bobbie Aanstad grabbed her younger sister and held onto the starboard banister. Something powerful began to stir in Bobbie at that moment, a terror that was beyond her ability to put into words, seizing her as she clutched at Solveig. Marianne had a vice-grip on the nine-year-old as well, and chances were that Uncle Olaf had a hold of Marianne as the boat slowly rotated toward oblivion.

"The panic was now universal," Hilton has reported. "The inflow of water and the worsening distribution of the weight of the passengers accelerated the movement of the ship to port, and she went into the river quickly, in not more than two minutes."

For those on board the *Eastland*, those two minutes encompassed an eternity. Like a bad dream in which all movement is retarded into torturously slow motion, the passengers lunged into awkward stampedes across the slippery incline toward the nearest hatch, companionway, or staircase. The strong trampled the weak. Well-dressed gentlemen trod over fallen ladies in their Sunday attire. Babies slipped from their mothers' arms and went sliding toward open gangways.

The screaming started then.

CLINGING TO a davit on the main level, a deckhand named Harry Miller heard the collective cry. Miller recalled later: "My mate and me heard them hollering on the deck around us and at first we thought they were shouting as usual to their friends on the dock. Soon we knew they were scared. So we hollered to them to climb the stairways to the upper deck."

The boat reached a list of 70 degrees. Nearly a thousand people, half of them women and children, made a mad lunge toward the stairs, clutching at anything that was nailed down, grabbing at the hems of skirts and coats and suits. Grown men started shrieking; women sobbed as they scuttled up the wet floor toward daylight.

Engulfed in the throng, the Sindelars scrambled for the grand staircase that lay just beyond their reach near the bar in the rear. Bodies crushed inward from all sides. Yet the family continued struggling: George in the lead, dragging his sons by the collars; Josephine clutching little William and her daughters, pulling them up the slick floor. The noise crashed down on them. Hundreds of keening voices bounced off the steel walls.

George made it to the staircase, which was already full of people. He tried to pull his boys through the bottleneck of frantic passengers, but it was futile. Bodies clogged the stairs. A magnificent piece of old-world craftsmanship by any standard, the staircase spanned ten feet at the base, with burnished mahogany risers and hand-carved newel posts. It was solidly built, stubborn enough to withstand incredible pressure from a desperate mob.

Josephine managed to reach George, and the entire family pushed its way upward.

"They jammed them going up," Miller recalled. "Women and children mostly, it looked like, in confusion, shouting, some of them crying."

The list reached 75 degrees.

AT THAT MOMENT on the hurricane deck, bracing himself against the starboard rail, Captain Pedersen lost his composure. The grizzled master of steamboats, the old leathery veteran, the unshakable rock, suddenly found himself going down with his ship. Temper flaring, panic turning to rage, he bellowed at the top of his lungs at one of the shipping company agents standing paralyzed down on the dock.

"FOR GOD'S SAKE OPEN UP YOUR GANGWAY!!"

The agent, a mild mannered gentleman named Martin Flatow, scurried toward the stern threshold. Hands shaking, he fumbled with the chain. Something splashed nearby. Then another splash. Flatow jerked.

Passengers had started leaping through the gangways—men in three-piece suits, women holding infants—all vaulting off the edges of the rising hatchways, diving through the narrow openings of half-doors. Crew members leapt off the foredeck and onto the dock. Their departure only hastened the capsizing. With each hairbreadth flight the starboard side lightened further, quickening the lean.

A rending noise pierced the chaos. On the dock near LaSalle Street, it sounded like the crack of thunder. One of the pilings had torn from the pier, the iron band snapping like a tinder stick.

THE EASTLAND'S port gangways plunged underwater as the lean worsened. The sounds inside the boat reached an incredible volume. "There was a roar and a scream," O'Meara recalled, "and a screeching of people."

The noise along the dock rose as well, as onlookers joined the passengers in their collective gasps and shrieks. All traffic stopped. On the upper deck of the *Roosevelt* people froze in place, the band halting in mid-song.

On the north side of the river, directly across from the *Eastland*'s berth, *Chicago Daily Tribune* photographer Mike Psaris stood behind his enormous wood-and-brass dry-plate field camera, and lined up a panoramic shot of the dock. The camera's trigger bulb gripped firmly in his right hand, Psaris prepared himself to capture the worst catastrophe in Chicago history as it occurred.

Objects plummeted into the river. Harry Miller, cowering inside a flooding gangway, saw a passenger go overboard. "A woman with a child in her arms jumped or fell off the rail into the water," he told the *New York Times*. "I jumped in after her to get her. In less than a second they began dropping in all around me. There must have been hundreds of them that jumped in. The water was thick with them. One hit me on the shoulders and drove me under."

The less fortunate found themselves trapped inside the ship as it made its final plunge.

THE INTERIOR of the *Eastland* changed suddenly, as if by the dark magic of a funhouse mirror. Floors became walls, portholes became skylights, and the gigantic influx of water turned the mahogany-trimmed rooms into sealed chambers worthy of Harry Houdini's worst nightmares.

The cabin deck erupted with water. Portholes gushed, and the shift in gravity tossed hundreds of well-dressed passengers of all ages and persuasions violently on top of each other.

"People were falling in the water all around us," Bobbie Aanstad remembered. Clutching her deck chair, she tried to avoid plunging into the knot of bodies and seething waters beneath her. "Everything seemed to give way, and my mother went down."

Bobbie's chair slipped out from under her, sending her sprawling to the floor. Adrenaline coursed through her as she clawed for the railing. Fueled by the sound of screaming and her Uncle Olaf yelling something that she couldn't quite understand, she grabbed at her chair in a futile attempt to hold onto *something*. It didn't do her much good: she slid across the hardwood deck, clutching the chair in her arms.

Bobbie slammed into a pile of other passengers who were charging toward the forward staircase. She cried out for her mother but her voice was swallowed up by the noise. She was thrown against a banister, and landing hard, she saw stars. Dizziness washed over her and threatened to take her down into unconsciousness. She fought to stay awake, and keep her head up.

Cool, greasy water coursed over her body, and in those frenzied moments, Bobbie Aanstad again felt adrenaline bolting up her spine. Call it survival instinct.

A POLICEMAN, John Lescher, scurried frantically up the weathered stairs near LaSalle Street. A member of the traffic squad, Lescher felt his heart racing as he vaulted the steps. He reached the top of the stairs and lunged across the stone threshold to an alarm box mounted on the corner of a building, nearly tearing the lid off it.

He slammed his hand down on the alarm, then stuck a whistle in his mouth and started madly blowing the whistle, unsure what good it would do.

INSIDE THE MAIN DECK, as the ship tipped 85 degrees and water crashed in, the doomed picnickers scrambled for air. Many eyewitness accounts, by rescuers, policemen, firefighters and divers, reported finding victims in each other's arms. Fathers and sons. Mothers and infants. Brothers, sisters. Friends. Neighbors. Coworkers. Captured in one last embrace, a final gesture of intimacy.

The Sindelars spent their final moments trapped on the main-cabin staircase—the "death stairs" as they came to be known—as the *Eastland* made its last rolling lurch into the river. At some point, George surely realized the seriousness of their situation, and a deeper resolve kicked in. The Sindelars were Freemasons, steeped in ritual, rites of passage, and symbolic gestures. George had always been proud of his membership. Even Josephine was active; she'd been in the Order of the Eastern Star for years. We will never know with any certainty, but Sindelar descendants believe that George and Josephine experienced a moment of purity, even peace, as death closed down on them.

"They were a very close-knit family," recalled Christine Harmon, a great-great-grand-niece. "They were a working-class, simple, loving family. They did everything together."

Crushed in the mob, their cries silenced by the explosion of water, the Sindelars faced eternity with their children pressed against them.

As the ship rolled over, First Mate Del Fisher, one of the few crewmen who remained until the last possible second, threw off his oilskin slicker and braced his foot around the rail. In that single horrible instant before the ship landed on its side, Fisher felt a tug on his arm and a pitiful cry behind him.

"HELP ME!"

He turned and saw a teenage girl howling with terror, her eyes blazing, her lovely crepe dress soaked and clinging to her. The moment hung suspended in time until Fisher finally acted.

"I grabbed her up in my arms," he told the coroner's jury only hours later. "And I pulled her over the rail with me, and we slid down the anchor, and that is the time she got over on beam."

* * *

PEDERSEN TIMED his escape perfectly. As the ship went over, he grabbed the starboard rail and casually hopped over the side, landing on the upended hull with a grunt. Evidently in all the excitement he had forgotten the cardinal rule among mariners that a captain always goes down with his ship.

He never even got his feet wet.

THE ENTIRE RIVERFRONT gasped in unison as the *Eastland* landed on its side with a muffled, faint thud—as though someone had simply jostled a gargantuan box full of glass. Those present couldn't believe their eyes or their ears.

"The boat just turned over like an egg in the water," one policeman reported. "Didn't even make a splash."

STANDING ON the opposite side of the river, in full view of the shocking spectacle, *Tribune* photographer Mike Psaris stood poised behind his camera, staring at the massive overturned ship, the broken railing, the piano floating on the currents, and all the arms flailing on the surface of the filthy water. It was all so horrible that Psaris, a veteran photographer who had seen it all and shot it all, could not even move a finger to take the picture.

＊

PART 2

Into Eternity

Every death, even the cruellest death,
Drowns in the total indifference of nature
Nature herself would watch unmoved,
If we destroyed the entire human race.

—Peter Weiss, *Marat/Sade*

＊

CHAPTER EIGHT

Down and Down

POLICEMEN ran for the nearest call boxes. *Eastland* crew members—some of them, at least—tried to help in any way they could. Deckhands crawled across the upended hull and loosened lifeboats from their stanchions. The boats crashed down on the water, striking some of the victims as they flailed for their lives. Other crewmen tossed life preservers onto the water. Mass chaos ruled; it seemed everything was happening all at once.

The noise shook the riverfront: the chorus of screams ringing out along the dock, the pitiful splashing of those who had been tossed from the decks into the water, and the frantic rush of the quicker-thinking onlookers. It was as though a vast bucketful of people—helpless babies included—had been emptied into the oily water. More than one witness saw tiny bodies bobbing momentarily, their little heads coming up once, maybe twice, then going under. Even skilled swimmers had a hard time of it. In the face of widespread terror, heroics did not come into play—animal instinct ruled.

"Most of them, it seemed, could not swim, or were dragged down by those that could not swim," deckhand Harry Miller told the *Tribune*. "They were going under and coming up and snatching at each other and hollering. Men, women, and children, all over that part of the river. The current carried some of them, those that could keep afloat, upstream some distance." The initial frenzy probably prevented many rescuers from getting to the victims. Onlookers stood dumbfounded for many moments by the frantic splashing and flailing, paralyzed with dread that they too would be drowned if they jumped into the water.

On board the *Eastland*, falling wreckage had trapped hundreds below-decks or on the starboard side. Others, making desperate attempts to escape, landed in oblivion.

"From my place on the dock, I saw a great many persons attempt to leap from the decks to safety," one witness told the *New York Times*. "But they did not gauge the distance correctly, and about a dozen of them landed on the bottom of the boat. Like rocks in a crusher they were ground to pieces between the bottom of the boat and the dock."

Amid these horrors, a few of the luckier ones—most of them on the hurricane and promenade decks—escaped without a scratch. "They caught hold of the rail and climbed upon the upper side [the hull] as the boat went over and sank on its side," a *Tribune* reporter witnessed. "James Belsan and Charles Schad were two of the rescued who didn't even get their clothing wet."

For the less fortunate who had been tossed into the dirty currents, clothing became deadly. Even in the shallow waters of the harbor, a wet woolen suit weighed as much as an anvil. Women sank under the weight of their fancy, layered garments. Sodden silk overskirts, satin blouses, shoes, even plaited hair, became chains of iron, dragging their wearers down into the cold, silt-fogged darkness.

"Miss Korn fell in the water, and I was just able to grab her hair," recalled a man who tried in vain to save his lady friend. "I held on as best I could, and supported another lady at the same time. Suddenly I felt the weight relax and found myself holding only a handful of Miss Korn's hair."

Other women found their elaborate dresses transformed into hideous bondage.

One passenger clung to the hull of the ship in her soaking Sunday best. Her mind racing with silent prayers, she heard a noise and looked up. Her husband Paul lay on his stomach a few feet above her. Their hands clasped. The woman tried to swing her boot up, but her beautiful dress clung too tightly to her body. Again and again she tried in vain to swing her leg. Finally: "Some blessed man gave my foot a boost. Paul could not have pulled me out."

The early moments of the capsizing saw many others engaged in violent, involuntary struggles to survive the rancid tide of filth. Decades of horse dung, sewage, and runoff made the water as noxious as acid. Victims gagged and went under. Others spat out mouthfuls as they fought to stay afloat.

"I went down and down," recalled Lillian Heideman, a young woman who had fallen from the hurricane deck. "Water rushed into my mouth and nose. Then I came up. A man pushed a plank in my direction. I reached for it; it slipped from my grasp, and down I went again."

Historians estimate that nearly ten thousand passers-by occupied the riverfront that morning, and most were struck numb by the surreal sight of so many hapless picnickers dumped into the water. Some bystanders managed to snap out of their horrified trance long enough to throw off their overclothes and dive into the river to help. One eyewitness "saw an Italian rush from a commission house, tear off all his clothing save his underwear, and leap into the river with a rope tied around his waist." But most only gaped, standing mute.

"Never, to my dying day, shall I forget the supreme horror of that moment, so fraught with terror," wrote the venerable *Chicago Herald* editor Harlan Babcock. "Many such scenes have been reported in connection with the sinking of the *Titanic* and

Lusitania . . . only the trapped passengers on the *Eastland* did not have the time to escape that did those on the doomed death crafts of the Atlantic."

As the seconds ticked away for those still trapped aboard the *Eastland*, Babcock's words proved far truer than any of the onlookers could have imagined.

BOBBIE AANSTAD dog-paddled frantically. Muffled pounding and shrill noises—screams perhaps?—assaulted her from all directions. Every few moments a hand clawed at her leg, threatening to drag her into the murk. Daylight shone from somewhere overhead. From the other side of the wall? How was that possible? Bobbie was dizzy.

She tried to twist around, but couldn't see very well. Her eyes burned as though they had ammonia in them, a result of the alkaline content of the river, rich with the proteins of local industries. A slice of soggy bread floated by on the surface of the water, then a half-empty box of Uneeda biscuits. The sight of those things—the sheer absurdity of a biscuit box trailing its contents like a mother duck with its ducklings—seemed to gird Bobbie. She realized she was treading water near the dining room. Strange mewling noises echoed in the dark hull from somewhere nearby, perhaps under the water or on another partially submerged deck. They reminded Bobbie of the sawing of broken violins.

Marianne's voice, garbled and waterlogged, suddenly called out over the noise.

Bobbie glanced over her shoulder and saw her mother about a dozen feet away. The sight would stay with the thirteen-year-old for the rest of her life. "I can see my mother holding onto my sister with one hand and onto the boat with the other as if it were yesterday," Bobbie remembered many years later.

Fallen wreckage lay between Bobbie and her mother and her

sobbing sister—most likely a piece of the dining room—and the top of Uncle Olaf's head bobbed in the shadows just beyond the women. The big Norwegian man took a big gulp of air, then dove under the water. A moment later Olaf helped a terrified woman get a hold on the slatted floorboards that had become the wall.

Marianne wanted to know if Bobbie was all right. Bobbie told her mother she was fine, maybe a little bruised, but all right. The threesome treaded water in silence for a moment. They listened to the commotion outside the ship. The frenzied shouts, the alarms, the boat motors revving. And those inscrutable mewling noises coming from somewhere inside the ship.

Luckily, Bobbie Aanstad had learned how to swim and tread water a couple of summers earlier. A neighborhood boy from Logan Square named Ernie Carlson had taught her. The Carlsons were a well-to-do family who lived down the street from the Aanstads. One time, out of the blue, the Carlsons had invited Bobbie's entire family to a summer retreat in Michigan. While visiting that lovely compound, Bobbie got to know the Carlson boy—a wiry young rascal with a perpetual twinkle in his eye. Among other things, the boy had shown Bobbie how to dog-paddle in place for many minutes.

Currently the Aanstads occupied an opening between the cabin and promenade deck, probably near the mid-ship stairway. The sideways orientation of the fallen vessel created a narrow cell not much more than eight feet wide. Below them was a tangled mass of chairs, bodies, and railings. Bobbie shivered. Muffled banging noises came from all sides.

Bobbie looked up. A narrow wedge of sky glinted through a gap twenty feet above them, taunting her. Thumping noises vibrated the other side of the bulwark. Were they rescuers or were they coming from below? Were they the last movements of the less fortunate?

Olaf Ness pierced the surface of the water fifteen feet away. Bobbie heard him before she saw him. Then came the sound of a gasping woman. Bobbie watched as Olaf gently helped the hysterical woman onto a broken railing, probably a balustrade, protruding from the sideways floor. "By the end of the day," marveled a *Daily Herald* reporter, "Olaf Ness had saved 27 people."

In those terrible moments, Bobbie finally identified those sawing violin noises bouncing around her. It was the sound of hundreds of people crying. Bobbie looked down and realized that the water level inside the chamber was rising.

PANIC SEIZED the docks. Screams rose. Luckless passengers, many of them non-swimmers, thrashed futilely in the putrid waters for a full ten minutes before any kind of organized rescue effort began. Women struggled to hold their infants' heads above the surface while men flailed and splashed against the swirling currents. One man, while making a desperate attempt to swim to safety, glimpsed a dark object flying through the air above him. Then another one. And another. One of these objects landed on the water in front of him. He grabbed it.

It was a small wooden crate.

The man held on and started paddling toward the dock. More crates splashed into the water around the accident site: empty chicken coops, egg crates, various packing boxes. Other passengers grabbed hold as best they could. Some of the wooden crates struck the weaker swimmers, driving them under to their deaths, but for many, the wooden boxes offered a means for survival.

Most of the crates belonged to the Cougel Brothers poultry market located at La Salle and South Water, less than fifty feet from the stern of the fallen *Eastland*. Hearing the pandemonium, and realizing a ship had listed over, the workers threw open their doors and came out with armfuls of the makeshift life preservers.

"One employee said he threw at least twenty-five chicken coops into the water, and estimated that 200 or more were thrown in by others," Hilton writes. "William P. Kearney estimated that 250 to 300 were thrown in, and that twenty to thirty passengers survived by clutching the coops that he alone had thrown in." These dilapidated boxes and crates, according to Hilton, "quickly became the principal life saving devices in the disaster."

Other objects landed in the water. Gangplanks, ropes, loose boards, ladders, empty shelves, even chairs and life preservers from the nearby tugs and the S.S. *Theodore Roosevelt* were all heaved in. The more robust among the neighboring teamsters and warehouse workers flung *themselves* into the fray. But it was woefully insufficient. People perished by the score.

"The surface of the river was black with struggling, crying, frightened, drowning humanity," Babcock recalled. "Wee infants floated about like corks. Shrieks and cries of 'Help!' from those in the water filled the air. Many sank instantly and were seen no more. Others tore off their clothing in the water as best they could and tried to swim to safety. Some succeeded. Others turned white, imploring faces toward the panic-stricken crowd on the bridges and piers, but before help could reach them sank to watery graves."

"I couldn't stand to watch," a secretary stationed at the nearby Chicago and South Haven office remembered. "I felt as if I were going to faint, and I ran away." Others gazed down in horror from the windows of neighboring buildings. David Durand, an employee of the H.F. Watson Company warehouse on the north side of the river, gawked at the horrors from his third-floor office. "God, the screaming was terrible, it's ringing in my ears yet," Durand told the *Tribune*. "The river was dotted with men and women shrieking and waving their arms for help as they were carried down with the current."

Durand's gaze fixed on one woman who had fallen from the *Eastland*'s hurricane deck. She went under for a moment, and Durand thought that she was gone. Then it appeared that she bobbed to the surface, but it was only the woman's big white hat that had torn loose in the chaos. "I saw her white hat float down the river," Durand recalled. "And that was all. I said, 'That's the end of her.'"

Confusion paralyzed many of the rescue attempts. "I started to throw life preservers off the *Roosevelt* into the river, so they could float down to the hundreds struggling in the water," recalled one stunned Western Electric picnicker. "One of the men on the *Roosevelt* jerked me back from the rail, telling me to 'cut that out!'"

THE CLOSEST emergency craft, the fireboat *Graeme Stewart*, sat docked at its Franklin Street berth only two blocks away. In post-disaster hearings, much was made of the speed—or the lack there of—with which the *Graeme Stewart*'s Captain Patrick Lyons responded to the ensuing calamity.

A passer-by, John Parotto, testified that he had hollered up at one of the *Graeme Stewart*'s crewmen only seconds before the *Eastland* capsized, warning him that something terrible was about to happen. The crewman replied that Parotto was crazy and that the crew of the fireboat was busy eating breakfast. And even after the *Eastland* went over, the fireboat was slow to respond.

"The captain," Hilton writes, "was accused of delaying on the west side of the Wells Street bridge for about ten minutes out of fear of a boiler explosion on the wreck." Lyons vehemently denied this, claiming that there were too many bodies in the water for him to proceed further east.

Regardless of the impediments, the response seemed to be much quicker along the neighboring streets.

Nurse Helen Repa, perched on a bench in the midsection of

a trolley car, heard the noise rising above the din of traffic on LaSalle Street. An in-house nurse at the Hawthorne works, Repa had been assigned that morning to work at the picnic in Michigan City. Every year, the company provided a hospital tent at the event for the usual battery of summertime ailments—sun burns, skinned knees, upset stomachs, turned ankles—and Repa had been put in charge of the operations. She had planned to take the *Roosevelt* across the lake, but as her streetcar ground to a sudden, unexpected stop, and the strange symphony of terror rose up in the distance, Repa felt her spine stiffen with alarm.

She pushed her way off the trolley, and discovered a mounted policeman blocking the line, having halted the streetcar about a hundred feet south of the docks. Activity swarmed around the cop. The horse tossed its head nervously.

Fearing something terrible had happened, Repa waved back the crowd and approached the fidgeting horse. She asked the policeman what had happened.

"One of the excursion boats has upset!"

"Which one?!" Repa wanted to know.

The mounted cop shrugged, and a bystander yelled, "Got to be the *City of South Haven*! Happened at the Chicago–South Haven berth. Gotta be the *City of South Haven*!"

"I'm with the group!" Repa told the cop.

"What group?"

"Western Electric, the group going out this morning! From the Hawthorne works, the picnickers!"

A motorized ambulance came screaming down Lake Street from the opposite direction. One of the first emergency vehicles on the scene, this ambulance was a plain box-type trailer carried on a model A–style chassis, with shaded windows and an open cab. In the time before sirens and chaser lights, the simple regulation red cross on the vehicle's side told bystanders everything they needed to know.

The cop waved the ambulance over, motioning wildly at Repa. No record exists of how the nurse rode the remaining single city block to the wharf. She may have hopped onto the attendant's seat in the cab. It is more likely, though, that she rode on the narrow running board—or perhaps even the "back step," as Hilton has suggested—the rest of the way.

The ambulance arrived at the dock sometime between seven-thirty-five and seven-forty, a mere five to ten minutes after the capsizing. Repa hopped off the running board and hastened down the weather-beaten steps, her heart drumming. She still couldn't see much over the sea of straw hats and derbies swarming the pier in front of the Hausman Building. The rain had slowed to a miserable gray veil.

The nurse pressed against the flow of survivors, who were just then shambling away from the fallen boat like waterlogged zombies, their ashen faces scanning the wharf as though unable to fully awaken from a nightmare. Repa pushed her way to the edge of the dock where she could see the torn piling lying bent and ragged near Clark Street, pointing like an accusatory finger toward the wreck. The ship lay roughly twenty feet away.

Ranks of people stood on the *Eastland*'s exposed hull, drenched and stunned and looking around, trying in vain to absorb the cataclysm. The noise on the water wrenched Nurse Repa's attention away.

"I shall never be able to forget what I saw," she later reported. "People were struggling in the water, clustered so thickly that they literally covered the surface of the river. A few were swimming; the rest were floundering about, some clinging to a life raft that had floated free, others clutching at anything they could reach—at bits of wood, at each other, grabbing each other, pulling each other down, and screaming! The screaming was the most horrible of all."

Repa got to work immediately.

* * *

FORTY MILES to the west, in Lockport, Illinois, word of the capsizing sizzled through telegraph wires, alerting engineers at the Bear Trap Dam. They sprang from their card tables and morning coffee, and rushed to the massive switch levers overlooking the dam. With a great, heaving effort they yanked the corroded levers, closing down the drainage canal and stopping the flow of the river's current.

AT THE ACCIDENT SITE, the last few unfortunates who were hanging from the starboard railing, beyond the reach of those on the hull, lost their grips. Mostly women, they began to plunge, one by one, into the water, their screams swallowed by the river. A few lifeboats, most of them launched from the *Roosevelt*, arrived far too late for many. Rescuers pulled one woman from the river clutching a baby that had already expired. She refused to let go of the tiny, still body. Several men spent agonizing minutes trying to pry the lifeless child from her arms.

"I saw strong men turn their eyes away and groan and weep," Babcock reported. "I saw others stagger and faint. I heard women ashore shriek out hysterically and saw them swoon. Others ran screaming from the mind-racking scene and were swallowed up in the fast-gathering, panicky, shouting, wild-eyed multitude. Thrilling and heartbreaking incidents happened so rapidly as to be kaleidoscopic."

Help eventually came, albeit slowly, and often in an unorganized, ill-advised fashion.

MANY OF THE riverfront businesses had private telephone lines, and the wires seethed with distress calls, as trembling fingers fumbled at rotary dials on candlestick phones. Calls went out for doctors from nearby hospitals, for nurses, and for firemen—anybody who had the slightest skill to contribute.

In a time before 911, EMTs, and paramedics, much of the emergency response became mired in nineteenth-century technology—the kind that steams and huffs and clops and defecates in the street. Chicago's fire department was not yet motorized. Their sluggish, primitive horse-drawn wagons, on wooden wheels, proved ill-suited to meet a disaster the magnitude of the *Eastland* capsizing.

The closest firehouse was only a block or so away: Station 13 at 209 North Dearborn, between South Water and Lake Street.

The air instantly filled with the trademark clanging of fire gongs. Although hand-cranked sirens were being used in other metropolitan areas (such as New York), Chicago firemen still employed these massive bells in order to avoid spooking the horses. Mounted on the side of each pumper, the gongs were operated by foot pedal. During a rare multi-alarm event such as the *Eastland* catastrophe, the dissonant ringing of gongs told all within earshot that help was on the way. Unfortunately, the enormity of the *Eastland* disaster had a strange kind of mortifying effect on many of the emergency workers, especially the police.

The cops at the scene dug their heels into the vagaries of protocol. They pushed back the onrush. They halted frantic family members. They shoved at hysterical women calling out for errant children. Reinforcements were rushing to the wreck from nearby beat-walks. Amid the frenzy, many bystanders felt, the officers did more to hinder than to help during those early moments.

"I saw at least twenty expert swimmers whom I know personally take off their coats and beg the police to let them dive in the river to rescue struggling men and women," recalled A. D. Coe, a welder who had hurried to the scene with his acetylene torch and three of his men. "The police obdurately refused but did nothing themselves to help."

A fast-thinking Western Electric employee named F. G. Hubbard had summoned the welder minutes earlier. Hubbard was a master mechanic at the Hawthorne works, and chances are, he had taken one look at the fallen boat from his vantage point on the dock and instantly understood that the only chance to save hundreds trapped below-decks was to burn holes in the damn thing.

"We had five burners," Coe marveled later, "one of them the largest in the United States. But the police wouldn't let us through."

The only thing burning at that point was time, and time was at a premium.

CHAPTER NINE

Daredevil Rex
and the Human Frog

"A BIG BOAT'S gone down on the river!"

At approximately seven-forty-five, while Western Electric picnickers fought for their lives eight miles to the south, a shrill cry pierced the placid air outside a small repair garage at 3812 North Springfield Avenue. The garage, a filthy, cluttered, two-horse affair, sat on a sleepy, tree-shaded neighborhood of Old Irving Park. A pair of hyperactive teenage brothers were huddled in this glorified shed, occupying themselves with a jumble of greasy, dismantled motorcycles.

The eldest boy set down his massive wrench and stood, wiping his hands in an oily rag. He cocked his handsome head as though trying to reckon whether or not he had just heard what he thought he had heard. The voice rang out again. The girl next door, daughter of well-to-do family that had their own telephone, kept squawking something about a ship turning over in the Chicago River.

The two boys looked at each other.

It is highly probable that something unspoken yet powerful

passed between the two Bowles brothers in that moment. Berwyn, the younger boy, standing in the rear of the garage, engulfed in shadows, knew exactly what was about to happen. The older boy, Charles, stood in the open doorway, silhouetted in the overcast light. He became very still. His eyes flared for a moment with a mixture of excitement, tension and fearlessness.

A boat's gone down on the river?

Like a bird dog suddenly on the scent, the elder Bowles scooped up the wrench and lunged across the garage to the nearest intact motorbike. Quickly tightening a few bolts, he hopped on board and kicked it into life. The engine sputtered and barked. Gears crunched, then engaged, and the tailpipe plumed black exhaust across the garage.

Charles Bowles yanked the throttle and roared out of the shadows of the garage, and reached the end of his block within seconds. Head lowered into the wind, eyes narrowed, the young man must have looked to a casual observer like an avenging angel as his motorbike screeched around the corner of Springfield and Waveland, then headed east toward Elston. The bike bellowed and complained as it rattled over the brick composite. The machine needed a new bearing, and the boy wasn't too sure about its engine, but that mattered little. This boy was a self-styled daredevil in an era when the word daredevil still meant something.

Eyes fixed on the gray horizon, back hunched over the battered gas tank, the young man focused on the mission.

"I'M BURNING TO DEATH! I'M BURNING TO DEATH!!"

The muffled, tortured sound of a man's death cries seeped through the iron wall and bounced around the flooded chamber of the *Eastland*'s 'tween deck as Bobbie Aanstad paddled furiously, trying to keep her chin above the rising water line and ignore the horrible screams. Ten feet away, her mother had somehow managed to keep a tenuous, slippery grip on some mangled wreckage—perhaps a broken banister, perhaps a bench damaged in the capsizing—while she simultaneously clutched little Solveig. But Marianne looked tired, and her grip was faltering.

Twenty feet away, Uncle Olaf tried in vain to save a drowning woman.

For nearly a half hour the Aanstads had been trapped inside the overturned boat, and Bobbie had been treading water for most of that time. Every bone and tendon in her lithe, eighty-pound body ached. Earlier she had searched in vain for something to hold onto. The water had risen over the other balustrades, and nothing else protruded from the ceiling or floor. Bobbie worried that if she grabbed hold of her mother, the weight would be too much for the weary Marianne, and all three of them would sink into the filthy rheum. They had no life preservers. Not even a stray piece of bread or biscuit to laugh at. The only things that floated by now were bodies.

Don't think about them, don't even look at them, Bobbie silently told herself, slamming her eyes shut. *There's nothing you can do for them. They're just tissue and cloth now. Just dead tissue and soaking wet cloth.*

Bobbie shuddered. She opened her eyes and glanced up at that wafer of gray sky barely visible in the gap above her. Pain stabbed her neck. She looked back down at the surface of the water in front of her. A woman, face down, floated nearby, her dress clinging to her twisted, pale body, followed by a young man not much older than Bobbie, also face down, his skinny arms splayed like withered branches. They probably had perished in the crush on the stairs and had since slipped free. Bobbie tried to fix her gaze on Marianne and Solveig in order to focus her thoughts.

"All I wanted to do was keep my eyes on my mother and my sister," Bobbie recalled later. "It was survival. I couldn't care about the others."

The pale bodies continued floating lazily in the enclosed air pocket like broken driftwood. *Please God*, Bobbie prayed to herself, *don't let them touch me.*

A sudden cracking noise made Bobbie jerk in the water, a muffled, rending sound that vibrated the hull like a kettle drum. Somewhere a man burned to death, howling like a skinned animal. An awful acrid odor like the smell of something burning on a stove mingled with the river rot. Bobbie's mind raced. She remembered the time she had been left in charge of the family while her mother was downtown cleaning offices. Bobbie had left the potatoes on the stove too long that night, and the stench had filled the two-flat. Uncle Olaf had come home from work early and had gotten so angry he had chased Bobbie through the house with a broom.

A realization suddenly jolted through Bobbie Aanstad: something—a sledgehammer or an axe or a crow bar—was striking the outer shell of the boat! Somebody was trying to save that poor burning man. And if they were trying to save *him*, maybe they would come for the Aanstads.

Oh please, God, please, please, please make the rescuers come.

TEARING DOWN the rutted macadam on his ramshackle motorbike, the misty wind tossing his sandy hair, the Bowles boy saw the first signs of upheaval. He zoomed toward the Ohio Street bridge, about a mile northwest of the accident site, its massive, soot-stained span reaching across the brown waters. He saw the flurry of activity both on the river and along the adjacent city streets. Tugs and Coast Guard boats churned through the currents, heading southward, engines grinding, men on the docks hollering, pointing, onlookers rushing eastward along the pedestrian walks and side streets. A regiment of horse-drawn ambulances and fire trucks clamored toward the Clark Street Bridge, gongs clanging like broken church bells.

According to Bowles family history, very few people noticed the young rider that morning as he lowered his head and shot across the bridge like a missile. But one thing is certain: he cut an imposing figure on that hurling motorbike.

His full name was Charles R. E. Bowles, but he went by the nickname Reggie, pronounced with a hard G (as in *reggae*). The pronunciation seemed apt, as though a soft G would have been an affront to this young man's masculinity. Wiry and compact, with perpetually tousled hair, he had a movie-star face: high cheekbones, wide-set eyes, aquiline nose, and delicate, almost feminine lips. But a certain leathery aspect to Reggie Bowles's appearance—the way his ears jutted, and the workman's tan—suggested a boy who had weathered tough times.

Born in Chicago on April 29, 1897, Reggie showed a mechanical aptitude from an early age. He liked to take things apart and put them back together. Growing up on the sparsely populated north side, the eldest of five kids, he proved a handful for his overwhelmed parents. He continually got into trouble, and relationships were exceedingly strained around the Bowles house.

This was not a happy home.

At a certain point, Reggie's mother gave up trying to discipline her eldest son—who had been running away from home regularly—and sent him to live with a couple of maiden aunts in Uniontown, Pennsylvania, possibly in the hope that their gentility would rub off on the child.

The women doted on the young boy, dressing him in Little Lord Fauntleroy outfits and parading him around town. These women, both Daughters of the American Revolution, put on airs that their mysterious ward was a descendant of royalty. Before long the headstrong Reggie extricated himself from the ridiculous situation in Uniontown and returned to Chicago.

He went back to school but found it stifling, and dropped out after the sixth grade. At age eleven he learned to swim. Apparently he learned the lessons well, as he became known among the neighborhood kids as a human tadpole. He worked a series of menial jobs, his mechanical aptitude blossoming, and when he was fourteen he managed to build a couple of primitive aeroplanes in his parents' backyard. At the time, the aircraft was a staple of a young American boy's fantasy life, and Reggie was no different. He joined aeroclubs, read all the journals, pulps, and magazines, and conducted makeshift test flights with less than spectacular results.

During one experiment, he hitched a horse to a plane and sent it galloping down a nearby lane. His ersatz aircraft threatened to take off for a moment, but then slammed into a fence, resulting in a broken nose and fractured leg for Reggie (and possible brain damage). But the boy remained unfazed. He hated his troubled home, and regularly dreamed of "flying out of there."

He started doing freelance repair work on motors, electrical wiring, and acetylene welders, and left home in April 1914 to work full time as a journeyman mechanic and electrician. But the fires in Reggie's belly made it hard for him to stay in one place. He fancied himself a risk-taker. However much he saw himself as a flying ace, a romantic figure of adventure stories, a man of action, he never dreamed he would see the kind of action he was about to encounter on the Chicago River.

A FEW MINUTES before eight, the waters boiled with activity, from the intersection of the north and south branches, to the mouth of Lake Michigan more than a mile away. In addition to the other steamships that had been preparing to launch Western Electric picnickers that morning—the *Roosevelt*, the *Petoskey*, the *Racine*, and the *Maywood*—the Dunham Towing and Wrecking Company had a virtual armada of boats now responding with fierce purpose.

"Dunham's tugs *Waukegan*, *Indiana*, and *Rita McDonald*

shortly responded," wrote Hilton. "The city of Chicago also responded with the fireboat *D.J. Swenie,* the tug *Chicago Harbor #4,* and the police patrol vessel *Carter H. Harrison,* which became the city's central authority for direction of the rescue efforts. The Erie Railroad's harbor tug *Alice Stafford* proved one of the most useful vessels . . . [and] the Merchant's Lighterage Company's *Commerce* also assisted in the rescue."

Fire departments mobilized with amazing speed, considering the level of technology at their disposal. Horse-drawn patrol cars and ambulance teams from several different hospitals made it to the riverfront in record time. Firemen hurried to the site with axes, ropes, spike poles, life preservers, tarps, blankets, gurneys, carbide lamps, and cutting torches. But regardless of how widespread and responsive the rescue efforts became, the disaster had a mind of its own.

In those horrible, critical minutes between seven-fifty and eight-ten, every decision, gesture, and action from anyone within shouting distance of the accident site, carried with it the profound weight of life-and-death consequences.

Reggie Bowles seemed to understand this on a primal level as he sped across the Clark Street Bridge in a thunderhead of black exhaust from the motorbike's failing engine, weaving along the edges of the crowd. Bystanders, too stunned even to notice him, blocked his path. He wove between knots of onlookers and steered the bike toward the southeast corner of the bridge. When he yanked the hand brake, the motorcycle went into a skid and nearly slid out from under him. Somehow the boy managed to hold on and not hurt anybody in his path.

The bike slammed into a brick rampart. The machine died, and Reggie sat there for one frenzied instant, staring down at his right hand as the chorus of screams echoed around him. He realized something then. Something that startled him. In all the excitement, he had forgotten to release his grip on the wrench he'd been working with; it was still clutched in his white-knuckled right hand.

Over the roar of the crowd Reggie heard horrible banging noises like pistol shots. He climbed off the bike, letting it fall to the ground where it had stalled, then craned his neck to see over the ocean of hats. Out on the river the massive spine of the fallen ship teemed with victims and rescuers. It looked like a prehistoric creature, a dead dinosaur covered with parasites. The river around it seethed with bodies and objects.

Adrenaline spurted through the boy's innards. He didn't drop the wrench. Instead he tightened his grip on it like a vice. He started down the steps, pushing his way through the crush of frantic bystanders.

"That's as far as ya go, son!"

A beefy patrolman at the bottom of the steps blocked Reggie's path: a giant, immovable object dressed in the trademark navy-blue woolen coat of the Chicago Police Department with its huge brass buttons and silver star the size of a crabapple.

"Lemme through!" Reggie shoved at the big man, "I'm an expert swimmer!"

"No ya don't," the officer growled and shoved him back hard enough to practically lift the skinny kid out of his boots. Reggie stumbled into a group of men, and as anger coursed through the young man's veins, he straightened up and fixed his gaze on the officer.

The cop had turned his attentions elsewhere. He was scanning the crowd along the edge of South Water Street, squinting against the drizzle.

"HEY!"

Reggie lunged. The officer had no time to react. Reggie swung his wrench.

The tool slammed hard against the cop's big, blocky head and regulation square-brimmed cap. It made a dull thwacking noise, like a cricket bat on a sandbag, and made the officer stagger sideways. The cop slipped on the wet planks and went sprawling to the dock, nearly knocking over a couple of his fellow officers like so many bowling pins. Reggie slipped past the jumble of confused cops, and vaulted off the edge of the dock, splashing into the cold water, the wrench still in his hand.

CAPTAIN PEDERSEN stood on the prow of the *Eastland*, watching his world unravel. The screams and splashing noises and whetstone sounds of axes striking metal filled the paunchy Norwegian's ears. In the moments before the ship tipped over, Pedersen had struck his head on the pilot house rail, and now his skull throbbed. But shame overrode any queasy feeling. A master of steamships must never lose control. Through the smoke and mist he now saw pandemonium raging across the exposed starboard hull of his beloved vessel.

Lying there on her side in the muddy river, the ship resembled a stretch of road congested with foot traffic. It wasn't even eight o'clock yet and already nearly a thousand well-dressed people stood on her hull, some of them soaked and dazed, some of them crazy with panic, some of the them trying desperately to help. Rescue workers lifted victims from the water and dragged them onto the side of the boat. Some picnickers dropped to their knees and sobbed impotently as drenched children were fished out, their tiny heads lolling in death.

Pedersen watched.

He tried to maintain some semblance of order in his brain. He needed to do *something*, to *react somehow*. He saw a traffic cop kneeling on the hull a foot away, lowering a rope through an eighteen-inch-wide porthole in a frantic attempt to help the trapped and dying out of the death cells inside the ship.

The traffic cop reported later: "We pulled three women through [that porthole] . . . and an elderly woman dressed in black was clinging to a beam under the same porthole. Just as I was throwing the rope through the porthole she lost her grip and sank back in the water. Her head sank beneath the water but one hand seized the rope. I dragged her to the porthole but was horrified to discover that the porthole was too small to permit her exit. I made three despairing attempts to extricate her but it was useless."

The cop urged the heavy-set woman to hold on to the beam until a cutting device could be found to widen the porthole. But the exhausted woman, numb from terror and moaning, finally let go and sank into oblivion.

The captain gaped at the turmoil, paralyzed with emotion, his bushy mustache twitching, his eyes stinging from the drizzle. The ship needed to be breached. Those still alive inside the wreck could not fit through the tiny portholes. Muffled cries and pounding sounds from within the vessel agonized the rescuers.

"We got one young girl's head and arms through a porthole," reported another policeman, "then managed to get her shoulders through. We could not go further. Then we put a rope around her and let her back into the water. Babies could be seen in the hold of the boat."

Finally the police relented and allowed welders onto the hull. Pedersen watched as the mechanics—many of them from the Oxweld Acetylene company, which happened to be working at a nearby construction site—dragged their gas tanks, masks, hoses, and torches across the steel shell of his "Speed Queen of the Great Lakes." Knees hit the iron. Masks snapped down. Flames spat from the tapered nozzles and people jerked away as sparks leapt from the metal surface.

Pedersen could no longer bear to watch.

The captain pushed aside a few picnickers, then rushed across the wet hull to the closest welder, who was just beginning to touch his flame to the ship. "Here—HERE!" Pedersen yelled, grabbing the man's arm, jostling the flame and sending sparks off into the air. "Stop that!"

The welder flipped up his mask, then looked up into the eyes of the grizzled captain. "Who the hell might you be?"

Pedersen identified himself and told him to cease and desist immediately.

"My orders are to save lives," the angry operator retorted. "Not to be careful of boats."

The mask went back down.

Pedersen saw other sparks blooming in the mist across the length of the hull, and he heard the clang of fire axes piercing the steel, sledgehammers striking weak spots, and crowbars prying at steel plates. He saw that they were about to cut into the coal bunker. Anger tightened Pedersen's chest, or perhaps something beyond anger. Perhaps *madness*. Captain Harry Pedersen was about to seal his own fate.

In front of thousands of witnesses, he began to rage uncontrollably.

Picnickers stared, aghast at the captain's behavior as he staggered across the slippery hull, moving from worker to worker, ordering each to stop, claiming he was still in charge. But the crowd soon found its own anger. "I could have killed that captain without the least feeling," mused one bystander who witnessed Pedersen's tirade. A group of firemen, when told to stop damaging the boat, responded with a barrage of obscenities. "He did not take our dare," one fireman recalled, "when we said to come near and try to stop us."

As quickly as the *Eastland* had gone down, the tide of raw emotions turned on the captain. Livid faces aimed their wrath at him. Women shook their fists and swore and sobbed that it was all his fault. Fear transformed to rage. Anguished men came at him with clenched fists.

"Drown him!" a woman shrieked.

Pedersen began to back off, stricken mute. Maybe the head injury had made him act irrationally. In post-disaster hearings, Pedersen repeatedly mentioned the throbbing pain in his skull as a reason for his less-than-exemplary behavior.

Whatever the cause, he had crossed a dangerous Rubicon.

A MAN IN UNIFORM observed the commotion on the ship from the edge of the dock. At first, he kept his distance—he had his hands full directing the rescue efforts—and he simply lingered there for a tense moment, looking on with fleeting interest. A sturdy, barrel-chested fellow, he wore the standard blue woolen frock coat of the police department, albeit with a few more stripes and bullion than the subordinates. He sported a handlebar mustache as thick as a paintbrush and was so stocky and robust in his bearing as to appear to lack a neck. Standing there, he looked like a hirsute bull, eyes blazing.

Acting Police Chief Herman Schuettler saw anarchy breaking out across the hull of the overturned ship, and Schuettler loathed anarchy. In his youth he had beaten back the anarchists at Haymarket Square, and later had made a name for himself in the Chicago Police Department as the architect of the city's first undercover unit. But Schuettler's cunning was matched only by his vigor.

Brought up on the bare-knuckle streets of the Levee, Schuettler got himself arrested when he was only seventeen for fighting with a teamster, and throughout his meteoric rise in the department, he continued to hone his toughness. About Schuettler a local historian once wrote: "Clubs, bricks, and stones were common weapons of offense, and Schuettler was as adept with them as he was with his knuckles." But the *Eastland* disaster truly tested the man's mettle.

Watching the furious picnickers surround Pedersen, Chief Schuettler made a snap decision. He would sort out the details later. People were dying, and this grizzled old steamship captain was, rightly or wrongly, about to be lynched.

Schuettler whistled at the closest tugboat—the *J. W. Taylor*—which only moments earlier had arrived at the *Eastland*'s bow to offer assistance. The tug's stern hovered five or six feet from the pier, and Scheuttler made the leap across the gap like a charging Angus, landing on the deck with a thump. He hurried past milling rescuers and climbed onto the *Eastland*'s prow. By that point the enraged picnickers surrounded Pedersen, and Scheuttler had to push his way through throngs to get to the captain. No record of their brief conversation exists, but the gist of it turned up in several news accounts.

"Excuse me, sir!" Schuettler said in a firm voice as he grasped Pedersen's arm.

"Let go, damnit!" Pedersen tried to pull away. "I'm running this show!"

"Not anymore."

"What?"

The chief locked his gaze on Pedersen. "Gonna have to place you under arrest, sir, if you please."

"You're what—?!"

Schuettler lowered his voice. "It's for your own protection, Captain. Your first mate, too. Now come along. Before something unfortunate happens."

The angry crowd made room as Schuettler ushered Pedersen across the bow toward the *J. W. Taylor*. People shouted obscenities in a mishmash of eastern European dialects. They called the captain a murderer, waved their fists and gave him the evil eye. One welder, at a certain point, told the captain where he could go.

"I told him to go to a place that is hotter than any torch flame," recalled J. H. Kista.

CHAPTER TEN

In the Grasp of Death

REGGIE BOWLES burst to the surface of the chilled, greasy river, gasping air, paddling with one arm, holding onto a young girl with the other.

Many sensations engulfed the wiry eighteen-year-old daredevil all at once: the arhythmic metallic drumming of the fire gongs; the dissonant symphony of screams from the adjacent bridges where helpless multitudes looked on; the cool, wet air on Reggie's face, blowing the stench of coal smoke and fish-rot up his sinuses; and a disconcerting, coppery taste of adrenaline in his mouth.

In his peripheral vision, Reggie saw myriad objects bobbing, dipping, and lurching. Overturned lifeboats, broken folding chairs, unoccupied life preservers, and rowboats filled with survivors dotted the river. Also in the middle distance, registering in the boy's brain in flashes and hazy shapes, the massive rescue vessels and steamships vied for position in the chaotic currents being stirred up by conflicting wakes. The *Graeme Stewart*, and lifeboats from the *Roosevelt*, like great, slow-moving leviathans, edged their way toward those who still thrashed on the surface. Scores of survivors continued to struggle in the water, but their number was dwindling. Far fewer heads bobbed in the currents than when Reggie had first plunged into the river only minutes earlier.

Reggie summoned all his strength, then started swimming for the north side of the dock, where he could see rescue teams gathered in front of a large brick building, beginning to treat victims.

The Reid-Murdoch building played a key role in the *Eastland* drama. One of the most prominent firms in the immediate area, Reid, Murdoch & Company, a grocery wholesaler, worked out of one of the largest structures on the riverfront. With its many balconies, windows, and large service doorways, it offered numerous unobstructed views of the disaster, as well as receiving areas for victims. The Reid, Murdoch workforce happened to be away that day on their own company picnic, leaving a "large, modern building virtually empty," as Hilton puts it, "immediately across the river from the wreck."

Paddling and kicking vigorously, Reggie moved through the water despite the young girl's heavy, sodden dress, her involuntary wriggling in his arms, and her pitiful attempts at garbled cries. He set his sights on the pier in front of him, ignoring the shrieks of horror all around him. It was as though he were shutting down his own emotions, cutting off his fear, as he had done many times in the past.

"Reggie had no relationship to fear," recalled his grandson, David. "He was a real tough, pugnacious kid." Other family members shared this impression. "He has never known the meaning of physical fear," Reggie's mother Emma once told a Uniontown newspaper. "He learned to swim at 11 years of age and took to the sport like a duck to water; within a year he had rescued two companions from drowning, and a year ago he rescued a baby from a burning building."

At last the boy reached the dock and with great effort lifted the gasping girl up to a nurse and doctor, who were diligently processing the victims. All around the area rescuers kept fishing survivors out of the river and laying them out on the dock as quickly as possible for treatment. Reggie treaded water for a moment, watching a local doctor practice a primitive version of triage.

Thomas A. Carter of the Chicago Health Department, one of the first physicians on the scene, treated many at that early stage. As head ambulance surgeon for the police department, Carter was the city's foremost expert in emergency medical procedures. But this event had already progressed far beyond the scope of everyday carriage accidents, factory mishaps, or beach drownings. The sheer numbers overwhelmed the doctor.

In that first hour, literally hundreds emerged from the river in all manner of distress. Carter went into a sort of hyper-focused state of concentration, moving from body to body, kneeling by each unconscious victim, injecting strychnine into the worst of them. The strychnine acted as a powerful stimulant, as well as a crude antibacterial to fend off the ravages of the pollution. Carter would feel each neck for a pulse. If a victim indicated no heartbeat, Carter called out to the attending nurses, raising his voice just enough to be heard above the din: "Gone."

If a person showed signs of life, the doctor called for a lung motor. Patented by The Life Saving Devices Company, a local firm, these machines resembled a large brass bicycle pump with a mask affixed to one end of the dual hoses. The mask was pressed down on the victim's air passages and the practitioner vigorously pumped air into the victim's lungs. Once heard, the noise of the lung motor in action was unforgettable, a macabre wheezing sound that vibrated the skull and set teeth on edge.

For a single instant, Reggie Bowles saw Carter apply this very device to the waterlogged girl he'd rescued. In that brief moment, as he treaded water and watched the medical team minister to the dying, Reggie Bowles pushed his terror further and further down into some dark place inside himself.

He whirled about in the water, then started swimming back into the vortex.

IN PRESS COVERAGE following the disaster, in articles published in the *Chicago Daily Tribune* and the *Fort Dodge Daily Chronicle*, reporters dragged out their hoariest cliches, waxing poetically about Reggie Bowles's heroic deeds. They christened him "The Human Frog" and called him a hero. This attention seemed to have a strangely formative effect on the young man, not all of it positive. But in that awful first hour following the *Eastland*'s plunge, no one had time to think about such things as bravery or heroism.

To Reggie's left, at the south steps of the Clark Street bridge and twenty-five feet away from the fallen bow, more physicians had arrived with more lung motors. "A score of machines clanked at the same time," a reporter later recalled, attempting to put into words a sound that was virtually indescribable—a desperate, rattling, breathy chorus of puffing noises mingling with the yelling.

A local Red Cross physician, Dr. M. K. Little, watched men with grappling hooks fish bodies from the river like so much detritus. Dr. W. A. Evans, the health reporter for the *Daily Tribune*, managed to get to the scene early and pitched in. Nevertheless, the influx of drowned and suffocated picnickers, many of them women and children clad in their saturated finery, their heads hanging loosely, took its toll on the rescuers. "The spectacles were harrowing," reported the *New York Times*. "Policemen wept as the bodies of women were taken out with their babies still clutching their bosoms in the grasp of death."

The presence of so many *female* victims defined the *Eastland* catastrophe in unexpected ways. Women had formed the backbone of the Hawthorne works. "Much of the women's work [at Western Electric] differed little from the traditional women's work in the household," wrote historians Stephen Adams and Orville Butler, "particularly the more repetitive tasks such as the winding, braiding, and sewing of wire." But 1915 was also a time of suffrage and changing attitudes. A year earlier, women in Illinois had won the right to vote, and the ladies of Western Electric had marched proudly in the parade at their annual picnic with suffragette slogans across their bodices. Throughout the *Eastland* disaster, the behavior of the women reflected a society in transition.

"In the crisis the women were stronger," the *Tribune* declared. "While men fought madly for their lives, the women and girls, after the first panic, quickly recovered. Either they clung patiently to rafts and bits of wreckage, or, if trapped in the hull, they waited calmly for rescue or death." And what if they were lucky enough to be rescued? The *Tribune* observed admiringly: "Their thoughts, for the most part, were of those not so fortunate."

"I did not lose my head at all," Mrs. John Schlemmer recalled to a reporter. "I saw a fat man was sinking and another woman and myself gave him a lift out of the water." Mrs. Schlemmer was badly injured, her head gashed and bleeding, but she refused treatment until she had made a frantic search of the hull for her husband.

"I saw a mother floating about with a baby on a life preserver," reported another picnicker. "I never saw anyone so contented as that baby was. Only the mother's dark head was visible above the water [beside it]. She did not struggle; she just depended upon the corks [preservers] to rescue them both."

Even in the midst of so much death, the women seemed more concerned with their children's lives than their own.

One unfortunate young lady made it to the dock only minutes after the capsizing, her slender form cold and drenched. She collapsed into unconsciousness. The doctor tried in vain to revive her. Finally the policemen stoically laid her lifeless form on a stretcher, covered it in a blanket, and started toward the Clark Street steps. At the top of the stairs, rows of ambulances and horse-drawn patrol cars awaited fatalities.

But as the officers trudged across the dock, a voice rang out behind them. "I saw the woman's arm move! She's alive! She's alive!"

The cops laid the stretcher on the planks and knelt down to take a look. They pulled the blanket down, and the woman's eyelids miraculously fluttered.

"My God, boys!" one of the officers cried out. "She *is* alive!"

They tenderly raised her to a sitting position, her face bloodless and dazed as she tried to speak. "What happened? Where am I?"

A crowd gathered around her.

"Madam, you're alive, you are," said the cop, wiping his moist eyes as the onlookers cheered. Several began to weep. "You're one of the first," the cop informed the girl, "one of the first that's been brought up that was not beyond help."

The woman suddenly jerked with a terrible realization: "Oh, no—my baby. My husband. Oh where do you suppose they are?! You don't suppose they were—?!"

"Madam, please—"

"He had the *baby*!" The woman yanked herself free and staggered back toward the water. The sad-faced officer held her back, but the tiny woman was inconsolable. "He had the baby! He had the baby! Oh why didn't I take the baby instead of carrying the basket?!"

For several agonizing minutes, the young woman struggled to escape the burly arms of the policeman. Finally, the woman extricated herself and ran back to the boat as a small body was being rooted out of a porthole. In a hellish, private moment of horror— a worst-case scenario for any parent—the woman grabbed the infant and realized at once that the child was hers, and was gone. Holding the dead baby in her arms, the mother swooned.

"She had her baby at last," a reporter from the *New York Times* sadly mused.

Other women, facing certain death, quickly and decisively made heartrending choices.

"My husband and I and the children . . . all fell into the water in a heap," recalled a grieving woman. "I am a good swimmer. I caught hold of my son, Harry, and my little girl, Helen, and clung to them and kept myself up in some way. I don't know how. My husband disappeared. I held Harry with my right arm and Helen with my left. I seemed to lose all strength in my left arm, and I had to let go of Helen."

The woman saved her son but lost both her daughter and husband.

Another female victim managed to get her baby on a floating deck chair but found the water too strong to save herself. She gave the chair a shove. "As the child floated away on the improvised raft," wrote the *Daily Tribune*, "the mother smiled and threw a kiss at it. Then she sank."

MALE PASSENGERS, in many cases, did not conduct themselves with nearly as much valor.

According to many eyewitnesses, some men shoved aside weaker women in order to flee the death ship. Even children were trampled by hysterical male passengers. In the aftermath, story after story surfaced of men panicking while women remained calm, and even after being rescued, many of these gentlemen stood stunned and helpless at the docks, unable to offer the most minimal assistance.

"Women and children first? Not on your life!" exclaimed a bitter crew member. "I saw men tear women and girls from where they were clinging to rails above the water in order to get to positions of temporary safety. There was nothing like chivalry. The stronger dragged down the weaker into the water and usurped their places, and usually the stronger were men and the weaker were girls and women."

"I saw two women come bobbing up to the surface not far from the shore piling," remembered a riverfront worker. "I jumped in to grab them. Some fat man, his face green with terror was making for them, too. I got hold of the women and started to pull them out. The fat man held onto the women's dresses, and I couldn't swim with the whole load. I yelled at him, treading water as I fought. He wouldn't let go." One of these two women eventually drowned, as did the fat man.

"All three of them might have been saved," the worker marveled later, "if that fella hadn't been scared into a frenzy."

AGAIN AND AGAIN Olaf Ness proved an exception to the rampant panic among males.

He broke through the surface of the water inside the prison of the *Eastland*, his square, handsome head drenched with river-slime as he gasped for breath, his eyes burning with urgency. He desperately treaded water, his right arm locked under the armpits of another partially conscious middle-aged woman. Ness scanned the shadows for a place to deposit the poor soul.

The overturned ship, filled with ammonia-laced air, was the scene of rending noises—the crack of timbers splitting, rivets popping, and metal shuddering. The ship seemed to be coming apart. The Aanstad women silently watched, Marianne and Solveig still clinging to that angular wreckage sticking out of the water six feet away, while Bobbie perched herself on a life preserver twelve feet beyond that, her slender legs dangling down in the dark, viscous water.

Olaf had located the errant life preserver only minutes earlier and had gotten Bobbie on it before the thirteen-year-old succumbed to exhaustion. Now Bobbie straddled the thing, holding onto the wall for balance. She could see very little across the length of the shadowy cell, her eyes stinging from the stench. She kept her gaze fixed on Olaf, her mother, and her sister.

Throughout that narrow chamber, victims floated like macabre icebergs, only the backs of heads and shoulders showing, a corona of hair floating gracefully like delicate sea anemones around the closest female corpse. Hats and stray shoes and broken chairs bobbed here and there.

Olaf attempted to pull the semiconscious woman toward the tangle of wreckage on which Marianne and Solveig rested. Every few moments the wreckage shifted slightly, making Marianne and Solveig jerk. As the big Norwegian man wrestled with the twitching dowager in his arms, the wreckage shuddered suddenly. "Olaf!—OLAF!" Bobbie screamed. "MOM IS FALLING!"

A terrible swishing noise swallowed Bobbie's cry as the wreckage gave way. It happened so quickly that nobody had time to react. The jumble of wood and iron slid under the surface, and Marianne and Solveig went with it, the younger girl's piercing squeal swallowed by the cold, black water. Olaf acted instinctively, letting go of the matron and diving toward his sister.

Bobbie watched, awestricken, perched on her battered cork ring. For one terrible instant, the rest of her family vanished under the water. Silence squeezed the chamber. Then Olaf burst to the surface with Marianne and Solveig both coughing fitfully but alive. Olaf managed to get them back to their original position. The wreckage had shifted under the water but was still partially connected to the boat; Marianne steadied herself on a jutting rail.

Behind Olaf, the gasping, unfortunate matron sank from view. Bobbie watched as the air bubbles gathered on the surface for a moment, then popped out of existence. A searing agony twisted inside Bobbie. She turned away and tried to will the repulsion and terror out of her brain by thinking pleasant thoughts. She remembered Ernie Carlson, that cute boy down the street who had taught her how to tread water.

Tears welled in Bobbie's eyes as the arc of her short life, in many ways a strange sort of rehearsal for this waking nightmare, flashed through her brain.

Born on July 28, 1901, in Trondheim, Norway, Bobbie had experienced severe respiratory problems as a young child. When she was two years old, her father packed a few giant trunks and launched the family on the arduous passage to America, even though the Norwegian doctors, skeptical that little Bobbie could survive the journey, had strongly advised him against it. For two weeks, Bobbie and her parents huddled in a dark, moldering steerage compartment of a giant ship "like animals." Along the way, Bobbie's bronchitis worsened, but Marianne refused to let her child succumb to the illness, wrapping the ailing toddler in blankets, and each day taking the child above-decks to breathe the salt air. Thanks to Marianne, Bobbie survived.

The previous year, Akim Aanstad had come over to the States to find work. He had secured a job in Logan Square as a tailor for Hart Schaffner and Marx, and that's where the family landed when they first arrived in Chicago. They lived in a little house on Diversey Avenue, and everything had been fine—for a while.

The winter of 1911 brought with it young Bobbie's near fatal case of diphtheria. The house had to be quarantined, and Bobbie underwent regular cleansings with disinfectant. Again, the little girl found herself huddling in a dark chamber not much better than the mildewed steerage of the ship on which she had emigrated, alone in her little sickroom, the windows shrouded by blankets.

Because of the quarantine at home, Akim decided to sleep at work. For weeks on end, the overworked father slept on the cutting tables at Hart Schaffner and Marx, shivering in unheated sewing rooms, while his daughter fought to survive at home. Akim developed a cold, which worsened, until pneumonia set in. He died shortly thereafter, aged thirty-three. Marianne Aanstad, who had already borne a second daughter, Solveig, became a single mother in a hardscrabble city. She spoke very little English, and had no income. As a result, when Bobbie recovered, she grew up quickly. She bore the brunt of the housework, and cared for her little sister while Marianne worked as a cleaning woman in various office buildings. Even after Uncle Olaf had arrived from Norway to help out—landing a job at Western Electric for fifteen dollars a week—Bobbie held the family together.

Such hardships strengthened the young girl's resolve. By the time she reached adolescence, she was amazingly self-possessed. Photographs show the joie de vivre on her face, the light in her eyes. Although very few records exist of her interactions with her family during their ordeal inside the *Eastland* that morning, it is highly likely that Bobbie shared her courage with her mother, sister, and uncle that day, surviving at all costs.

The trouble was, nobody had any idea how high those costs would eventually rise.

THE *EASTLAND*'S exposed hull swarmed with firemen, welders, and dazed survivors, the latter trying to help but more likely just getting in the way. Sparks from arc flames shot up at dozens of sites. Ropes bullwhipped across the *Eastland*'s steel surface, plunging down portholes and open gangways. Struggling against the effects of the intermittent drizzle, crews of firemen threw giant tarps across parts of the slippery hull in order to provide traction, while other exposed areas were strewn with ashes from the fire boxes of adjacent tugs for the same purpose. The mist turned the ash to a gray, mottled gunk.

The rescuers realized that time was running out. The window of opportunity to save anyone clinging to life inside the fallen ship was rapidly closing.

Stricken survivors wrapped in city-issued blankets trudged off the side of the ship, two abreast, like zombies, onto adjacent tugs and fireboats positioned around the *Eastland*. The crunch of their footsteps in the ash and cinders made rhythmic tattoos. It is likely that Bobbie Aanstad heard all this commotion vibrating the dark entrails of the hold.

Along the south dock, between LaSalle and Clark, firemen and volunteer workers laid down makeshift bridges hewn from metal pontoons and planking in order to connect the *Eastland*'s starboard hull to the pier, making access easier for the rescue workers. While water churned and voices penetrated the steam and smoke, doctors, nurses, reporters, police photographers, coast guard officials, shipping company personnel, teamsters, stevedores, commission house workers, tug boat crewmen, and clergymen arrived from neighboring areas and tramped across the creaking, yawning makeshift bridges and onto the crowded hull to help in any way possible. But deaths outpaced the recoveries tenfold in what the *Tribune* would later refer to as "a wholesale slaughter of innocents."

Nearby hospitals such as Henrotin and the Eye and Ear Clinic at Wabash and Franklin dispatched teams and equipment. John J. O'Connor, the director of the local Red Cross, immediately began planning relief efforts. The city coroner's head physician, Thomas Springer, arrived at the scene shortly after eight and established a position near the Clark Street steps. It was Springer's grim task to quickly examine fatalities in order to determine the cause of death. As each pathetic bundle arrived by tug or across a bridge, and was laid at Springer's feet, the doctor knelt and quickly pinched the victim's neck. Suffocation was the verdict in most cases, either from drowning or from the crush inside the death boat. Then began a somber process that would define the rest of the day.

Coroners tagged victims' toes, then sent the bodies to be taken to temporary morgues. The complicated process of identification began in earnest. Since there was no passenger manifest, Springer knew it would be difficult. But he also rejoiced whenever he was able to revive a person thought to be dead. A sort of jury-rigged "bucket brigade" of stretcher bearers formed along the river to rush those clinging to life to the nearest hospital.

Ironically, the closest major medical facility, Iroquois Memorial on Market Street, where many of the injured were taken, had gotten its name from another famous disaster. On December 30, 1903, a few blocks south of the river, a fire broke out backstage at the elegant Iroquois Theatre during a gala production of *Mr. Bluebeard*, a popular musical comedy. In a panic, the audience stampeded the exits and found them locked. In less than half an hour, nearly 600 people lost their lives. For years the tragedy had stood as Chicago's worst disaster in terms of death toll . . . until the morning of July 24, 1915.

BY EIGHT-FIFTEEN the faces of onlookers began to reflect a deeper horror. A huge percentage of the 2,500-plus passengers had simply vanished, either swallowed by the river or trapped in the unseen tomb of the ship.

"As a consequence of the abruptness of the capsizing, there were few examples of laborious or prolonged escapes," Hilton writes. And even in those rare instances of adventurous escapes, the survivors usually turned out to be crewmembers. "Sailors knew what to do on a capsizing ship," Hilton explains, "the passengers, typically, did not."

Tens of thousands of onlookers pushed forward on LaSalle Street, fighting the police in order to see, straining the limits of the Clark Street Bridge. "The bridges creaked uneasily under the weight," witnessed one reporter, "in spite of the desperate efforts of the cordon of black-rubbered policemen, who shouted, 'Keep Moving!' until they were hoarse in a frantic attempt to adjust the strain to the weakened girders. Clubs, threats, and the combined authority of the mounted squad had absolutely no effect on the horde of stunned humanity that clung to the guard rails like limpets and peered down from every vantage point."

On the river, time ran out for many.

Exhausted stragglers bobbed and thrashed one final time before going under. Some bystanders leapt into the river in frantic, last-ditch attempts to save the weak and dying. A young watchman on the *Petoskey*, Peter Boyle, dived into the breach and was not seen alive again. Even an unemployed man who was down by the river that morning, contemplating suicide, suddenly felt compelled to join the fray. According to the *New York Times*, this "gloomy" man ended up saving nine people, until he had to be dragged out himself, near dead from exhaustion.

The chaos was insurmountable. There were simply too many victims flailing and clawing at the crates and timbers and life preservers, and too many disorganized rescue attempts occurring at once. Workers tossed nets downstream into the channel to catch victims stolen by the current. Desperate patrols paddled back and forth in rowboats and dinghies, grasping at anything that moved. By the time the giant clock-hands on the Reid-Murdoch tower reached eight-twenty, a staggering number of fatalities had accumulated, and a sort of mass dread had settled in over the scene.

AMID THE PANDEMONIUM on the starboard side of the fallen *Eastland*, a group of black-clad men appeared in almost ghostly procession. They came from the steps near LaSalle Street. The police let them pass without a word. These men in dark frockcoats moved with a somber urgency as they negotiated the pontoon bridge, and then staggered across the slimy hull of the wreck, clutching their rosaries and vials and bibles. Father P. J. Fitzsimmons from Holy Name Cathedral, the administrator of the archdiocese, led the group. Father Thomas Kelly from Precious Blood parish was there too, along with Fathers O'Hearn, Wolff, Dunne, Mullaley, and O'Callaghan.

The priests gave each other silent nods and spread out among the throngs of victims. O'Hearn found an opening in the hull, and with the aid of a fireman leaned down into the darkness. Witnesses later reported at least a dozen different strangled voices offering whispered confessions. Fathers Wolff and Dunne stood on either side of the procession of victims being hauled away, anointing foreheads with dabs of holy water and uttering ancient words under their breath, barely audible above the uproar:

Jesus, Mary, Joseph, I give you my heart and soul.
Jesus, Mary, Joseph, assist me in my last agony.
Jesus, Mary, Joseph, may I breathe forth my soul in
*   peace with you.*
From a sudden and unprepared death, deliver us,
*   O Lord.*

CHAPTER ELEVEN

Too Harrowing
for Any Viewer

THE COLD, foul-smelling water pounces on a drowning victim like a predator, slashing at the face, flooding the nasal passages. The throat closes (a process known as "laryngospasm") and the body seizes up. Sounds and sensations become muffled, blurred. Weight displacement begins, and the victim eventually slips beneath the surface.

The oxygen-starved brain begins hallucinating in the dark, and involuntary struggling and thrashing only make matters worse. The body sinks further into darkness and oblivion. Death is imminent.

Without oxygen, a person becomes "clinically dead" within four minutes. However, the brain can survive well past this deadline. At least up to six minutes beyond it, and in many cases up to ten. After ten minutes without oxygen, brain damage is almost certain, but there are exceptions. Cold water, for instance, has a major impact on the process.

A condition known as "hypothermia," or a loss of inner-core body heat, often precedes death by cold-water drowning. This process has hidden benefits. When the face is submerged in water that is less than 71 degrees Fahrenheit—such as that of the Chicago River—the so-called "diving reflex" slows the body's processes so that oxygen-bearing blood is diverted to the heart and the brain. For this reason many of the *Eastland* victims were completely revived, without brain damage, as long as 45 minutes after the initial plunge into the water.

A TERRIBLE SORT of assembly line had begun on the *Eastland*'s ash-strewn hull. Firemen pulled limp bodies through holes in the ship while doctors offered a frenzied sort of triage, sending each victim to its appropriate station. Policemen became stretcher-bearers.

The first bodies were taken by tugs to the S.S. *Theodore Roosevelt*, which had been evacuated in the moments following the capsizing. Almost immediately Dr. Springer saw the need for additional morgue space and designated the basement of the Reid-Murdoch building to serve this function. Most DOA's were tagged as death-by-asphyxiation, and bodies accumulated quickly. By eight o'clock a dozen victims lay strewn across the floor of that grocer's dark, damp cellar. Fifteen minutes later, scores of them lined the planks. The sheer volume of fatalities made documentation and identification tremendously difficult. Confusion gripped the scene. More than one death certificate arrived prematurely.

Hypothermic individuals can often appear dead. They turn blue, are cold to the touch, and appear not to be breathing. They also exhibit many other death-like symptoms such as dilated pupils, lack of pulse, uncontrolled bowels or urination, penile erection, lividity, even false rigor mortis. In the mad rush to save as many passengers as possible, coroners' assistants misidentified several of the living as corpses.

The psychological toll began to set in among rescue workers, especially the police. Notwithstanding their alleged bungling of crowd control and rescue response, policemen were forced to serve multiple functions, from morgue attendant to medical orderly. Within 45 minutes of the capsizing, they showed signs of mental exhaustion.

"Policemen's hands began to swell as they handled scores and hundreds of the victims of some awful criminal negligence," reported the *Daily Tribune*. "They worked like automatons, however, mindful that someone's precious lifeless clay was being removed from the maw of this death orgy."

At his chaotic, bustling command post near the Clark Street steps, Dr. Springer gave orders for a second temporary morgue to be established on the water. Within minutes, workers from the county coroner's office hurriedly gathered materials and began erecting tents on a floating barge on the north side of the river. Ghostly white canvas flapped in the wet breezes, resembling a battlefield hospice from the previous century. It was now approaching eight-thirty.

The tragic brigade of dead bodies shifted. Police started hauling the deceased toward the floating morgue, and the crowds looked on. Somebody had to tell the world what was happening here. Somebody had to spread the news of this grave event.

BULLETINS WENT OUT almost immediately over every available medium. Wire services telegraphed the news to bureaus across the country. Facts were scrambled. Death-toll estimates varied greatly. Many early accounts went out via telephones, and many of these calls were made by newspaper reporters.

In July 1915, Chicago had twenty-one newspapers. In addition to the major dailies—the *Daily Tribune*, the *Herald & Examiner*, the *Daily News*, the *Evening Post*, and the *Whip*—the city boasted publications geared specifically for African-Americans, Bohemians, Italians, Swedes, Poles, labor, and the bigger metropolitan communities such as Hyde Park and Calumet. Each and every one of these organizations covered the *Eastland* disaster in some fashion. Both the *Chicago Evening Post* and the *Daily News* arrived early with a platoon of photographers; much of the visual record that survives today is drawn from this coverage. Bureau chiefs from out-of-town papers rushed to the scene. But no single organization invested more resources, or responded more quickly, or covered the disaster in greater depth than the *Chicago Daily Tribune*.

Begun in 1847 with a circulation of 400, the *Tribune* rose in power in tandem with Chicago itself, alongside the great Hog Butcher for the World. In 1860, the paper, led by its charismatic chief, Joseph Medill, virtually engineered Abraham Lincoln's ascendancy to the White House. The *Tribune* became the "Voice of the Union," and prompted Medill to quip: "A good many swear *at* it, but swear *by* it notwithstanding." The newspaper established its own paper mill and became the first news organization to establish a wire service. By 1915 its giant steam-powered printing presses at Madison and Dearborn Streets churned out a half-million copies per day. Most important, the paper excelled at covering calamities of the scope of the *Eastland* disaster.

On the morning of July 24, 1915, the managing editor was a portly, kind-hearted man named Edward "Scotty" Beck. Admired for his gentle nature and even temper, Beck had made a name for himself covering the Iroquois Theatre disaster twelve years earlier as city editor. When the news of the *Eastland* capsizing reached Beck at his breakfast table, he instantly sprang into action, marshalling his considerable news-gathering staff and resources.

The paper's staff set up extra phones at the paper's headquarters, as well as extra shifts of operators. Every available employee came to work that day to assist in giving out information to panicked citizens. Down at the docks, Beck convinced a riverfront business owner, J. C. Oram of Oram Printing, to hand over his building to the squad of *Tribune* reporters already at the scene. Next door to Oram, the travel agent for the Chicago and South Haven Steamship Company ceded his trunk phone lines to facilitate transmissions of the latest news from local hospitals.

By eight-thirty, Beck's people arrived at the side of the fallen steamship, installing phone lines so that a direct connection could be made between the paper's headquarters and the site of the wreck. The city's telephone and telegraph lines were taxed to capacity as word began to spread with brushfire speed. "The load of wire work," reported one witness later in the day, "was said by employees [of Western Union] to be as great as that resulting from the Ohio floods."

A motion picture crew arrived at the scene and began photographing the most heartbreaking, stomach-churning images imaginable. In the days following the disaster, out of respect for the victims' families, city officials censored the movie footage, its grim scenes of death and destruction deemed too harrowing for any viewer to endure.

OTTO MUCHNA puffed on his Panola, gazing out the open doorway of his tidy little carriage garage at 2716 South Central Park Avenue. Situated in the quiet, westside neighborhood of Lawndale, Muchna's funeral chapel was more than five miles due west of the chaos now occurring on the river. For most of those early hours of July 24th, it might as well have been a million miles away as Otto Muchna had been holding court among his drivers, talking about everything under the sun *but* shipwrecks.

The conversation that morning was casual, maybe even a little "salty," considering the somber vocation in which they were engaged. Muchna spent a lot of off-time with his hearse drivers, telling jokes, sharing morning smokes. Contrary to popular myth, immigrant undertakers of this vintage compensated for all the daily challenges and routine sorrow of their trade by leading amiable lives.

"They weren't morbid," Otto's grandson, Roy Muchna, recalls with a smile. "This was their job. At the picnics and celebrations, they had a good time. They formed associations. There was a lot of socializing. They did a lot of things as a group, and they drank a lot of beer."

Early twentieth-century undertakers provided an integral thread in the tapestry of Chicago's immigrant culture. Tiny, family-run funeral chapels were located practically at every corner. Immigrants themselves, and sensitive to the needs of their brethren, the undertakers provided comfort at this most delicate moment in a family's history.

In a typical privately-owned funeral parlor, the father did the embalming, and the mother handled the makeup and burial attire. Most undertaker businesses were multi-generational, and they made house calls. Wakes took place in the home. Coffins sat in modest living rooms, displayed next to the hearth, the tick-tock sound of ice dripping beneath the funeral bier blending with the soft hush of sobbing.

On that cool July morning, Otto Muchna seemed like the last person on earth one would associate with death. Surrounded by his drivers, he stood tall in his little garage, leading the conversation between puffs of his fragrant stogie. A rangy, olive-skinned man with a lantern jaw and prominent nose, he wore his pomaded dark hair swept straight back, as though he were facing down the perpetual gale winds of sadness that blew past him every day. He had an elegant mustache that seemed to evolve according to his social stature. His wedding photographs reveal a finely groomed young man, his mustache a mere pen-line across his upper lip. Later pictures show a luxurious, bushy growth—the mustache of an earl or a viscount.

Born in Chicago on January 13, 1883, the eldest son of Bohemian immigrants, Otto lost his mother at an early age and was raised by his father, who passed away when Otto was fourteen.

At that point Otto went to stay with his older sister, Anna, who lived in the Lawndale district on the city's west side. Anna's husband, John Cervak, was a respected local undertaker, and it was there, living with the Cervaks, that Otto first learned the funeral parlor business.

At that time, the Cervaks had a little storefront funeral chapel at the corner of two busy streets in a predominantly Bohemian area. Fascinated by the trade while still a teenager, Otto helped his brother-in-law with all aspects of the business, from the preservation of bodies with arsenic, ice, and sawdust, to the operation of wakes in the homes of the bereaved. Otto soon took over the family business, and cemented his destiny.

This was a watershed time for mortuary science, which had just begun to modernize. In the late 1890s, the use of formaldehyde in the embalming room had become the new standard for preserving the deceased. (Until that time, practitioners used arsenic to kill bacteria, which made forensic autopsies next to impossible.) At the age of nineteen, Otto became one of the first (and youngest) Chicagoans to qualify for an embalming license under the new guidelines for mortuary safety.

In 1903, Otto married his neighborhood sweetheart, Mary Juranek, took possession of the Cervaks' little chapel after John and Anna relocated, and later had three children. The Muchnas became a fixture in their community. Otto's sister-in-law, Jenny Juranek, worked as a cable winder at the Hawthorne plant, and pitched for the Western Electric ladies' softball team, known as the Bloomer Girls. Accordingly, the Muchna family knew all about the annual Western Electric picnic, which had been a big topic of conversation around the Muchna dinner table that July. However, nobody expected such cataclysmic news when Mary's pallid face appeared above the Dutch door connecting the chapel to the garage.

"There's been a boating accident," she uttered.

All heads turned. Otto's eyes narrowed as he pondered his wife's bloodless stare. "An accident?"

"Anna called—it's Jenny." Mary's hand fluttered to her mouth in terror. "One of the picnic boats has gone down. They don't know if she was—"

Mary's words choked off, and the men looked at each other. Otto Muchna's expression turned stony. He stubbed out his cigar, went to his wife and put his arm around her. He assured her that her sister was fine. Mary trembled, which was out of character for her. Normally rock-steady during a calamity, she was a woman of quiet dignity and humanity. But this was different— this was her sister.

"What happened?" Otto wanted to know. He began to realize just how grave such a situation could be for a ship packed to the gills, loaded with friends and neighbors. But Mary had no details. All she knew was that the *Eastland* had turned over, and things didn't look good.

Behind Mary, within the shadows of the chapel, the phone started ringing again.

"Where are the kids?" Otto asked her, his stoic expression unchanged.

"Otto and May are inside; Jerry's down the street, playing with the Illich boy, making wooden boats."

"Better gather him." Otto nodded toward the chapel. "And you better see who's calling. Could be something else about the accident."

Mary turned and hurried back into the chapel.

Otto whirled toward his men. They were standing there, calm and still, like soldiers awaiting orders. Otto told them to prepare the horses, and get the hearse ready to travel. Otto knew he would have to take a trip down to the docks to find his sister-in-law, and god-only-knew what else.

The men sprang into action. They grabbed bridles off hooks,

threw open stall doors, urged horses out of their cubbies. Metal bits and chains jangled. Horses snorted. The men worked quickly, without speaking to each other, until they heard Mary's cry: "She's all right!"

Mary appeared in the doorway, her eyes wet. "That was her! That was Jenny. She's all right. She says she's wet but alive and all right!"

"Where is she?"

"She's at Iroquois Memorial, and she's all right."

Otto went over and gave his wife a hug. Mary was still shaking. Otto held her, stroked her hair, murmured that it was okay. But Mary was rattled. She looked up into Otto's eyes, and he could tell by her expression that all was not well.

"It's bad, Otto. Could be a thousand gone."

Otto took a deep breath, then nodded. "Go get Jerry. I'll head on down the river, pick up Jenny and maybe see what I can do to help."

ABOVE THE Reid-Murdoch building, its giant scorched-brick garret overlooked the accident scene, its clock face displaying the time: eight-thirty-five. Down below, the surface of the black water appeared almost still. The bobbing heads had vanished. The tugs and fireboats burrowed against the hull of the *Eastland* like pilotfish, as stunned hordes of soaked picnickers stood on the decks, dripping with rancid water, looking on. The chorus of snoring lung-motors and crackling arc welders filled the air as helpless multitudes watched from bridges and piers, held back by an army of men in sodden blue uniforms and rain-slick coats.

Fewer and fewer bodies dragged from the water or from the guts of the ship showed any signs of life. Only an hour had passed since the capsizing, but already a terrible dread pressed down on the scene. The crowds grew silent, and their silence fed the anguish. Survivors began to realize what may have happened to entire families such as the Sindelars.

"The virtually instantaneous nature of the disaster in the passengers' perception constituted a very random element in their survival," Hilton surmised. "This, in turn, explains one of the worst aspects of the disaster, the extent to which it knifed through families and groups of friends, quickly killing some members while leaving others with physical injuries no worse than bruises."

The lucky ones escaped death with a stunning randomness. One man survived because a nail caught the collar of his coat. Others were tossed to safety. Stories abounded of "near misses"—people deciding at the last minute not to board the *Eastland*, people delayed, people directed by ticket-takers to board a different ship. Stories of incredible coincidences pervaded the news coverage. A gauge tender aboard the *Eastland*, a man named John Elbert, provided the *Tribune* one of these amazing yarns.

"I was up on deck when she settled on her side, and got safely over," Elbert explained. "I knew there were a lot of people imprisoned in the lounging room in the rear of the main deck." Wasting little time, the crewman quickly ripped off his shirt and crawled back down into the guts of the wreck. He found more than fifty people trapped in the saloon area, clinging to life preservers. One by one, Elbert helped them back through the companionway, saving dozens.

In later interviews, Elbert credited his twelve years of experience in the navy for his swimming skills. He also gave another explanation for why he was so fearless in the face of such calamity, an explanation hotly disputed by many and questioned eighty years afterward by historians such as George Hilton, who could find no documentation on the subject.

The reason, according to Elbert, that he was so hardened to

shipwrecks, was because he had served on another boat that had experienced its own brand of catastrophic failure, the *Titanic*.

E. K. PLAMONDON stood on the edge of the dock near the crowded threshold of the Reid-Murdoch building.

Dripping wet, his woolen vest clinging to his back and his straw boater long gone, the middle-aged man wiped tears from his eyes as he gazed toward the east end of the pier. His nephew, W. J. Plamondon, was emerging from a cluster of survivors, his arm around his stunned, soaking-wet wife. The older man rushed to his niece and nephew. The threesome embraced amid the chaos, and stayed that way for some time, tearful yet thankful, until raw emotion broke them down as they hugged each other.

For once, luck was with the Plamondon family. Seven of them were on board the *Eastland*, including E.K.'s wife, his two daughters, and his brother Ambrose, and all of them survived. The daughters were taken to St. Luke's Hospital. Ambrose recovered on the other side of the river after single-handedly saving three women. The Plamondons' stroke of good fortune was long overdue: they had seen much tragedy within their family in recent years. E.K.'s cousin Charlie had lost a daughter in the Iroquois fire of 1903. And only a couple of months prior to the *Eastland*, that same cousin, Charles Plamondon, had perished along with his wife in the cold waters off the coast of Ireland during the sinking of the *Lusitania*.

THE DRIZZLE momentarily ceased, and for the briefest of moments, the sun came out.

For many present that day, this strange incongruity went unnoticed. But for some, the sunlight felt like a travesty—a sort of macabre grace note at the end of one of Chicago's ghastliest hours.

A reporter for the *Tribune* noticed something floating on the water, reflecting the light. "Rays of gold dust yellowed a tangled bit of hair that floated on the water for a moment," wrote the reporter, haunted by an aching sadness. The object became a symbol of many things: the tragic loss of life that was just beginning to register; the speed with which the disaster had come and gone; and that horrible point in all great tragedies where rescue becomes recovery.

The tangle of hair slowly sank from view.

*

PART 3

City of Constant Sorrow

Grief can't be shared. Everyone carries it alone, his
own burden his own way.

—Anne Morrow Lindbergh,
Dearly Beloved

*

CHAPTER TWELVE

That Final Parting Embrace

THE *EASTLAND* disaster attracted every able-bodied diver within a fifty-mile radius. Freelancers rushed to the scene with their breathing rigs, slamming through cordons in their ramshackle trucks. Among them were Charles Gunderson of Gunderson & Son Submarine Divers, and Arthur Loeb, the self-proclaimed King of the Bell Divers. These staunch, grizzled, fearless men had torsos like tree trunks and granite constitutions, calloused by years of punishing duty. "I am the only man in the world with a broken blood vessel on my forehead and a fractured skull," Loeb once asserted. But not a single one of these tough-willed men had any idea what they were about to find under the surface of that black river.

One of these divers, Iver Johnsen, balanced himself on the creaky, floating platform just below the dock east of the wreck, waiting impatiently for his helmet, a huge rounded bell with little barred windows on three sides, to be lowered over his head by a tender. One of the first divers to arrive at the Clark Street pier, Johnsen wanted to get in the water as quickly as possible. The noise bothered him—all the clanging and crying. A tall, big-boned young Dane, Johnsen had a bushy, ginger-colored mustache, and was decked out in heavy-duty canvas diving gear. One of the best known "hard-hat" divers on the Great Lakes, he usually employed his son, Walter, as the tender, and on that fateful morning the tradition continued.

Young Walter crouched nearby, readying his gear. A slender man, his boyish face narrow and earnest, he helped Iver put on the standard knit under-cap of most hardhat men. Then Walter turned his attentions to the bulky helmet. The Johnsens had non-verbal, almost extrasensory ways of communicating: a series of nods, hand gestures and obscure signals. On that tumultuous morning, with all the noise and turmoil on the docks, these signals proved especially useful.

In 1915, scores of full-time divers were employed in Chicago to do salvage work and bridge repairs on what was essentially nineteenth-century technology. A primitive version of a diving apparatus had been in use since the eighteenth century, and over the course of the next 200 years the physical principles had not changed that much. The *Eastland* divers utilized a modified version of the "closed suit dress" first introduced in 1830 by the German inventor Augustus Siebe. Made of layers of canvas and rubber, the suit covered the divers almost completely from head to toe, except for the hands and helmet area. A leaden bib covered the chest and shoulders in order to support the massive metal helmet, and extra weight was carried in the belt for stabilization. Even the shoes bore heavy blocks of lead that would not have seemed out of place on Frankenstein's monster.

The Johnsens made their final checks quickly. Surface teams got into position, flinging air hoses in coils along the dock. Each diver connected himself to a pair of umbilicals—a hose for air, and a rope for signaling trouble. One hard yank meant they had run out of oxygen or they had gotten caught or they needed to come up immediately.

Iver noticed a third diver standing on the dock beyond Walter, preparing to go under. His name was Harry Halvorsen. A tall, burly, chiseled-looking man, and one of the city's veteran hard-hats, Halvorsen had a reputation for being a diplomat, a man who could keep things running smoothly between the divers and the cops. It is likely that Iver Johnsen, at some point, gave Halvorsen a terse, quick glance—maybe a nod or a wink—to acknowledge the gravity of the situation and to assure him that the Johnsens were ready for anything.

The helmet snapped down over Iver's head, muffling the noise and clamor around him, and darkening the light into narrow nimbuses from the viewing portals. Wing nuts clicked. The sound of Iver's breathing filled his ears. He signaled his son, then signaled the firemen, then climbed slowly down the steps of the floating platform and went into the river with a gurgle.

Everything went silent, dark, and cold.

Iver paddled and moved his legs in order to orient himself. He hit bottom almost immediately; at only twenty-three feet, the river would never give anybody the bends, and it was a soft impact, like landing in a bowl of oatmeal. Iver blinked and rotated his body toward the wreck.

Ghostly objects appeared. As Iver's eyes adjusted to the murk, he began to discern things floating weightlessly past his helmet. Cigarettes, bread, a shoe, pieces of waterlogged wood. He moved forward slowly toward the looming black monolith. The first sign of the ship's sideways bow came into view.

Deadlights.

They appeared out of the haze like signposts, and Iver recognized them immediately: closed portholes partially buried in the silt of the river bottom, probably those on the port side of the forward saloon. The sailors called them "deadlights," and it was standard operating procedure to keep them closed during certain maneuvers. The number and condition of these closed portholes came into play during criminal proceedings after the disaster.

Iver found his way into the wreck.

He entered through the forward portion of the hull, probably through a submerged stairwell, and immediately noticed his surroundings changing. The ambient light dimmed, and the muffled thumping and crackling of rescues-in-progress up above him vibrated the swill. Shapes loomed. Ruined fixtures, broken benches, and furnishings reached up at Johnsen like skeletal arms. The diver moved more cautiously now, careful not to snag his lifeline on the twisted wreckage.

The first body came into view, a teenage girl wedged between a pile of chairs and the cabin wall. Clad in a brightly colored party dress, now dulled by the dark dross of the underwater world, her body swayed in the shifting currents. Iver secretly girded himself as he peered through his glass lens at the girl's wan face, contorted in asphyxia.

This was going to be far more difficult than repairing bridge pilings.

Johnsen extracted the limp form as gently as possible, working in the near dark, trying not to register the soft surfaces of her dead body on his fingers. He pulled the victim back through the stairwell, soldiering through the muck as a man might slog through a dream. Other divers materialized: Barney Sullivan and Halvorsen moving like phantoms on either flank. Another corpse, a boy, perhaps, moved off the port-side stern. Johnsen urged his sad bundle toward the surface.

Iver Johnsen would not meet Reggie Bowles for several more hours, but the Human Frog from Old Irving Park had already made his presence known to many.

* * *

"It was strange how many of them drowned hanging tight to some object below water," recalled the deckhand Harry Miller. "Some I hooked down at the bottom, others halfway up, others only two or three feet below the water. I could tell by the pull it took to tear them loose that they had their hands gripped onto a rail or a table or some other fixed object down below the water." In many cases, as it turned out, the "other fixed object" was a loved one.

"Sometimes they had to put two bodies on the same stretcher," a local journalist reported. "Death had so tightened that final parting embrace, indulged in as the gray river water leaped up to meet those who had left home early and exclaimed in light hearted satisfaction when they found they were still in time to garner a seat on the shady side of the boat, the side that now lies buried in the river ooze."

The pathos of the recovery was matched only by the gruesomeness. Due to the violent abruptness of the capsizing, the furniture and the various unbolted items sliding down upon the victims, the accident had mangled bodies beyond recognition. Falling debris tore scalps from skulls and sheered extremities from torsos. The leeching effect of the river made the revelations of the dead especially surreal. Mutilated bodies appeared blanched and bloodless, like waxen dolls, their gashed visages still adorned by neatly buttoned Arrow collars or delicate lace chokers.

Firemen and police repeatedly hooked female victims buried down in the silt, then dragged them up by the sashes of their skirts, onlookers audibly gasping as the young ladies' privates glared in the gray light.

"I wondered dully why they waited for stretchers at all," recalled Gretchen Krohn, a renowned Chicago writer of that era. "All the bodies carried past were so rigid that poles to carry them by seemed superfluous; and the pitiful shortness of most of them!

Wet, clinging curls that swept the dock punctuated the line so frequently that even helpers groaned. Children, and yet more children; and when it wasn't a child it was a young girl of 18 or so."

The instantaneous nature of many fatalities had another disquieting effect: death had embossed ghastly expressions onto many of the dead faces.

"Has it ever been your unhappy lot as a youngster to drown a batch of particularly unwelcome kittens?" wrote Krohn in a fit of rhetorical delirium. "Or have you ever plunged a wire rat trap into water? Imagine that expression of trapped animal terror transferred to the face of a human being, and then so firmly stamped by death that the pattern has set."

The recovery teams worked with as much decorum as possible in such abysmal conditions. Firemen struggled across the slippery surface of the hull in grim silence. Along the pontoon bridges, divers communicated wordlessly and shared concealed flasks of whiskey to steady themselves between plunges. With varying degrees of success the stretcher bearers tried to keep their pitiful human cargo covered with tarps and away from the prurient gazes of the crowds.

"The tarpaulin sheets!" Krohn opined. "They were the travesty that put the final keen edge on this ghastliness. After all these poor bodies had been trampled on and then drowned, or drowned and then trampled on, they covered them up with tarpaulins to keep this poor, wet earth from getting any wetter."

CAPTAIN PEDERSEN sat bolt upright on a bench aboard the *Graeme Stewart* fireboat, where Schuettler had ordered him held for the time being. The captain's head throbbed, and his gnarled hands kept working in his lap, wringing convulsively, involuntarily. His first mate, Del Fisher, sat next to him. Although no record exists of their conversation at that point, the two likely had little to say to each other. The infernal noise outside the boat kept them silent and sheepish and defensive.

At some point after nine a.m., Chief Schuettler gave orders that the steamboat master and his right-hand man be moved to City Hall where Cook County Coroner Peter Hoffman and Assistant State's Attorney Charles Case were waiting to question them. Twenty policemen filed on board the *Graeme Stewart* and took Pedersen and Fisher into their custody for the short journey across the Loop. They rode in a horse-drawn patrol car surrounded by a dozen or so mounted police, and made the journey as quickly and discreetly as possible, but discretion proved difficult, considering what was occurring on adjacent streets, not to mention the escort of twenty cops.

Before the procession got far, the patrol car encountered a roadblock formed by what the *Tribune* described as "a mob." Hundreds of furious onlookers and victims' family members, galvanized by the madness on the river, pushed toward the patrol car. Batons came out. People started shoving. Pedersen, sitting in the rear of the car, partly visible through the open doorway, tried to remain stoic.

Finally a desperate, unidentified man broke through the mounted cordon and reached the rear of the car. Before officers could intervene, the man pried open the doors and found Pedersen sitting stiff-jawed in the shadows. The attacker got off one solid blow to the Captain's ruddy face before policemen tore the man away and clubbed him into submission with batons.

AT THE ACCIDENT SITE, the lingering problem of identifying the dead began to weigh heavily on the minds of recovery workers.

Most of those who were fortunate enough to survive, clinging to chicken crates and life preservers, had already been conveyed to local hospitals or wrapped in blankets on the pier. Already traumatized, these passengers now joined the thousands of desperate families pacing the docks, frantically searching for loved ones along the hull and in the temporary morgues set up on the barge and in the Reid-Murdoch building. Frantic mothers pushed their way through the clogged hallways of the warehouse, desperately seeking the familiar face of a lost child or a missing husband in the dim passageways where the corpses lay.

Complicating matters was the fact that the first several dozen bodies recovered had been transported by spare horse patrols to remote funeral parlors or neighboring hospital morgues, and were unaccounted for. By late morning, the deceased had been scattered throughout the city.

Exhausted nurses tried futilely to keep order. Women bumped into each other, their eyes wide with terror, mumbling, letting out little squeaks of agony. "Mothers fell across the biers of children whom they had sent away a few hours before on what was intended to be a day of pleasure," wrote the *New York Times*.

"Nearly every room on the lower floors of the warehouse contained bodies," reported the *Tribune*. "The remaining space was filled with crowds of policemen, rescuers, friends and relatives of the dead, and a corps of fifty embalmers." The embalmers had already been at work for some time in a furious attempt to stave off further decomposition among the waterlogged dead. Temporary curtains went up to separate the crowds from the rattling, dripping business of the undertakers. But the turmoil along the docks, as well as the nature of most of the drowning deaths, made such considerations secondary.

"Speed was important, and time was of the essence," explains Jon Austin, current director of the Museum of Funeral Customs. "Immediate removal from the water and immediate embalming was ideal in order to prevent the blood from coagulating in the vascular system. Coagulation would have made it very difficult for the undertakers of that era to drain the blood and properly prepare the body for viewing."

Workers from the office of the county coroner made valiant attempts to keep order. They affixed tags to stretchers of the deceased, beginning with "A-1," and numbering them accordingly, up to "A-100," then beginning again with "B-1" and so on. Descriptions were entered into logbooks before the embalmed bodies were placed in "ambulance baskets"—oversized wicker containers with lids—for discreet conveyance to mortuary homes. But the fact that so many of the dead had already been taken to funeral parlors scattered across the town made the process agonizingly slow and imperfect.

Emotions crackled. Something had to be done to bring order to this awful process of identifying the dead. The situation required leadership, and perhaps a little something extra, something verging on iron-clad resolve.

TWO FIGURES emerged during those early, tragic hours on a tide of righteous indignation of almost biblical proportions: Cook County State's Attorney Maclay Hoyne, and Cook County Coroner Peter Hoffman.

Of the two men, Hoyne was the younger and the wealthier. Born in 1872, the scion of an old-money Chicago family, he studied law at Northwestern University and entered the bar in 1897. A mere five years later, he had risen to senior partner at what would become one of Chicago's most prestigious law firms: Hoyne, O'Conner and Hoyne. A staunch Baptist, he was elected state's attorney in 1912 running as a Democrat, and immediately started building a reputation for himself as a tough-minded reformer—perhaps *crusader* was a better word to describe him.

With his patrician bearing, pursed lips, and fussy little oval eyeglasses, Maclay Hoyne resembled a young Franklin Roosevelt.

One year after the *Eastland* disaster, Hoyne solidified his mythic status by conducting a raid on City Hall itself, exposing the corruption in Mayor "Big Bill" Thompson's well-oiled political machine. But it was the *Eastland* disaster that provided Maclay Hoyne with his earliest role on the national stage.

Hoyne had been roused from his Loop office only moments after the capsizing, and by noon that morning came face to face on the north bank of the river with Coroner Peter Hoffman. At fifty-two, Hoffman was nine years Hoyne's senior, and was a bit coarser, a tad rougher around the edges. Born into a working-class family, Hoffman had attended public schools and had gone to business college. He'd been a grocer, had worked for the railroad, and in 1898, he ran for Cook County Commissioner and was elected by the same people to whom he had once served coffee each morning on the Chicago Northwestern. But Hoffman had bigger fires burning in his belly. In 1904 he launched a successful campaign on the Republican ticket for Cook County Coroner.

A big city coroner in 1915 served a unique function. Unlike medical examiners or pathologists who are required to have advanced medical degrees, the county coroner served what was ostensibly an administrative position based on English common law. In a major metropolis such as Chicago, the coroner required no professional credentials other than supervisory skills, but those he supervised included a vast team of specialists, assistant coroners, and physicians. Hoffman was well suited to the task.

A stout, round-faced man with a head of thick, wavy, unruly brown hair, in early photographs Hoffman gives off the appearance of a bull about to charge. With his huge walrus mustache and eyes glimmering with confidence, he was not a man to be taken lightly. As he aged—and his girth spread and his hair grayed—he seemed to grow even more steadfast. In a photograph in a safety pamphlet published around the time of the *Eastland* disaster, Hoffman stands with back rigid, huge belly jutting defiantly, an accusatory finger pointing out at the reader. The terse title reads: *I Am Trying to Make This County Safe! Are You With Me?*

On the morning of July 24, as Hoffman stood on that beleaguered dock, this same stubborn rigor straightened his spine.

Hoffman and Hoyne stood side by side, surveying the scene, surrounded by underlings and other city officials, including Acting Police Chief Schuettler, Assistant State's Attorney Michael Sullivan, Dr. Springer, Dr. Evans, and a cadre of assistant fire chiefs and deputy coroners. The group huddled in the drizzle, their straw boaters and hard bowler hats pulled low over their grim faces. The clock tower above them ticked away the minutes as the dock writhed with mania. Hoffman realized that a central facility was needed for the temporary warehousing of the dead. The consolidation of bodies would be necessary for the bereaved to have a chance to identify loved ones in an orderly manner with some degree of certainty.

Hoyne suggested the Coliseum. The Romanesque assembly hall, used in 1915 as a meeting facility for the burgeoning business community, was on the west side of town, not far from the river and large enough to serve as a temporary morgue for so many fatalities. Hoffman agreed, and Hoyne sent one of his assistants to secure the facility.

While the group waited, they assessed the scene. They observed the divers in action, saw the sparks and plumes of smoke coming off the hull from the arc welders, and witnessed limp, sodden bodies of children being extracted through the jagged maws. The crackling and the yelling and the low sobbing of thousands bearing unspeakable loss chilled the men worse than the drizzle.

As Hoffman stood on the dock, listening to Dr. Springer tick off the litany of death, something must have snapped inside the burly coroner. Witnesses who observed the man at the site remember him being "wet with rain, and with perspiration dripping from his face."

Hoffman turned to his group and announced that he was going to get to the bottom of this horrible tragedy, and he would do so immediately. He would require the services of five men to serve on a special jury. Then he named the men he wanted, one by one, his voice booming over the noise: Dr. William Evans, health editor of the *Tribune*; Colonel Henry Allen, Department of Public Works; William Bode of Reid, Murdoch & Company; Henry Moir, president of the Morrison Hotel; J. S. Keogh, general manager of the McLaughlin Company; and Eugene Beifeld, manager of the College Inn.

"As each man was named," the *Tribune* later reported, "assistants hurried to telephones and asked if they would accept the responsibility of fixing the blame for the disaster."

Minutes later, Hoyne's personal assistant returned to the scene with more bad news: the Coliseum was currently in disarray, torn asunder by decorators in preparation for a meeting scheduled for August 3rd. The building's agent offered an annexed section for use as a morgue, but it was doubtful that the annex provided enough space.

At that point, one of the deputy fire chiefs—his name is unknown—suggested an armory building on the near west side as a possible facility. Hoffman and Hoyne concurred that an armory would be ideal, and the coroner's assistants were immediately dispatched to the 2nd Regimental Illinois National Guard Armory on Curtis Street between Randolph and Washington, about fifteen blocks from the scene, in order to prepare the space for the horrendous gathering of human remains.

CHAPTER THIRTEEN

Somebody Made
a Big Mistake

THE LITTLE BOY materialized in the murk.

Through the fogged goggle of Halvorsen's diving bell the child looked ghostly, otherworldly, like a broken little porcelain doll caught on part of the twisted wreckage in the submerged main deck. The child, dressed in a sailor suit, could not have been more than five years old. A jolt of anguish coursed through the diver's heart.

As Halvorsen drew near, stretching his lifeline to its limit, a glowing object came into view near the child's lifeless yet tranquil face. Through the helmet's window the object looked like a firefly hovering there. Halvorsen reached for the boy, and realized that the firefly was a little crucifix floating in the dark current. Halvorsen gently tucked the icon into the dead boy's shirt. Then, with great care, despite his exhaustion, the diver carefully extracted little William Sindelar from the wreckage.

No one knows exactly what happened to the bodies of the Sindelar family immediately after the capsizing. It is believed that the family died together, in a cluster, in the main cabin. They probably died instantly, not from drowning but from the crush of the throngs pressing into the stairwell. The configuration of the dead shifted and jostled during recovery. The bodies of Josephine and George, Jr., were missing until three days after the capsizing. For the team of divers, as well as those participating in the recovery effort, finding William Sindelar became a milestone.

Halvorsen carefully made his way back to the surface with the body in his arms, and tenderly handed it to the firemen. The sheer pathos of a little boy in a sailor suit being fished out of the abyss seemed to signal a turn in the energy level. Fatigue started taking hold. Nobody put it into words, but the signs were present in the faces of all the grizzled rescuers. As William was borne away on a stretcher, a metal flask was passed discreetly among some of the divers. Downtrodden and exhausted, Iver Johnsen, a teetotaler, bit down on his last plug of Copenhagen snuff.

Although the whiskey burned their throats, made their eyes water and tightened their bellies, the girding effect was insufficient. The job had worn them down. The divers were not looking at each other anymore. No more jaunty signals or brazen leaps into the mire.

Even the sound of a "human frog" bursting out of the water nearby did nothing to penetrate their weary stoicism.

REGGIE EMERGED, gasping, lifting more bodies from the water, laying them as gently as possible on the pontoon bridge at the feet of firemen and policemen. Some victims clung to each other, bound together in death, drenched clothing intertwined. Reggie couldn't look for too long. If he looked for more than a second he started feeling bad inside, and that slowed him down.

"HEY!"

He ignored the barking baritone. He had already recovered two dozen bodies at that point, most of them women and children, and the anguish was working on him. Every fiber of his spindly body ached. The beginnings of hypothermia tightened his joints. With his skinny arms and legs and his dearth of body fat, he would soon succumb to the chill.

"HEY—YOU! BOY!"

He kept ignoring the voice.

Turning back to the wreck and preparing to dive under again, he took a deep breath of air into his throbbing lungs. One reason newspapers called Reggie a "human frog" was his capacity to stay underwater for long periods of time. He could hold his breath for up to three minutes, although it was getting more difficult with every dive. The combination of exhaustion, cold, and mental anguish was threatening to knock Reggie out.

A meaty hand grabbed his shoulder just as he was about to dive.

"Hold your horses," said the deep voice.

Reggie Bowles turned suddenly, looked up, and saw a big cop standing over him.

Dressed in a black rain slicker, the drizzle dripping off the brim of his cap, the officer had a strange expression on his face— a mixture of stern, paternal anger and something like admiration. One of the key supervisors at the accident site, Major Funkhouser, who worked directly under Schuettler, said, "Time for you to knock off, son. Let the professionals take over."

"Let go!"

Reggie yanked himself away, then dove back in. The wreck loomed like a sleeping whale.

Reggie Bowles madly searched the muck for the opening through which he had been entering. Plenty of bodies still lay in the innards of the ship, and Reggie would not give up until they had all been taken out.

NEWS OF THE calamity spread across the land. "Steamboat *Eastland* sunk at the dock," announced one frenzied dispatch addressed to Honorable Woodrow Wilson, President of the United States, Washington D.C., going on to report, "1000 lives lost." Wilson was at his summer retreat in Cornish, New Hampshire, but the moment he learned of the disaster he wired his secretary of commerce, William Redfield, and ordered an immediate investigation.

Published death tolls varied, the *Tribune* wire service claiming 1,200 at first, later revising the numbers throughout the day. Other news bureaus reported anywhere between 900 and 1,800 fatalities. As only about 300 had perished in Chicago's Great Fire, and the Iroquois Theatre fire claimed approximately 600, the gravity of the disaster quickly became apparent.

Chicago's mayor, a flamboyant career politician named William Hale Thompson, had left town a few days earlier to attend the Panama Pacific Exposition in San Francisco with Illinois governor Edward F. Dunne. The event, celebrating the 1914 opening of the Panama canal, had been a gala international gathering. Organizers had planned a "Chicago Day" on the 27th, featuring a dinner, reception and ball. But news of the *Eastland* rocked the contingent and spread a pall over the entire event. Governor Dunne found himself "grieved beyond expression," and Mayor Thompson ordered a special train to be provided by the Overland Limited that afternoon for his immediate return.

"I am shocked and grieved by the news from home detailing the horrible disaster," the mayor told attendees before departing. Thompson had once been a passenger on the *Eastland*, and had been spooked by its unstable feel. From that point on, he had refused ever to ride on the boat again. "I consider it imperative for me to return to my post," he went on, "and city officials here will return with me."

As the mayor's train started for home, thousands bowed their heads while the band of the 1st Regiment of the Illinois National Guard played "Nearer My God to Thee." "Tears ran freely in the cosmopolitan audience as the hymn was sung," wrote a visiting *Tribune* reporter.

While Thompson lit out across the high desert, the acting mayor back in Chicago, Commissioner of Public Works William

Moorhouse, dealt with the shock and tumult overtaking the town. Moorhouse responded swiftly and decisively to the catastrophe, immediately releasing relief funds as well as ordering that "all places of amusement in this city, including theaters, parks and other pleasure resorts, be closed and remain closed for two days as a mark of respect to the dead, so suddenly snatched from life."

Moorhouse also took charge of the scene. He arranged a command post between his office and the recovery operation, and ordered wooden panels erected along the Clark and Wells Street bridges to block the gazes of the morbidly curious.

Across the lake, in Michigan City, the sad little lakeside park lay silent and still under the changing sky, all garnished and trimmed for a celebration that would never occur—on that day, or ever again. An advance party of Western Electric workers had been there for two days, preparing the town, and when the news reached them, they sat stunned in the deserted amusement park. Colorful floats sat unused in storage at the Indiana Transportation Company's warehouse. Restaurants remained empty, their shelves brimming with extra supplies. The Vreeland Hotel, prepared for a gala banquet, sat vacant in eerie silence.

Mary Clark, a lovely, fair-haired eighteen-year-old who had been voted prettiest girl at the Hawthorne plant, was appointed the queen of the festivities and planned to lead the parade. She now lay dead in the Chicago River in one of the sunken berths of the *Eastland*.

Word of the disaster reached St. Joseph, Michigan. Hearing the news, W. H. Hull, general manager of the company that owned the *Eastland*, had a nervous breakdown and collapsed at his home. After being placed under the care of a physician and sequestered in his room, Hull refused to speak to anyone other than his family. A few miles away, hundreds of residents of St. Joseph and the neighboring city of Benton Harbor mobbed the company's headquarters, demanding information about friends and relatives on the *Eastland*.

The news reached far-flung wire bureaus. Telegrams zipped over the transatlantic cable, and within hours wire reports had apprised the entire war-torn European continent. The British had their own problems at the time, with German submarines blockading waterways, the Kaiser sinking ocean liners, and zeppelins raiding major cities. But the world in 1915 seemed somehow to be shrinking. Countless European families had children and grandchildren in Chicago in search of the American dream, and many villages were stung by the news.

In Poland, then under attack by both German and Russian forces, people marveled that such a tragedy could happen in the United States, where so many Polish emigrants had gotten jobs at Western Electric. "In the heart of a peaceful country, and in the heart of a peaceful city, where all precautions are supposed to be taken for the safety of men, women and children," wrote one Polish journalist, "the lives of a thousand persons, on pleasure bent, have been snuffed out."

Other Eastern European countries, many of them the homelands of *Eastland* passengers, reacted with similar emotions. Hungary sent off a special message to Chicagoans from their minister of foreign affairs. In Vienna, U.S. Ambassador Penfield was deluged with inquiries and expressions of sympathy.

Lloyd's of London, who carried insurance on the *Eastland*, responded immediately. While victims were still being hauled out of the boat, Lloyd's cabled its U.S. representative, T. C. Warkman of Milwaukee, and dispatched him to the scene. Warkman jumped on a train, and by mid-afternoon had checked into the Hotel LaSalle, and by five o'clock was making inquiries.

William Rolph, the mayor of San Francisco, in the throes of hosting his own international exposition, dropped everything and boarded a train for Chicago to help in any way that he could.

An early postcard of the *Eastland*. (Eastland Disaster Historical Society)

A moonlight excursion. (Eastland Disaster Historical Society)

Postcard depicting the Hawthorne works. (Eastland Disaster Historical Society)

Hawthorne assembly-line workers, ca. 1913. (Eastland Disaster Historical Society)

Washington Park in the early 1900s. (Courtesy LaPorte County Historical Society, Inc.)

A parade of suffragettes from the Hawthorne works, ca. 1913. (Courtesy Lucent Technologies and Ron Steinberg)

The 1914 picnic: "Sit down, you're rockin' the boat!" (Courtesy Lucent Technologies and Ron Steinberg)

Postcard of the *Eastland* in happier times. (Eastland Disaster Historical Society)

The Aanstad family
(*clockwise from top:*
Uncle Olaf, Bobbie,
Solveig, Marianne).
(Courtesy the family
of Jean Decker)

Borghild "Bobbie"
Aanstad: "Never
stopped loving the
water." (Courtesy
the family of Jean
Decker)

Five-year-old William Sindelar. (Courtesy Christine Harmon and the family of George and Josephine Sindelar)

Josephine Sindelar's watch. (The family of George and Josephine Sindelar)

The *Eastland* minutes after the capsizing. (Eastland Disaster Historical Society)

Emergency pontoon bridges. (Eastland Disaster Historical Society)

Welder cutting holes in the downed *Eastland*. (Chicago Historical Society)

Reggie Bowles shortly after collapsing on the dock. (Courtesy David Bowles)

Diver Arthur Loeb inside the sunken *Eastland*. (Eastland Disaster Historical Society; photo by Jun Fujita)

Fallen *Eastland* covered in victims: "An unparalleled paradox." (Chicago Historical Society)

The procession of victims exiting the scene. (Chicago Historical Society; photo by Jun Fujita)

The sideways promenade deck shortly after accident. (Eastland Disaster Historical Society)

A man being lifted through a hole in the hull. (Eastland Disaster Historical Society; photo by Jun Fujita)

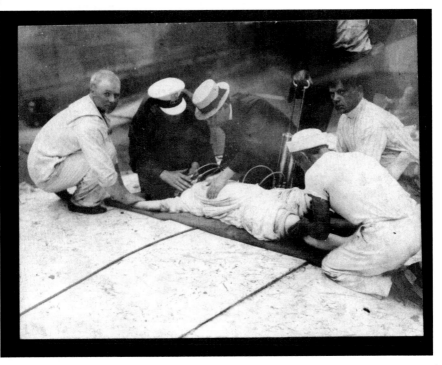

Unidentified female victim being treated with a pulmotor. (Eastland Disaster Historical Society; photo by Jun Fujita)

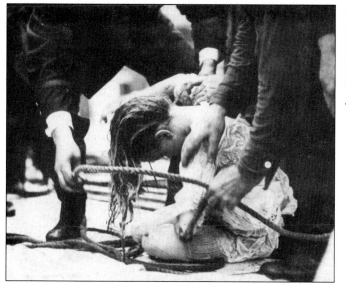

An unidentified fatality just before removal: "Wholesale slaughter." (Eastland Disaster Historical Society; photo by Jun Fujita)

A fireman carrying out his sad duty. (Eastland Disaster Historical Society; photo by Jun Fujita)

Diver Harry Halvorsen. (Chicago Historical Society)

Principal divers (*from second-to-left*: Charles Gunderson, Iver Johnsen, Harry Halvorsen, Barney Sullivan). (Chicago Historical Society)

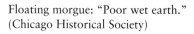

Floating morgue: "Poor wet earth."
(Chicago Historical Society)

Overflow of bodies: "Most were
simply assigned numbers." (Eastland
Disaster Historical Society)

Undertaker Otto Muchna.
(Courtesy Roy Muchna)

Otto Muchna's business card.
(Courtesy Roy Muchna)

2nd Regiment Armory building: "Clearing house of the dead."
(Chicago Historical Society)

Lines outside the armory. (Chicago Historical Society)

Inside the armory: "Strong men broke down and fled weeping." (Eastland Disaster Historical Society; photo by Jun Fujita)

The recovery efforts continuing through the night: "An unearthly glow." (Chicago Historical Society)

Sindelar coffins at a mass funeral. (Eastland Disaster Historical Society)

Mass funeral at St. Mary's of Czestochowa. (Eastland Disaster Historical Society)

Hawthorne works draped in bunting: "Black Wednesday." (Eastland Disaster Historical Society)

"We in San Francisco can never forget the wonderful heart opening of Chicago in our hour of trouble," he told reporters, referring to the Great Fire of 1906, which had been caused by an earthquake and had raged for three days, destroying practically the entire bay area. "Our city," he went on, "is at Chicago's command, financially and otherwise."

Other U.S. news organizations started processing the event immediately for next day's coverage. "A carnival of death!" cried streetcorner news hawks in Milwaukee. "It is too soon to apportion blame," a *New York Times* editor wrote that afternoon, "but some things are indisputable: The *Eastland* had a bad record." In Montgomery, Alabama, typesetters for the *Advertiser* laid out giant headlines: "TERRIBLE DISASTER AT CHICAGO!" In St. Louis, outraged desk editors at the *Globe Democrat* surmised, "Surely men have not been building ships for 3,000 years without discovering some way to prevent a steamer sinking at the wharf, with its precious freight, in absolute calm."

In Washington, D.C., as the afternoon dragged on, the first assistant inspector general, Dickerson N. Hoover, Jr., mustered only a brief yet terse statement to the horde of reporters: "Somebody made a big mistake."

OTTO MUCHNA wiped the sweat from his brow. He didn't like to perspire while he worked but the heat had a way of collecting in the small and airless carriage garage behind his funeral chapel, despite the blocks of ice beneath the makeshift gurneys. Chilly rain had only added to the midsummer humidity, and the ice would soon be gone, leaving only a fog bank of pale vapor in the charnel house. The handsome Bohemian worked in silence—a mixture of decorum and professionalism—his sleeves rolled up, his tie still neatly snug against his neck. He finished washing and disinfecting the teenager, then prepared to inject the embalming fluid.

He paused and gazed down at the body of a young girl lying waxen and bloodless on the table before him. Partially clad in a sheet, her face darkened from bruises and encroaching lividity, she didn't look much older than Otto's sister-in-law, Jenny. Otto knew the girl's parents. Both members of Otto's church, they had called the Muchna chapel earlier that afternoon to ask if Otto could provide burial services for their daughter.

Otto had said yes, of course, as he had said to almost a dozen other local families who had lost someone in the capsizing. As the afternoon waned, the workload had become almost overwhelming. Otto had already made a half-dozen trips to the temporary morgues at the accident site, and had been forced to remove the rollaway doors that connected the adjacent workroom to his garage in order to accommodate the numbers of dead. He normally washed the carriages in the workroom, but now it held rows of bodies, lined up like milestones in the ice fog. Otto used the doors as temporary gurneys, and propped each door up on one end with a crate in order to keep the livor mortis from collecting in the heads of the deceased.

At only thirty-two years old, Otto had been a licensed embalmer for nearly half of his life. A natural perfectionist, he knew that many of the families were going to want open-casket viewings in their homes, and he knew it was up to him to make the deceased presentable. This sort of pressure might have undone many an ordinary man, but Otto worked in a sort of altered state—as did many of the undertakers that day—which allowed him to focus intently on the job at hand, ignoring the exhaustion, the sorrow, and the horror.

Thank God Jenny had survived, he thought. Otto had picked his sister-in-law up at Iroquois Hospital earlier that day and had heard her tale on the buggy trip on the way back to Lawndale. The young Western Electric "Bloomer Girl" had been thrown into the river when the boat went over and, grabbing hold of an enormous box camera floating by in the water, she had been able to survive in the filthy currents long enough for rescuers to reach her in a rowboat.

Putting it out of his mind, Otto began the embalming process.

A large glass bell jar full of formaldehyde hung on a stand above the operating table, glimmering in the low light. Otto injected it into the girl's body through the brachial artery in her arm, using an instrument known as a percolator. In this premotorized era, embalming was a hand-operated job, but otherwise virtually identical to today's techniques. The percolator resembled a large stainless steel cake-decorating device, with a piston-plunger, and a nipple connected to a hose. The blood was forced out of the corpse as the gravity-fed fluid was injected.

It is likely that Muchna's makeshift operating room deposited the blood, river water, and other liquid human byproducts through a drain in the floor. Most of the bodies Otto treated that day were drowning victims, and their cavities required some time to clear. To a trained ear, all this draining made an unmistakable noise: a soft, rhythmic sucking sound that was almost tranquil.

Otto had completed the fluid exchange and was about to begin the cavity treatment when the sound of the telephone ringing inside the adjacent chapel reached his ear. Mary Muchna, who had been applying makeup on the deceased inside the chapel, appeared once again in the inner doorway. "They've identified another one for us," she said, her voice flattened from exhaustion. "They've got them all in one place now."

Otto looked at her. "All in one place? Where?"

"Armory building on Washington Street. Washington and Curtis."

Otto nodded. Most of the day he had been traveling back and forth from a temporary morgue at the old Shenandoah Garage at Jackson and Damen, where many Lawndale residents had been summoned to identify their loved ones. It sounded as though the powers-that-be had succeeded in consolidating the remains in one place. Otto told his wife he would return as soon as humanly possible.

Wiping his hands and lowering his sleeves, Otto called to one of his grooms. The assistant quickly tacked and prepared the freshest mare for another journey downtown. Out in the enclosed driveway, metal bits jangled, and leather harnesses creaked. The big horse snorted, its hot breath cooled by the icy draft from the carriage house. The groom clucked his tongue, and the mare backed up to the funeral carriage parked along the side of the drive.

The carriage itself looked like a giant coffin, set on massive springs and great wooden wheels, its burnished rectangular body featuring ornate moldings and carvings—curtains, fruit, flowers, all meticulously sculpted. The front had an upholstered seat and two big decorative gas lamps flanking the cab.

Otto sighed as he put on his dignified wool coat and readied himself for the journey. If his exhausted horses didn't rest soon they'd surely start going lame, and that would be bad for business. But Otto didn't have the luxury of worrying about such things. He had to keep going, had to do what was required.

As he climbed into the driver's seat, he noticed a small figure crouched in the shadows of a half-ajar door at the end of the drive.

The little fair-haired boy in the baseball suit huddled behind the wooden slats, watching everything with keen interest. Little Jerry was Otto's middle son, and only a few short hours earlier had been sailing wooden boats in Lawndale's swollen drainage gutters with his pal Frankie Illich. Now the boy seemed entranced by all the excitement, not to mention the strange, low tones with which all the adults were speaking to each other.

Otto gave the boy a wink, and a sad little smile, then climbed onboard the carriage. He took the reins and gave the mare a snap, and the horse dutifully jerked its head, then started clopping toward the exit at the end of the drive.

THE BEST ROUTE to the armory was via Kedzie Avenue, a busy, cobblestone artery running through the blue-collar encampments of Douglas Park and Altgeld.

Otto Muchna pushed the horse as hard as possible through the drizzle. A heavy gloom hung in the air among the street vendors and motortrucks as they went about their normal Saturday afternoon business. Word-of-mouth news of the disaster had spread to every quarter of the city. Every newsie, tavern, druggist, and greengrocer seemed to be conducting business with a hushed sort of sorrow.

It took the undertaker a half hour to make the five-mile trip to Washington and Curtis.

The 2nd Regiment Armory sat at the corner of a densely populated area on the near west side of the city. As Otto approached, he got his first glimpse of the building's dark brick turret rising above the street corner. Although the armory had been built in the late nineteenth century with strictly utilitarian purposes in mind, the design had a quintessentially Victorian-era feel. Squeezed into a crowded sector of apartments, row houses, and restaurants, the two-story pile of stone and brick sat like a fortress. The building was made of the darkest-colored brick in the area—compared to its flagstone neighbors—as though the structure had somehow been stained by its sad destiny. The shingles of the conical turret dominated the facade, with large stone dormers protruding along the pitched roof, reaching nearly a hundred feet down perpendicular blocks. The central entrance formed a huge round archway with the words 2ND REGMNT. ARMORY embossed in stone.

Directly across the street lay a rubble-strewn vacant lot, a sad refraction of the desolate, barren madness about to afflict visitors to this doomed place.

Parking the hearse-carriage next to an ambulance, tying off the weary horse, Otto negotiated a tense cordon of uneasy policemen in order to get inside the building. The morbidly curious had already descended on the place, and coroner Hoffman was struggling to maintain order and dignity.

Otto showed his credentials, then followed an officer through a side door and into the armory.

The air felt cool yet stifling in that main drill hall. Otto immediately recognized the telltale odors of formaldehyde and death, as well as the familiar breathy sounds of embalming percolators already working busily behind tarps drawn across the corners of the huge open room. A narrow balcony-walkway wrapped around three sides of the hall, and a pall of crestfallen silence hung heavily in the air. For years the armory had housed munitions and practicing honor guards—a storehouse for instruments of war— and now Death had found the building in the shape of fancily clad corpses brought through its side doors in wicker caskets.

Coroner's assistants laid the bodies unceremoniously on the floor like so many pieces of cordwood, while Hoffman and his team supervised the agonizing process. Otto watched these sullen men with something like awe as they directed each casket bearer to remove the body, gently lay it on the floor, and cover it with National Guard–issued blankets. "They were laid in rows of 85," Hilton writes. "Most were simply assigned numbers. Their possessions were placed in large envelopes marked with their respective numbers." Already there were hundreds, with more streaming in.

Otto heard the cries of the bereaved outside the entrance, penetrating the mist, wailing to get inside the building. It was going to be a very, very long night.

CHAPTER FOURTEEN

Sackcloth and Ashes

THE HOURS CRAWLED by for Bobbie Aanstad and her family. According to a combination of oral history and public record, the Aanstads huddled in a pocket of noxious air and cold water, located between the cabin and promenade decks, for the entire afternoon without relief. Due to the awkward angle of the cavity in which they huddled, they remained unseen and unheard, despite their periodic cries. But throughout those terrible hours, they could hear the recovery operation continue unabated.

They heard the muffled rending of metal around them, the thump of ropes hitting wreckage behind the bulwark, the metallic tapping of divers burrowing beneath the wreck, and the cries—all too rare—of rescuers finding a victim clinging to life in the *Eastland*'s belly. The diver Halvorsen found one such stalwart victim late in the day, on his tenth descent, deep in the recesses of the ship.

"He was up over my head," the diver later told reporters. "And except that my line fouled, he would have died there. I looked up to see where the trouble was and saw him perched in the wreckage of the companionway. I guess he had used his last strength to crawl there. He must have felt himself slipping.

Anyway, there he was, straddling a stanchion and propped up so his head would stay out of the water whatever happened. It flashed on me that maybe he was alive, and I climbed up after him."

Halvorsen knew the man was alive the moment he touched the body. "He wasn't like the rest," the diver explained. "He was sort of limp, but not stiff."

Halvorsen frantically uprooted the man and hastened him to the surface, where the medical team sprang into action, retrieving the lung motor which had long been retired from service. As the grizzled diver stood with his helmet under his arm, catching his breath on the docks, watching the doctors struggle to revive the man, a sad realization suddenly rippled through the crowd. The man had expired.

"That's eight hundred and twenty-one," the diver uttered, putting his helmet back on, taking a weary breath, then splashing back into the river.

Chances are the Aanstads heard muffled evidence of those desperate, last-ditch rescue attempts all afternoon. "At times it was so still," recalled one survivor, "that the feet walking over the boat's side above our heads sounded as if we were on the inside of a big bass drum."

Few records exist of conversations between Marianne and Olaf, or between Marianne and her two girls, during those harrowing hours trapped in that hull, but it's highly likely they kept talking. Whispered prayers, perhaps. Maybe soft words of encouragement from Marianne. Perhaps Olaf kept them alert and hopeful.

Certainly Bobbie contributed to their survival through the sheer force of her personality. Perched on that ragged, cork lifesaver, bracing herself against the vertical floor of the ship and shivering convulsively, Bobbie simply refused to believe that they would perish there. Every muffled thump, every creaking rivet, could be their deliverance. But with each passing hour it was getting more difficult even to speak. Bobbie's nerve had begun to falter. Hypothermia and the torturous nature of waiting, of struggling to survive, enveloped in cold slime and surrounded by floating corpses, had begun to break her down.

Hypothermia occurs when the internal temperature of the body dips below 95 degrees Fahrenheit. Breathing becomes labored, shallow, and slow. The heart rate also slows and grows faint. The victim pales and starts to shiver violently, accompanied by a loss of coordination and slurred speech. Left untreated, the shivering stops, but debilitating muscle stiffness sets in, and the victim becomes drowsy and weak. Vision blurs. There is a desire to be left alone, to simply shut down and give up. Without immediate treatment advanced hypothermia can render a victim unconscious, induce cardiac arrest or coma.

The Aanstads hadn't yet reached that stage but with each tantalizing noise—each thump, each bang, each wrenching sound—their spirits shrank further toward submission.

Bobbie gripped the ruined floor as best she could, trying in vain to suppress the horrible shivering. Once again she found her racing thoughts returning to a single image in her mind, a single moment of joy to help squelch the fear. A secret mantra in her head: . . . *Ernie's lesson* . . . *Ernie Carlson's lesson.*

At that moment, in her imagination, Bobbie Aanstad traveled back to a warm summer afternoon a couple of years earlier. On a placid lake in Michigan. The sky a deep cornflower blue. Cottony clouds dotting the horizon. And that rascally little neighbor boy, giggling as he instructed young Bobbie in the art of treading water. . . .

BY LATE AFTERNOON, the intermittent drizzle added to the rescuers' anguish. "Everything oozed moisture," wrote one onlooker. "The bodies dripped. The policemen and other men carrying the stretchers had no free hands to reach up and wipe away the perspiration that streamed down their crimson faces. The rain dripped into [the ship's] hold and down the rubber coats of the rescuers."

But the moisture, in many ways, turned out to be the least of the workers' problems. Throughout the afternoon, sparks from the arc welders touched off small fires on the side of the boat. As a result, pockets of methane rising out of the filthy river water ignited. Fire belched through open portals. The drizzle mixed with ash and soot, choking survivors and workers alike. Hand extinguishers, primitive and ineffectual even for 1915, were used to quell the fires as much as possible. At one point, panic spread through the recovery workers that the ship might explode. "It was reported that there was a fire still further back in the hold," recalled one rescuer, "and that the hull might blow up at any minute. Lines of firehose stretching away endlessly seemed to bear out the rumors."

Unbeknown to most bystanders, however, a single, selfless act only hours earlier by the *Eastland*'s chief engineer had averted an explosion. Erickson had lingered on the capsized vessel, and as the water roared in around him, he managed to open the injectors on the ship's massive boilers, cooling them down gradually. "Had there been no water in the boilers," explained a crewmember, "the onrush of cold water from the river would have caused a certain explosion. Erickson did all in his power [to avoid that]. He stayed in the engine room until the rush of water from the side made him stand in it up to his neck." But the chief engineer—at that moment, sitting in jail—received no credit for heroic deeds.

Human spoor had touched nearly every surface. "The few that were resuscitated were desperately nauseated," recalled one worker. Vomit clung to the hull, dripped from the poles of stretchers, stained the dresses of stoic nurses. The odor mingled with coal dust, methane, and the coppery smell of blood. Many of the survivors bore impact injuries, and triage proved messy. Inside the ship, conditions were worse. "Because of the turbid condition of the water in the vessel," observed a *New York Times* reporter at the scene, "it is black, and filled with debris such as luncheon baskets, chairs, furniture and other articles."

Human depravity also polluted the scene. Morbid souvenir hunters descended on the river, scrambling for a shred of material or a piece of wreckage associated with the disaster. The police, already stretched emotionally to the breaking point, fought off the greedy interlopers with firearm and fist. But they kept coming. "Pieces of porthole glass, wood, or any other part of the boat which could easily be carried away were taken," wrote the *Tribune*.

Opportunistic pickpockets cruised the temporary morgues and rows of human remains in search of valuables. A detective named John Buckley noticed one such young ghoul robbing a well-dressed corpse. "I recognized this fellow as one I had arrested once before," the detective told the *Tribune*. "He pretended to be helping take out the bodies. When I caught him with his hand in the pocket of the clothing of one of the bodies, I grabbed him."

"Many of the bodies bore evidence of being searched," the *Times* reported. "Pockets were torn away, cut open, turned inside out; parts of jewelry had been taken from some bodies; bits of earrings, a lavaliere torn off its chain."

Near a row of bodies awaiting transport, one detective sergeant stood in the mist and pointed out evidence of theft to a cluster of stunned reporters. "If I could find the man who did that," the cop announced, fingering his revolver with one hand, pointing at one of the ransacked victims with the other, "I'd shoot him dead." The detective indicated signs of pilfering and said, "Here, you see, a watch has been broken from that chain. There's a tie with the stickpin gone. You can tell a ring's been wrenched off that dead finger. It's a shameful crime." Heads bowed in a mixture of revulsion and despair.

By late afternoon the recovery workers began to crumble under the tremendous strain.

Fred Swigert, one of the firemen who had been at the scene from the earliest moments, found himself part of a bucket brigade—lifting body after body from the hull, gently handing them off to stretcher bearers. Swigert had been at it for nearly three hours, and his limbs had grown numb. His hands and back ached. His mind had gone blank. In the words of one observer, he had become an "automaton."

Then one of the divers handed up a body of a little girl, "her flimsy dress a pitiful, clinging shroud." Swigert placed the body on a stretcher, paused, and looked down at the child's blanched face. The fireman gasped. Rearing backward suddenly, jaw trembling, Swigert tried to say something but couldn't get any words out. He staggered for a moment, then collapsed onto the weathered planks, unconscious.

The girl was his daughter.

Others had difficulty absorbing the magnitude of the tragedy. The horrors assailed members of Coroner Hoffman's jury, faced with the grim task of viewing the dead and tabulating the human cost. They shouldered their way through the throngs in front of the Reid-Murdoch building, trying to remain objective, but sorrow spread like a virus. One member of the jury had to excuse himself and flee to his home in order to avoid a full-blown breakdown in front of his peers. The signs of fracturing resolve were everywhere, even among the stony ranks of the city divers.

They had been recovering bodies for hours. Bone tired, Charles Gunderson resorted to using pike poles to remove many of the victims he discovered wedged in the wreckage below-decks. "Four were women," observed one reporter. "The fifth, a boy of eight, in a bedraggled Indian suit—killed by criminal paleface negligence." Gunderson found the boy's mother only inches away, dressed in a white corded suit, white stockings, white slippers and pearl earrings. The sight of her did something beyond articulation to the veteran diver's spirit.

The *Eastland*'s two bartenders, Ed Bartlett and LeRoy Bennett, were found next. The former boxers and fast friends had died together in the bowels of the ship. One of the divers found the men with their arms around each other's shoulders, an eternal bond of friendship that began twenty years earlier when they fought each other to a draw at Kerwin's saloon.

The discovery of the boxers tore through the divers' hearts. They had no more whiskey to staunch the sadness. It was time for a shift change. Iver and Walter Johnsen knew it. Gunderson knew it. Even George A. Saunders, Sr., a later arrival among the dive team, knew it was time to change divers. And when Harry Halvorsen emerged finally from the black depths, dripping with slime, one of the firemen knocked on the top of his helmet, which was how the surface team had been communicating throughout the day with the divers.

The fireman cupped his hands around the top of Halvorsen's bell and yelled that it was time to quit and bring in a fresh team for the evening.

Halvorsen did not argue.

ON TOP OF A nearby building, a janitor appeared in the shadows of a fire exit. He carefully held the door open and allowed a small group of spectators up onto the roof to watch the terrible spectacle.

Admission was ten cents.

REGGIE BOWLES burst from the water near the stern of the fallen ship. Ears ringing, chest heaving with pain, he reached out for the dock, but his vision blurred, and he misjudged the distance. His hands brushed the edge of the planks and he slipped back under.

Cold silence enveloped him again, and he let out a garbled, inarticulate gasp. His voice sounded like a muffled depth charge in his ears as he writhed and thrashed in the cold darkness, swallowing another brackish mouthful of river water.

He struggled and managed to make it back to the surface. He got his slippery, numbed hands around an iron rod protruding from the wreckage, and held on as best he could. He coughed up a lungful of water. Anger seethed in him. He was empty handed again, and it was killing him. He wanted so badly to recover just one more body.

He had witnessed terrible things that day, things which would have disturbed the sturdiest of minds. From the guts of the boat he had pulled a man with his hands clasped together in death, frozen in prayer. He had recovered a boy "with his fingers gripped between his teeth." In total Reggie Bowles had removed thirty-six bodies from the *Eastland* over the past eight hours, each more pitiful than the last.

Reggie's fingers began to slip, the fight draining out of him. He considered just letting himself go, sinking into oblivion with the rest of those poor folks in that flooded hold. It was not as though he would be missed—his mother had been trying to get rid of him since he was a little boy.

As his grip finally gave way, something held onto him. A vice-grip of iron, like a crane hauling him back up into the light, held the collar of his shirt. As Reggie blinked and coughed and strained his neck to see who or what had rescued him, a broad-shouldered sailor came into focus.

"You all right, son?" the sailor said, lifting Reggie onto the dock. Reggie landed with a thud on the weathered planks. The sailor was a navy reserve man, his uniform soaked and stained with blood.

Reggie managed a nod as he sat there dripping on that dock, catching his breath. The sailor nodded back at the boy, then hurried off to help someone else. It took immense effort for Reggie to hold his head up. His skinny, sinewy limbs felt like dead weight. He trembled convulsively. His lips were blue. If he rested for a few minutes, perhaps he could marshal enough energy to go back in.

The chaos swirled around him. A jumble of voices and noise filled his ears, steam and sparks flickered in his peripheral vision. He tried to stand but the flow of adrenaline had depleted him, and the water in his ears had stolen his balance. His body was limp, and when he tried to rise to his feet, his knees buckled. Dizziness washed over him and he staggered backward. Then a shade drew down over his eyes, and everything went black.

"Hey! Kid!"

A voice pierced the darkness, and Reggie found himself lying supine on the weathered boards of the dock where he had collapsed. His eyelids fluttered for a moment before focusing on a burly figure hovering over him.

"Kid!"

Reggie blinked and tried to sit up. His body felt leaden, and as though his head were filled with cement. How long had he been lying there? The sun hung low on the horizon, the shadows lengthening. Blinking fitfully, Reggie gazed up at that huge, uniformed figure towering over him.

"I'm puttin' you under arrest," Major Funkhouser informed the boy. Then the big cop knelt down close, and he glared at Reggie. "Don't make me pull my revolver."

Reggie was nonplussed. "Arrest?! But I was just—"

"No arguments!"

The major signaled one of his officers. The patrolman came over and awaited orders. The major looked up at his underling. "I want you to put this young fellow under arrest. Use my motor. Take him to the squad house."

"Sir, just let me rest a bit," Reggie pleaded, finally getting his bearings. "And then I'll go back in because, see, I can stand it when the professional divers cannot, because they keep stimulating themselves with whiskey, and the effect wears off, but I don't touch it."

"I said no arguments."

The officer helped Reggie stand. Reggie glanced up and down the dock, saw the procession of stretchers, and the dozens of bodies lined up on the pier, each covered with damp, stained linen. The boy could think of nothing to say. He let out a weary sigh and nodded at the officer. The cop took Reggie by the arm and started toward the LaSalle Street steps when Funkhouser called out to them.

"One moment!" Funkhouser went over to the two men and spoke in low tones to the officer. "There are some dry blankets in the back of the motor."

The major and Reggie Bowles made eye contact then. The major smiled sadly. "When you get to the squad," he added softly, almost under his breath to his patrolman, "make the boy some soup."

SOUP WAS OFFERED to others, as well as sandwiches, coffee, first aid, cots, and blankets. Merchants along Water, Clark, and LaSalle Streets opened their doors and offered places for survivors to congregate. Max Hyman, a local clothier, sent his son Leo to get food, and his Clark Street store welcomed the victims and their families. Mandel Brothers, Marshall Field and Company, Carson Pirie Scott & Company, and the Adams Express Company all lent vehicles and facilities to the recovery workers. The Sherman and LaSalle hotels, as well as the Weegham and Thompson restaurants, sent sandwiches to the scene. Nobody wanted to leave. Pockets of shocked survivors lingered under awnings, inside storefronts, and along the wharf, vexed by the grief and inexorable pain. Broken families huddled near the backs of ambulances and patrol cars, hoping for some word that their kin had been located.

The American Red Cross—the Chicago branch officially formed only months prior to the *Eastland* disaster—played a critical role in relief operations. By late afternoon, John J. O'Connor, the local director, was in the midst of organizing a campaign of unprecedented aid.

The Reid-Murdoch building became a base of operations for the Red Cross, and O'Connor personally supervised the scene, handing out food and drinks to workers, accommodating every request for space and nursing assistance. Red Cross nurses became fixtures at the scene, their starched regulation uniforms luminous in the overcast light, their presence scattered among the gray, teeming throngs. In almost every photograph a white-clad woman bearing a trademark cross insignia is visible. "A crowd of willing but ignorant volunteers kept getting in the way," recalled one nurse, "and made our attempts at resuscitation almost useless."

By dusk, as the chances of finding anyone alive became almost nil, the Red Cross workers became the principal disseminators of information, both at the scene and, later, at the temporary morgue in the armory. Many of their dispatches, however, were either inconclusive or just plain wrong.

Late in the day, for instance, the American Red Cross reported that all of the bodies "above water inside the hull" had been removed, an assessment that proved premature.

CHAPTER FIFTEEN

The Rustle
of His Spectral Robe

BOBBIE AANSTAD heard a noise. She craned her neck up to see into the cone of dwindling light from the gap between the two decks. Her body, still straddled precariously on a piece of floating cork, shivered convulsively, her senses almost completely numbed. She couldn't smell the rot anymore, or even feel the cold, but she could still see, if barely.

Her family huddled next to her—Marianne still clutching Solveig around the waist, the older woman's white fingers still holding onto a broken balustrade; Uncle Olaf bobbing a few feet away in the narrow channel, taking shallow breaths—all of them merely waiting to die. In the far reaches of the air pocket, other survivors floated, holding on to wreckage, too exhausted to do anything but hyperventilate. Most of them were women, the majority saved by Olaf Ness.

The Aanstads had been trapped for almost eleven hours. Miraculously they refused to give up hope, despite the forces working against them. Late-stage hypothermia brings on a tremendous temptation to loosen one's grip and gently go under. It can almost seem preferable to survival. Survival means having to lift oneself up, to struggle, to breathe in more air. Giving up means peace and quiet.

But that scratching sound from above, on the starboard side of the ship, kept tugging at Bobbie's attention. It sounded like fingernails dragging across slate, a flinty, rusty noise. It sent more chills down Bobbie's spine, but at once the chills transformed into something like feverish excitement: Bobbie could see movement.

Nobody knows exactly when or how Bobbie got her first glimpses of a heavy rope slithering its way toward her. In interviews, years afterward, Bobbie spoke of the rope almost casually. But on that horrific afternoon, as the rescuer's rope dangled in that shaft of pale light, banging off the side of the floor, then the ceiling, and appearing mere inches above the heads of the Aanstad women, Bobbie let the emotion pour out of her. Marianne surely cried and murmured prayers of thanks. Bobbie wept, and Solveig sobbed as well, as her Uncle Olaf reached for the slimy rope, grasping it with bloodless fingers.

It took great effort, given the fatigue that had set in, for Olaf merely to maintain his grip. Muffled voices bounced off the steel hold above them, and Olaf hollered back at them, jerking the rope as hard as he could, signaling to them that they had survived, and dear lord, yes, these survivors were ready to come out!

Solveig went first. Olaf boosted her up the rope, keeping one arm around her waist. She couldn't have weighed more than seventy pounds, but exhaustion made the task arduous. He coached her to hold on as tightly as possible, gave the rope another tug, and yelled up at the rescuers to lift her out. Bobbie watched through her tears as her sister was raised like a tangle of soaking laundry up a dumbwaiter. Years later, Bobbie regularly told family members of that day, and mentioned that this was the last time she saw her sister for quite some time. After being hauled from the narrow opening, Solveig somehow got separated from her family.

Olaf wanted to send Bobbie next, but Bobbie wanted her mother to go. Marianne insisted that her oldest daughter go next. A weary debate ensued. Finally, out of frustration, Bobbie relented and allowed her uncle to wrap the rope around her.

The trip up through the topsy-turvy wreck made Bobbie think of being born. She held onto the rope as tightly as she could, her chilled, aching limbs scraping the metal convolutions of the ship as she rose. Pain throbbed throughout her body but the exhilaration kept her alert, her neck arched upward, her faltering gaze locked on that source of dusky light. She was going to make it—they were all going to make it. She felt almost giddy with nervous energy as she reached the opening cut in the side of the *Eastland*.

As she emerged, and got her first glimpses of the ship's hull, her euphoria died. Something switched off inside her. As she was dragged onto the hull and checked over by a nurse, Bobbie gaped at the rows of bodies arrayed across the hull, lined up hundreds of feet into the distance, nearly the entire length of the ship—scores of them, maybe hundreds. Pathetic human remains bundled in linens. It was a sight that would stay with her for the rest of her life.

"There were so many people lying there," Bobbie remembered years later. "You couldn't tell if they were dead or alive."

At length, Marianne and Olaf emerged from the hull. Marianne searched in vain for Solveig, while Olaf, refusing to leave the scene, went off with the firemen and continued to work well into the night with the recovery crews. Weeks later, the coroner's office awarded the young Norwegian, along with scores of others, a special medal for heroic behavior.

"IN THE NAME OF GOD!" Coroner Peter Hoffman boomed into his megaphone. "I ask you to go away and let those seeking relatives and friends come in and identify their dead!"

Hoffman stood just outside the entrance of the armory on Washington Street, fifteen blocks from the sunken *Eastland*. Dressed in a somber suit, his barrel chest jutting, the coroner fidgeted with adrenaline. Darkness had closed in around the city, the gaslights spitting on along the parkways, the shadows settling around the massive brick pile of the armory, where thousands yelled and jockeyed for position as policemen shoved them back. Emotions ran at an extremely high pitch. The disorder made it difficult for the bereaved to enter the building and identify their next of kin.

For a while, after all the bodies had been collected and laid out across the floor of the armory's drill hall, Hoffman and his team had tried to screen visitors. They had run a phone line from inside the building out to a taxicab parked at the head of the queue. Western Electric employees interrogated each interested party over the phone, partly to spare the visitor the heartache of searching for a loved one who had already been identified, partly to weed out the "morbidly curious" (as Hilton calls them), for depraved thrill-seekers had become an enormous problem. By ten o'clock that night, Hoffman and his men had a potential riot on their hands, which led to the coroner's decision to allow entrance to anybody who desired it.

"Listen carefully, please!" Hoffman called out to the throng milling around the dark street. "You will all be allowed to enter forthwith. All that we ask is that you form a single line. We will admit twenty persons at a time."

The crowd shifted. With the help of the police, a line formed that reached back to Carpenter Street. An uneasy silence settled over the queue. Mothers wrung their hands and dabbed their faces with wadded handkerchiefs. Fathers stood stoic and stiff-backed in their woolen suits and bowler hats. Black umbrellas clustered here and there, forming a somber shroud over much of the line.

Among the gathering stood Robert Magnussen. A longtime Hawthorne works employee, Magnussen hovered near the front of the line. He had been waiting all afternoon to get into the temporary morgue, and anguish and frustration had worn him down, but somehow he managed to maintain his composure. He kept telling himself that it wouldn't be long now. Magnussen had been on the *Eastland* with his wife and two children. When the boat tipped over, he got separated from his family; when he was lifted to safety, there was no sign of them.

A policeman near the armory's entrance gave a signal, and the next twenty were admitted.

Magnussen shuffled through a vestibule and into the main drill hall. The central room reeked of death and disinfectant, and filled with a low din of whispers. Bodies lined the floor in narrow rows, less than thirty-six inches between the heads of one row and the feet of another, allowing only enough space for a single viewer to pass. Magnussen started down the first aisle when his world suddenly collapsed.

The body of his wife lay in the first row. The sob blurted out of Magnussen without warning as he gazed down at her. Attendants hurried to him and held him by the arm as though he might collapse at any moment. His voice, barely audible, uttered her name repeatedly, tears starting to track down his face. Notations went into logs as Magnussen continued down the row of victims.

"On he went bravely," wrote the *Tribune*. "While passing another row he stopped again. There was Robert, Jr. Magnussen's knees weakened under him; his eyes were blind with tears; but there was still another."

Somehow Magnussen willed his body to keep moving. He passed row after row of nameless victims. Finally, at the end of the last row, he found the crumpled body of his daughter Irene. It was too much for him, and he collapsed. A policeman rushed over and held the grieving man upright. When Magnussen managed to get back on his feet, he turned and stumbled across the hall toward a group of officials standing near an embalming table. Deputy Coroner Samuel Davis came forward and tried to calm the grieving father. Magnussen had difficulty speaking but managed to make a request that the bodies of his wife and children be gathered together. It wasn't right that they were so far apart. The deputies nodded, and hurried across the room to comply.

"His wish fulfilled," reported the *Tribune*, "he knelt down slowly beside the three and prayed."

THE PROCESS CONTINUED throughout the wee hours of the night. As each group of twenty entered the hall, accompanied by coroner's attendants who would kneel by bodies in question, and slowly lift blankets to expose the dead. "Face after face was uncovered," one reporter witnessed at the scene. "Strange eyes, glazed and fixed, look up at one; this one is bruised, that one distorted; and after the searcher has looked at many victims he comes at last on the one sought." A moan or cry of recognition echoed intermittently across the cavernous drill hall. Some anguished seekers fell to their knees and wailed. Nurses helped downtrodden brothers or mothers or husbands back across the rows of dead, toward administrative stations or one of the exits.

As each body was identified, a Western Electric volunteer called out, "Identified!" Assistants then took the remains to an enclave established in one corner of the drill hall, where coroner's physician Springer would record the cause of death, in most cases drowning or suffocation, before finalizing certification. The volume of cases was so great, and the assembly-line aspect of the process so relentless, that Hoffman ordered rubber stamps be brought in that evening that read: DROWNED, JULY 24TH, 1915, FROM STEAMER EASTLAND, CHICAGO RIVER AT CLARK STREET.

Western Electric brought twenty additional telephones into

the armory, and the constant ringing kept piercing the silence of the morgue, providing a harsh, metallic counterpoint to the proceedings. The psychological pressure on those present reached unprecedented levels.

"Tears were in every eye," observed one reporter. "Mothers and daughters, wives and husbands, fathers and sons, collapsed beneath the strain of the great life tragedy in which they found themselves forced to play leading parts."

Physical considerations and human needs became secondary priorities. Workers went without sleep or meal breaks. "Four policemen act as waitresses," one reporter observed at the scene. "They distribute coffee and sandwiches and pieces of pie wherever they are needed. Attendants eat without knowing they are eating, judging from their preoccupied manners, and the fact that they do not interrupt their work."

Outside, in the darkness, the graceless shadows of adjacent buildings pressed down on the grieving throngs. The silver flicker of gaslights found an occasional broken face, caught in stunned silence. "There are lines of men and women extending for blocks in all directions," observed a *New York Times* reporter. "Chicago has seldom seen crowds like these—crowds without any gaiety, without boisterousness, without much talk—crowds with solemn, wistful, staring, tear-stained faces. Chicago is used to happy crowds. These people are desolated."

Neighboring residents provided ice water to those standing in line. Many of those waiting to enter the armory fiddled with handkerchiefs and dabbed their eyes, their composure breaking under the strain. Some tried to cut in line. Others collapsed in paroxysms of sorrow before even gaining entrance. The mounted police and patrolmen kept order as best they could, balancing the grim charge of keeping things moving with the delicate process of comforting the anguished.

Coroner Hoffman immersed himself in the brutal task at

hand. "I'm so busy trying to meet immediate needs that I haven't had time for anything else," he told a reporter at the scene.

Hoffman's righteous rage had already started festering, and would surface over the next few days, but on that horrible night he somehow managed to maintain a steely focus, balancing several priorities: record keeping, respect for the bereaved, and handling the decomposition problem brought on by the summer warmth. "The problem of caring for these bodies, and helping these poor people find their relatives and friends," he explained, "is what we should look after now. But you can be sure that we shall have a most rigid investigation."

Despite the inhospitable hour, children darted among the crowds. Although minors were not allowed inside the armory, the Red Cross provided temporary facilities for their care while their parents went inside. Near the main entrance, a number of benches filled an improvised tent, and volunteer nurses turned the niche into a makeshift nursery. "Women and girls from homes in the neighborhood volunteered as nurses," wrote one reporter. "At one time, seventeen children under four years old were on hand."

Police Captain Thomas Meagher heard the children crying at one point, frightened by the gruesome proceedings. The captain dispatched one of his men to help. The tender-hearted officer went in and sat down amidst the infants and toddlers, entertaining the children for hours. "The first thing one of the babies wanted was the policeman's badge," wrote the *Tribune*. "The baby quit crying when the policeman handed it over."

A few dead children lay inside the armory, some scattered among the rows of ragged bundles on the floor of the drill hall. Others, mostly infants, were segregated into their own tiny row at the end of the room. Viewing this grouping broke more spirits than any other task. "The sight of the babies lying in rows away from the others," observed one witness, "brought tears to the eyes of most women as they passed, but they wept quietly."

A local man named Otto Brandt experienced this misery first-hand. A brawny laborer from Congress Park whose sister, Mary Braitch, had been on the *Eastland* that morning with her family, Otto knew it was up to him to identify the victims. The Braitches had been separated when the ship capsized, and Mrs. Braitch had survived. But when she got home that day, she had immediately contacted Otto. "I know that at least one of my babies must be alive!" she had told her brother. "God would not take everything from me. You must come back and tell me at least one has been spared. God does not need all. He would leave me *one* I know." The words had stamped themselves on Otto Brandt's brain like a fiery brand.

"You must bring one of them back alive with you tonight!"

Now Brandt stood still, keeping a lonely vigil over one corner of the morgue. He couldn't find the strength to move or pray or do much of anything but stand and stare down at the floor. "I have to go home and tell her," he moaned, his voice reduced to the whimper of a small child. "On the floor at Brandt's feet," wrote the *New York Times*, "lay John Braitch, his sister's husband, and beside John Braitch lay 9-year-old Frederic, 12-year-old Gertrude, little Annie, 7 years old, and Marie, only 6 months old. The body of Rose, 4 years old, has not yet been found."

Unfortunately, days later, Rose was found dead in the bowels of the *Eastland*, her mother's worst nightmare realized.

THE HOURS PLODDED. The shuffling mourners came and went. Morgue attendants tagged each body, then lifted it into a mortuary cot or an oblong basket, and carried it away.

At the end of one row an anonymous seven-year-old boy lay pale and silent in death. He was number 396. Nobody came to identify him. Nobody came to weep over his limp form. He lay there at the end of that row throughout the night, unclaimed, forgotten. But he had not died in vain. His death symbolized something far more tragic than a mere boating accident.

Within a few short days, the death of number 396 would bring captains of industry and leaders of men to their knees.

IN THE DARKNESS outside, doors slammed. Drivers clucked at their teams. Horses snorted, and reigns snapped. One by one the hearses pulled away, as each tagged body was transported to local funeral parlors. More carriages arrived, backing their payload bays up to the armory's side exit. The procession continued throughout the night.

Otto Muchna worked alongside these conveyers of the dead. He had been at it since late afternoon. His horse foamed at the mouth with exhaustion, the steam rising from the animal's sweat-damp hindquarters in the chill darkness. Otto felt as tired as his horse, but Muchna, ever the perfectionist, refused to give up or to neglect a call from a family in need. These were the relatives of neighbors and fellow Bohemians. Compounding these considerations was the unexpected crisis occurring within Otto's westside community.

They were running out of caskets.

In 1915, even a teeming metropolis of 2.5 million people had no provisions for such a glut of deaths. The undertakers had access to a limited number of receptacles, and by the middle of the night, after hundreds of bodies had been conveyed to homes and chapels across the west side for visitation, the supply had dwindled. Undertakers like Otto began turning to alternatives such as wicker ambulance baskets and temporary containers. The emotional impact of such a hardship overwhelmed these quiet professionals.

As Otto started out for home, another shattered body stowed in the rear of his hearse, he felt an uncharacteristic stab of emotion in his gut. *Running out of coffins? How could something like this happen? How could such a terrible thing like this boat careening happen in a modern, vibrant city?* Never before had Otto Muchna felt such shock, dismay, or seething anger.

The outrage spread like a virus.

Back inside the armory, as the mourners trudged up and down the aisles, the phones jangled, and the occasional keening of a grief-stricken mother razored through the air. Cook County Coroner Peter Hoffman smoldered. "In the name of decency, I ask you to let the mourners be!" he shouted now into his megaphone, addressing the few still haunting the building, wandering the room trying to get a glimpse of something lurid. On the floor, one victim had come uncovered in the confusion, revealing a contorted cranium partially sheered in half by falling wreckage. Attendants hurried to replace the covering before any curiosity seekers could get a look.

"They were a peculiar lot, those morbid onlookers," wrote the *Tribune*. "Some passed in through the entrance six and eight times . . . women carrying babies in their arms, fathers leading children by the hands . . . and some even protested when the police refused to let youngsters view the bodies. There was one man, unshaven and collarless, who took a comb from his pocket and combed his hair before passing the bodies." Such behavior added a macabre layer to the sorrow. Even worse, it slowed the process.

"I will arrest anyone who has entered this armory without reason other than the satisfaction of morbid curiosity!" Hoffman continued booming through his bullhorn. The coroner's anger extended beyond that of a mortician offended by the desecration of solemn proceedings. Hoffman's anger, albeit currently directed at ghoulish intruders, sprang from a deeper well of outrage. It was the anger of a lawman confronting banal evil. The object of Hoffman's rage would ultimately be those responsible for such hellish anguish.

Some time later Hoffman huddled in a corner of the armory with the five men that would make up his inquest jury. "You are to make a thorough and impartial investigation," he told them under his breath, his eyes burning with urgency, "and put the blame where it belongs."

CHAPTER SIXTEEN

An Unearthly Glow

"THE OLD EASTLAND, its livery work done, lay wearily on its port side less than fifty feet from where it started," wrote the *Tribune* of the ghostly sight that haunted the riverfront that night. "More than half the boat was submerged. Over all, emergency electric lights flared and flickered, casting an unearthly glow on the faces of the dead as they were brought forth and placed on stretchers."

Few bodies remained in the wreck. Workers had recovered most of them, and yet the divers continued their work through the predawn hours, through that sullen, lifeless stretch of time that is neither night nor morning. As the disposition of the workers deteriorated, the area became almost silent. Only the crackle of arc lights and sizzle of oxygen flames could be heard echoing over the black surface of the water. A few feet off the stern, barely visible in the shadows, the ship's giant propeller blade protruded from the surface of the river.

Commonwealth Edison had supplied the recovery team with enough power and illumination to continue working around the clock. Workers had strung cables across the exposed starboard side, and more than a hundred tungsten lamps on metal stands went up on the hull. On the roof of the Reid-Murdoch building, ten carbon-arc spotlights shone at key points, trained on the wreck. The silver shafts of light crisscrossed each other and gleamed off the white iron, sending impossibly long shadows into the dark canyons of buildings along the wharf.

Work lamps burned inside the wreck as well, casting an eerie yellow glow through the open portholes and jagged openings cut earlier in the day by welders' torches. "Strings of electric bulbs made the interior a blaze of light," wrote the *New York Times*.

Divers worked as best they could under these conditions, burrowing through the flooded cells inside the ship, moving in and out of shadows. When they brushed against a body, or found a limb poking out from wreckage, they hurriedly paddled back to the nearest opening and signaled a fireman or a physician. The surface team then rooted the body out with pike poles and hooks. The work progressed slowly, and the second team of divers neared its point of exhaustion.

William "Frenchy" Deneau, one of these stalwart night divers, took a *Tribune* reporter with him on one of his last dives. Over subsequent days, the journalist wrote of the horrors he witnessed that night in those black depths in and around the *Eastland*: "As we sank, the green, slop-laden river water sank below the three windows of my helmet. Every second, it seemed, a piece of bread, a scrap of cloth or some other object from the *Eastland* floated within my view. Several times I felt a piece of submerged wreckage strike my rubber suit." The reporter tried to enter the hull but after only a few minutes terror and throbbing pain from the air pressure squeezing his skull overwhelmed him. Finally the writer clamored to be lifted out.

Two blocks to the west, city workers labored silently, pulling shredded catch nets from the river, the webbing tangled with all manner of remnants from the disaster. Throughout the night, passing emergency tugs had torn the nets at Randolph Street, Wells Street, and other points due west, and now the nets had to be replaced. As the men worked in pools of gaslight and nitrogen lamps, the detritus from the capsizing tumbled to the dock at their feet. Countless items shimmered with the river slime: loose change totaling nearly 3,000 dollars, jewelry valued at nearly 4,000 dollars, men's and women's clothing of all descriptions— handbags, pocketbooks, billfolds, mesh bags, shoes—cameras, picnic baskets, a cornet, and a bass drum.

A city custodian arrived, and the sad inventory of these objects began in the shadows along the river. But the sorrow shared by those workers cataloguing the personal effects of the dead was surpassed by those grieving in other parts of the city.

THE DISASTER hit Cicero, Illinois, the hardest. In 1915, the west-side village was essentially a company town, and the company of record was decimated by the *Eastland* disaster. However, very few natives of that community realized the gravity of the situation until the hours just before dawn.

"One large house in which dwelt two families of workers in the factory was without a light tonight," one witness told the *New York Times*. "Neighbors said that every resident of the place was dead."

The tragedy devastated street after street of small row houses and tidy yards. "For blocks there was hardly a house which had not felt directly the shock of the *Eastland* disaster," one reporter observed. "Many of its residents were employees of the Western Electric Company."

For those restless enough to maintain their night-long vigil, the evidence of loss mounted steadily. Every few minutes, a black wagon appeared at the end of a street and pulled up to a dark house—a harbinger of disaster in the guise of an ornate funeral carriage or patrol cart. In a single block there were nineteen dead.

"All night long," recalled one witness, "crowds had thronged the streets, going sorrowfully from house to house to learn of the death of a son, a daughter, a mother, a cousin." Before daybreak, Hawthorne residents reeled from the mounting death toll. Literally hundreds from that one small enclave met their demise on the *Eastland*. The devastation reached deep into surrounding areas. "In the communities of Morton Park, Warren Park, Grant Works, and Clyde, all bound by ties of blood into one huge Polish family, nearly 200 were mourned."

The Sindelar house sat empty and silent that night.

The dark, lifeless quality of that modest home at 4735 West Jackson spoke volumes of the tragedy. Neighbors kept watch on the place as though Josephine or one of the kids might show up at any minute, soaked to the bone and full of tales of adventure. But most knew the truth: George, Sr., George, Jr., Sylvia, Adella, and William were all lying on the floor of the 2nd Regiment Armory building, their bodies awaiting transport to a local mortuary. Josephine and Albert were as yet among the missing. But few of the Sindelars' loved ones, friends or neighbors expected them to be alive.

In fact, Josephine Sindelar's body lay still buried in the flooded wreckage, floating not far from her eight-year-old son. They were among the last bodies remaining underwater. For nearly twenty-four hours the divers had been passing within inches of their remains, oblivious to their presence. In the end, Josephine and Albert would not be found for another two days, their bodies obscured behind mangled wreckage and water so filthy it was nearly opaque. Only Josephine's beloved turnip watch, its dull gleam barely visible, offered divers a sign of her presence.

It was merely a pocket watch—a simple American Waltham—the kind anybody in 1915 could pick up for a few bucks at the Fair Store, but for Josephine Sindelar it had always held a deeper significance. It was a watch that had been handled so lovingly, fingered by tiny hands, its gold plated housing burnished by years of use. When brought out for special occasions, it provided an elegant grace note to Josephine's dressiest ensembles. The watch was a part of her identity, and would one day serve as a sort of totem for her descendants. The watch would survive the generations, along with Josephine's spirit.

Its hands were frozen at seven-thirty-one, the exact time of the capsizing.

THE SKY LIGHTENED over the accident site, exposing the darkened hull of the *Eastland* like an open wound. Arc lights fizzled out; gas lamps were snuffed. For the first time since dusk, workers got a clear glimpse of the ravaged starboard side, riddled with jagged openings, strewn with dirty canvas as well as cinders and ash from the fire boxes of rescue tugs. Barrels, axes, ladders, and stools lay upended here and there, remnants of the frantic rescue operation. Talk began of raising the boat, and of dismantling pieces in order to get to any bodies still trapped below.

A black despair hung over the scene. The mobs of onlookers had thinned. A second shift of divers, brought in from Milwaukee, had reached the end of their tour, having removed most of the bodies that were accessible to the reach of their pike poles and ropes. A fresh contingent of firemen arrived from the south. Their grim expressions fixed, their heads bowed in somber silence, they filed down the LaSalle Street steps without much ceremony. More police arrived bringing the number of cops in the immediate area to 500. A regiment of guards was placed on a zone encompassing the two city blocks adjacent to the fallen *Eastland* in order to maintain some semblance of control.

As the morning wore on, the paralysis of shock and anguish turned to action. At City Hall, Acting Mayor Moorhouse called an emergency meeting in the office of the commissioner of public works. J. J. O'Connor of the Red Cross was present, as well as officials from the Western Electric Company and a representative from William Thompson's office. The central issue was relief. As there had yet to be a tally of the dead, the amount of money this would cost was left undetermined, although 200,000 dollars was mentioned as a starting point. It was decided that fund-raising would be limited to Chicago; no general nationwide appeal for funds would be made.

"We must show some pride in this matter," urged Thompson's assistant, James Pugh. "Chicago is amply able to take care of this and to apply the funds necessary to relieve the suffering caused by this appalling disaster. We will get plenty of money from individuals, and the officials of the Western Electric Company have responded nobly to the situation."

In fact, the Hawthorne works had become something of a central clearinghouse for information. Relief workers turned the factory's employment office into a telephone station to coordinate information with personnel records, as well as to field questions from frantic next-of-kin. The shock of such a calamity had a galvanizing effect on staff.

Margaret Condon, the plant's chief switchboard operator, had planned on going to the picnic, but once the accident occurred, she returned immediately to the factory to supervise the phones. She ended up working continuously for thirty-four hours until she collapsed from exhaustion. Other operators pitched in throughout Sunday morning and well into the afternoon. Some of these women had lost relatives in the disaster and insisted on working the phones in order to distract them from their grief.

Six miles to the east, an urgency bordering on the feverish blazed at the criminal court building. Police had ushered into the office of Maclay Hoyne twenty-nine crewmen from the *Eastland* including Captain Pedersen, First Mate Del Fisher, and Chief Engineer Joseph Erickson, to be questioned by the state's attorney himself. Tired and rattled, the crewmen had spent the night in jail, under the close guard of Hermann Schuettler, the human bulldog, and his toughest prison guards.

Hoyne grilled the sailors, anger glinting behind his round spectacles. The state's attorney demanded to know why the *Eastland* ran for two years out of Cleveland rated at only 652 passengers for its regular service across the lake. He also wanted to know why it had only been allowed to carry more than 652 within a specified distance of the shore. Why was the government reluctant to allow this boat its full load of passengers in the open water?

Hoyne paused and waited for an answer. The room remained silent for a long while. After an awkward exchange of glances, the grizzled captain spoke up, breaking a silence he had maintained since his arrest the previous morning. "I'll tell you what you want to know," Pedersen said, "but I want you to know one thing before I do."

Hoyne asked what that was.

The captain replied in a low voice, his own anger sparking in his eyes: "I will not be made the scapegoat."

CHAPTER SEVENTEEN

Coffins in Every Mirror

THE *EASTLAND* had settled in the silt. This made the prospects of moving it daunting at best. It lay too close to the wharf for 360-degree access, and scores of victims remained buried within. Adding to these difficulties were the simmering politics going on in hearing rooms across town.

The owner of the ship, the St. Joseph–Chicago Steamship Company, wanted to get the salvage operations under way as quickly as possible. Under federal law, the owner of any vessel that has become a major obstruction to a navigable waterway is required to remove said vessel within thirty days. Such an undertaking is a massive and convoluted job, involving the installation of giant ballast tanks in order to make the wreck buoyant enough to be raised into an upright position. As early as Sunday afternoon, the owners of the *Eastland* had begun negotiations with the Dunham Towing and Wrecking Company to initiate the process.

The second camp in this evolving drama, Chicago's local officials, had other ideas. Avenging angels Hoffman and Hoyne did not want their key article of hard evidence to be dismantled and carted away without a rigorous and timely examination. On

Sunday, Hoffman brought his jury to the site and toured the hull. Sober men in suits and derbies staggered up the side of the fallen metal giant, peering down into it, making mental notes of the scene. Hoffman, near collapse from a sleepless night at the armory, worked on sheer adrenaline. No detail, no matter how minute, would be overlooked.

By Sunday afternoon Hoyne had spoken to enough witnesses to begin formulating a theory. This theory initiated not only a series of legal skirmishes with the federal government, but led ultimately to the undoing of the criminal proceedings. "The United Sates inspection service is directly responsible for this disaster," Hoyne announced to stunned reporters. "And now they are either here or on their way here . . . for what? To investigate their own service and their own officials? Chicago should be warned against this. The inspection service of the United States government has been an open scandal with seamen for years. Now is the time to inspect the inspectors. Chicago and every public official here should demand that and nothing less."

His words touched off a brushfire of emotion across Chicago. The wounded city had no patience for dissembling or prevarication, and Hoyne's plain talk was just the tonic it needed. The Sunday papers had already blanketed the town with gruesome tales of death and destruction. The west side was shrouded in grief, paralyzed with the shock of immense loss. Chicago was poised to aim its wrath at a big target, and the federal government was it.

U.S. Secretary of Commerce William Redfield was already on his way to Chicago to supervise the public hearings. A brusk, no-nonsense man who saw no conflict of interest in his presence, Redfield had the imprimatur of the President of the United States behind him. Redfield arrived late Sunday and immediately made an official seizure of the wreck, putting the vessel under federal control. This proclamation did not sit well with locals. To make matters worse, Redfield enlisted the aid of the already infamous Judge Kenesaw Mountain Landis, to whose district court the future federal criminal case would ultimately be assigned.

Landis had been a protegé of Teddy Roosevelt. Tart-tongued, jingoistic, and impatient with the subtleties of politics, the judge had the posture of a bantam rooster with a jutting chin and hard eyes. "Quite often, when dissatisfied with the progress of a case," wrote the *Tribune*, "he would glower at a witness, transfixing him with a long menacing finger and piercing eyes, and take the questioning out of the hands of attorneys." Years later, Landis added another layer of infamy to his resume as the commissioner of baseball during the Black Sox scandal, barring for life eight members of the team for fixing the 1919 World Series.

In those anguished days following the disaster, the judge and his contemporaries—Redfield, Hoyne, Hoffman, Moorhouse, Thompson, Schuettler—all found themselves swept up in a whirl-wind of controversy that pitted local authorities against federal authorities, management against labor, the big man against the little man.

AT THE ACCIDENT SITE, the recovery process slowed to an agoniz-ing pace. More than 300 people remained missing or unac-counted for, and in many cases, people who were feared dead turned up Sunday afternoon at their homes. Numerous passen-gers had fled the scene without identifying themselves. A few were never found. The record-keeping varied greatly among the different agencies tabulating the dead.

Inside the wreck the divers worked methodically, slowly, pulling the occasional body from the deepest recesses of the ship every hour or so. The mood was sullen, pained, the urgent hys-teria of the day before replaced by a sort of laborious piece work.

By Sunday afternoon, according to the *Tribune*, "ghouls" lined the riverfront. The morbidly curious crowded the edges of the Clark Street bridge and peered down from the rooftops of adjacent buildings in order to get a glimpse. The spectators seemed only to add to the heartache and sorrow that pressed down on the scene.

Commercial traffic on the river had dwindled almost to zero. A few contract ships plied their way past the wreck in grave silence, heading out the mouth of the harbor to points north and east, such as Milwaukee, Benton Harbor, and Holland. "In each instance, it was the same story," wrote one reporter. "A light load of heavy-hearted people."

The S.S. *Theodore Roosevelt*, the *Eastland*'s sister ship, made a futile attempt to continue its service as though nothing had happened. Steaming slowly eastward from its dock near Clark Street, the *Roosevelt* passed within inches of the wreck. "Instead of the usual happy crowd of 2,500 aboard," wrote the *New York Times*, "there were fewer than 500 sober visaged passengers, who, as they passed the *Eastland*, either turned their eyes away or gazed at the hulk with looks akin to horror." All moonlight cruises were canceled. Excursion companies reported less than 20 percent of the usual number of Sunday passengers.

Acting Mayor Moorhouse's appeal for nonessential businesses to close down was taken seriously in all quarters. Taverns shuttered their doors and put up wreathes. Amusement parks were silenced. Major-league baseball games, three of which were scheduled for that weekend in Chicago, were canceled. Ironically the games probably would have been called off due to inclement weather. "The weather," Hilton wrote, "served as a perfectly appropriate setting for what was rapidly developing as the worst day in loss of life in the city's entire history."

UNDER BLACK SKIES, Cicero residents came out of their homes and stood in helpless vigils in front of the houses of victims. On their way to mass, neighbor women passed the homes of grieving friends and coworkers, and paused to hold each other in horror. Many fainted in the streets.

"In every church prayers were offered for the dead," observed one local reporter, "and after the services the members of each parish went from house to house to mourn with relatives and friends. The door of each house of death stood open, and men and women entered silently to kneel before the candles."

"Six of our congregation lost their lives," one minister told his congregation on Sunday. "We do not blame any unkind providence on the part of God, but we do blame those who made and operated a boat which so easily could be overturned."

Many of the bereaved families were Catholic, and the wakes were held in the homes. "A coffin in every mirror," wrote another reporter visiting some of the homes in Cicero. "No matter where one looked, the coffin was there, reflected in the mirrors, on the walls, and from the door panels." Votive candles burned in virtually every corner. In some homes, the ceaseless dripping of ice beneath the bier brought to mind the cruel passage of time. Flowers arrived throughout the day. Outside, these delicate, futile symbols of death fluttered in the bluster of passing rainstorms.

"On each house where there was a dead person," recalled one survivor, "they had what they called crepes—a spray of flowers and a ribbon. Probably every third, maybe fifth house, had these crepes." And as the number of icons grew, the collective sorrow pressed down on the little village. An out-of-town reporter visiting Cicero on Sunday noted the weight of grief that permeated the atmosphere around the factory. "Kolin Avenue, two blocks from the Western Electric company, is a street of weeping and distress," he wrote. "In that part of the avenue nearest the plant, almost all of the houses are occupied by workers at the Western. And there are not many houses in that vicinity into which the *Eastland* catastrophe has not directly reached. A pall of general grief hangs over the entire neighborhood."

A series of uninvited visitors only added to the torments of these grieving families, as members of the Health Department feared a typhoid epidemic. "Persons who fell from the decks of the boat into the river undoubtedly swallowed some of the polluted water," the health commissioner announced to the press on Sunday morning. "They are in danger of typhoid fever, and the Health Department is going to attempt to ward off the disease." The commissioner ordered a house-to-house canvass.

On Sunday afternoon, physicians from the department and numerous local hospitals arrived in motorcars, interrupting wakes, alarming grieving widows, and generally adding a troubling new layer to the anguish. Chicago had seen its share of epidemics. Only a few decades earlier cholera had wiped out thousands; Chicago's medical community was not about to let that happen again. Doctors offered their assistance free of charge, and addresses were published in the *Sunday Tribune*, alerting survivors to the various stations throughout the city where they could receive vaccinations.

A wave of opportunistic crime compounded the misery. Grieving residents, distracted by the horrors all around them, left their doors open, and their homes often went unattended. Widows and widowers found themselves alone and vulnerable to all manner of exploitation.

"A new breed of thief made his appearance in the grief-stricken homes of Hawthorne and Cicero," wrote one reporter. "They appeared at the open crepe-draped doors and stole softly into the candle-lighted death rooms. Once inside, they knelt beside the mourners, and taking advantage of their hysterical condition, robbed them of jeweled pins or necklaces."

These thieves had no shame. They often stood before the home altars, leaning over caskets, pretending to pay respects to the deceased while deftly removing rings from dead fingers and brooches from funeral dresses. Anything that wasn't nailed down was stolen, including furniture, pictures on walls, candlesticks. Thefts reached such a point that on Monday afternoon, Chief Mongrieg of the Cicero Police Department stationed extra patrols outside the town's forlorn little bungalows to guard their contents.

Loan sharks posing as representatives of various relief funds convinced bereaved wives to sign fake "receipts" which turned out to be contracts binding the signers to pay exorbitant rates of interest. Corrupt undertakers forced expensive coffins on destitute widows and orphans. Fraudulent employment agencies preyed on impoverished mourners, asking for hundred-dollar fees in return for nothing.

The police had their hands full throughout the week, ferreting out scam artists. The health commissioner himself stumbled upon one of these swindlers, an undertaker named Frank Roda who had charged a woman five times the customary fee to bury her husband. "It was extortion," the commissioner told the *Tribune*. "I think this man's license should be revoked."

Through it all, the bodies kept arriving from the east, in Black Màrias, funeral carriages, and drays, as if off an assembly line. A collective anguish drew down over the community like a black shade. Many of the men repressed their sorrow, refusing to talk about what had happened. One of these men was a janitor at the Hawthorne works named John Salak.

Salak and his wife had been on the *Eastland*, but as was the case with so many, they had been separated during the capsizing. Salak's wife had not survived. The janitor kept his grief bottled up. His brother had tried to help, but Salak rebuffed all acts of kindness.

"Let me alone," Salak kept saying to anyone attempting to connect with him.

Two days later, police found the janitor dead in his bungalow on Kildare Avenue, a gas tube in his mouth.

* * *

ON SUNDAY, the area around the Hawthorne works resembled a ghost town. "Through the daylight hours," observed one reporter, "the district around the Western Electric plant at Hawthorne presented the appearance of an almost deserted city. Only the occasional rumbling of a hearse or an ambulance through the streets suggested the ghostly situation to the casual observer."

Inside the factory, the 100 volunteers who had been staffing the makeshift information bureau neared exhaustion. The names of victims had filled the huge bulletin boards tacked to the walls. The phone lines established between the accident site, the armory, and the plant, rang ceaselessly—but the number of volunteers was dwindling.

"Those who stood in front of the bulletin boards and gazed weary eyed at the lists of dead, missing and survivors posted there," recalled one reporter, "could be counted in groups rather than in crowds. There appeared to exist a universal desire in the neighborhood to get the news from as near the seat of the accident as possible."

The president of Western Electric, H. B. Thayer, arrived in Chicago late Sunday from New York, and immediately went to a meeting with Moorhouse in order to discuss relief. But a more pressing problem for Western Electric was the confusion over the passenger list.

Around the same time Thayer was huddling with the acting mayor, the plant superintendent, H. F. Albright, sent a terse notice to each and every employee:

> The shops and offices of the company will be open at the usual time on Monday, July 26th, in order that a complete and reliable list may be compiled of the survivors. It is hoped that all employees who can do so will report to or advise their department heads.

* * *

BY MONDAY MORNING—another dreary, overcast day—shock had set in around the city. The overturned ship seemed to radiate despair up and down the riverfront. A small contingent of divers continued prodding the depths of the wreck, but it appeared that most, if not all, of the victims had been located.

Josephine and Albert Sindelar were among the last bodies pulled from the hull.

BLAME U.S. OFFICIALS cried the morning headlines in the *Tribune*, taking their cue from Hoyne's dogged fixation on government negligence. A popular political cartoonist, John T. McCutcheon, offered a torpedo labeled GREED slamming into the *Eastland*'s hull, with a legend underneath that said, "Fired without warning." Harrowing accounts of the capsizing filled the pages of every daily newspaper, describing acts of heroism as well as cowardice.

It seemed the shellshock of the previous two days had turned to a citywide outrage. A disaster happened, in front of thousands of eyewitnesses, right here in this great city, and now something had to be done, not only to ensure that something of this magnitude never happened again, but also to punish those responsible.

In Cicero, the Hawthorne works opened its massive doors in solemn silence. This was a place that was almost never quiet, never still, but on that Monday, as the stunned workers filed through the Twenty-second Street entrance, the tableau that greeted them, the vaulted iron ceilings and rows of nitrogen lamps shining down on the shop floors in somber silence, must have given off an almost cathedral-like atmosphere. Only a hundred or so employees showed up for work that morning. For the first time since the accident, the devastation was visually evident to company officials.

"On one bench where twenty-two women had worked," recalled historian Betty Carlson Kay, "only two had survived." This tremendous loss penetrated every corner of the plant. Out of the 800-plus who had perished on the *Eastland*, more than 600 were Western Electric employees. Entire departments were decimated. Cable rollers were still. Molding machines sat idle. Checkers went from department to department, counting the number of people missing from benches and desks. "Only in a few departments was there any effort to operate the plant," noted one reporter. As Monday wore on, company officials dealt with the aftershocks as best they could.

One unexpected challenge was the onslaught of desperate job-seekers. Hundreds descended on the factory Monday afternoon in search of work in the aftermath of the disaster, but company officials were preoccupied by more pressing matters of relief. "Four special policemen were assigned to turn away the job hunters," wrote the *Tribune*. "The employment office was besieged by a crowd of 500, which remained even after repeated announcements that no new employees would be taken on."

Rumors circulated that Western Electric officials were trying to procure from victims' families "documents fully releasing the company from all claims for damages in connection with the accident." But no one was ever able to substantiate the stories. The ill will toward the company was merely another symptom of the desolation and helplessness permeating every quarter of the city.

People were looking for somebody to blame.

ON TUESDAY MORNING, Chicagoans awoke to newspapers brimming with names of identified dead. Entire pages were filled with lists of Western Electric employees "missing and possibly dead." Headlines expressed the wounded psyche of the town. HUNT GUILTY TODAY, crowed one headline. PUNISH CULPRIT NO MATTER WHO, shouted another. DAYS OF DREAD, exclaimed the *Tribune*. "The city is suffering the shock of the greatest man-made disaster in the history of the country," wrote one editorial. But the deepest wounds were to be found in Cicero.

As the last of the bodies were conveyed from the morgue on Washington Street to the various undertaking establishments, the little factory town prepared for the largest number of simultaneous funerals in its history. "The situation took on a ghastly aspect," observed one reporter, "when it was found that there was a shortage of caskets in the city, and a large number of funerals may have to be postponed on this account."

Undertakers from neighboring communities offered extra coffins. Cemetery managers braced themselves for the imminent flood of burials. Several local cemeteries offered graves free of charge for *Eastland* victims whose families were unable to afford them. A call went out to clergy across the state, asking all available ministers to come to Cicero to assist their brethren in the impending funeral ceremonies. A spirit of communal need spread throughout Chicago. Funds poured into relief agencies. Flags billowed at half-mast. Most businesses closed down in observance of the coming funerals. Taverns, theaters, grocers, and retail stores shuttered their windows and locked their doors.

Funeral services were scheduled for the next day.

AT DUSK ON TUESDAY NIGHT, a lone city official sat in his office, staring at cluttered shelves and tables. His name was De Witt C. Creiger, the Chicago city custodian.

He gazed at piles of personal belongings left in his office: coins, soggy dollar bills, family heirlooms, hats, shoes, handbags—countless items of clothing, still damp, folded neatly and stacked on tabletops. All of it as yet unclaimed.

ON THE WEST SIDE of the Loop, morgue attendants in the armory prepared one of the last unidentified bodies for removal.

In life, Number 396 had been a small, delicate-boned boy with prominent ears, full of laughter and vigor. In death, he had become "Little Feller," the name the police and morgue attendants assigned to him. The moniker resonated deeply with the anguished citizenry. For days, newspapers had bemoaned the fate of "Little Feller," the personification of all that was lost in so impersonal a tragedy.

No immediate family members survived to identify the boy's body. Little Feller's parents had both been lost on the *Eastland*, and the lack of a passenger manifest had left the tiny form in limbo, as forsaken and discarded as the handbags and hats stacked on the tables of the custodian's office. The coroner decided on Tuesday to have the body removed and transported to Sheldon's undertaking rooms at 912 West Madison Street, with the hope that somebody from the community, a neighbor or extended-family member, might visit the funeral parlor in the next few days and recognize the boy.

The coroner's attendants moved Little Feller with utmost care and tenderness. The staff at Sheldon's received him with the dignity and attention accorded to royalty. It wasn't long before the tiny body was identified by a couple of neighborhood boys.

"That's him! That's Willie! Willie Novotny!" cried a seven-year-old boy named William Cech, standing before the boy's remains. "I know it's him. He was wishin' me and my brother Walter could go along with him on the boat!"

William and Walter Cech lived next door to the Novotnys, and played with Willie Novotny practically every day. The children were classmates, and the Cech boys had recently attended Willie's seventh birthday party. The entire Novotny family—Willie's father, mother, and sister—were lost on the *Eastland*. The neighbors were certain that the pale body at Sheldon's was the youngest Novotny, but the police were skeptical.

"Get Willie's grandma down here," urged Walter Cech. "She's all that's left of 'em next door. She'll tell you!"

The elderly woman was summoned to the funeral parlor. Arriving in a police car, sobbing uncontrollably, the grandmother immediately handed the undertaker a parcel. The package contained a small pair of brown Knickerbocker pants, never worn. "If it's Willie," she murmured, her voice cracking with grief. "He's got on pants like these. It was a new suit he went to the picnic in, and two pairs of pants came with it, and these are the others."

The pants matched. Little Feller had a name.

The total number of identified dead increased by one.

CHAPTER EIGHTEEN

Black Wednesday

BELLS TOLLED on Wednesday morning.

The chimes rang out over rooftops, echoed past flags (still flying at half-mast), and reverberated across the streets and rows of brownstones draped in black. A sea of black umbrellas stood in somber silence, as pedestrians paused and bowed their heads while funeral processions passed. Men removed their boaters and stood motionless at street corners. Women hushed their children as the melancholy sound of horses' hooves clopping across the cobblestones filled the air.

The official day of mourning had begun, and before it was over, nearly 700 victims of the *Eastland* would be "borne to their last rest."

So many funeral processions crisscrossed Cicero that the town ran out of horses. Otto Muchna put more miles on his carriages on that one day, shuttling the dead from chapel to cemetery, than on any other day in his long and respected career. Exhaustion nearly put him in the hospital. "It was too much for him," remembered his son. Florists were cleaned out. Churches swelled to capacity with mourners spilling out onto the streets. Gravediggers worked extra shifts, but the requirements outpaced all preparations. Businesses donated motortrucks to carry the dead. Marshall Field's allowed thirty-nine of its largest transport vehicles to be used as hearses. Western Electric provided delivery trucks and open automobiles. Cemeteries were overbooked.

"The bell towers were ringing every fifteen minutes," recalled one historian, "tolling another life gone."

Seven of those chimes signaled the passage of the Sindelar family—George, Adella, Sylvia, George Jr., and William—now reunited for eternity with mother Josephine and son Albert. Early Wednesday, Josephine's family, the Dolezals (who had also lost a second daughter, Josephine's sister, Regina Dolezal, in the accident) arranged for the transportation of the bodies on an open motorcar provided by Western Electric. Photographs survive of the procession: seven white coffins stacked precariously on the rear of a Model T festooned with crepe and flowers. Wreaths and sprays of flowers were placed on top of the uppermost coffins. A black-suited attendant rode on the rear running board, steadying the assemblage. Onlookers stared open-mouthed at the heart-wrenching image of miniature, child-sized white coffins stacked on the larger counterparts below, en route to the Veritas Masonic Temple.

It is likely one of the surviving Dolezal women clutched the golden turnip watch in her moist palm that day, as the Sindelar coffins were slowly hauled away on their short journey to the temple services.

No record exists regarding the whereabouts of Reggie Bowles that morning. At the accident site, the recovery operation came to an unceremonious close. The previous day the *Tribune* tallied the identified dead at 824, with five bodies as yet unidentified. With no further need for heroics in the filthy river, most likely the young Bowles boy returned to work in his garage on Wednesday morning. He might have seen a funeral procession or two pass his northside neighborhood, and he might have paused from his work to ponder the tragedy in which he played a tangential role. One thing is known: according to family records, Reggie suffered a bout of typhoid fever after his experiences in the river.

Nor do we know exactly where Bobbie Aanstad was that day. Chances are she was back in Logan Square. She might have attended one the *Eastland* funerals with her Uncle Olaf, who had lost so many friends and co-workers in the disaster, but she could just as well have remained close to home that day. The trauma of enduring eleven hours in the wreck weighed heavily on the girl as well as on her sister Solveig, who rarely spoke of the incident from that day forth. Somehow, Bobbie managed to maintain her amiable spirit, possibly through sheer force of personality. "She observed the grief from afar," explained Bobbie's daughter-in-law, Jean Decker, remembering stories of that sad day—"Black Wednesday," as it came to be known to many Chicagoans.

MEANWHILE, the Hawthorne works sat nearly empty. Huge funeral bunting swept across the entrance, large wreaths festooned the stone ramparts that flanked each door, and the rows of medieval-looking windows that stretched up and down Twenty-Second Street were also draped in black. "The towers and the principal gates were creped in flowing streamers of black and purple," wrote one reporter. "Few workers seemed to be about, and these crowded the windows constantly to watch the various processions pass."

By noon that day, funeral masses were underway at many of the Catholic churches.

"May the angels lead thee into paradise," chanted Bishop Paul Rhode from the crowded high altar of St. Mary's of Czesto-chowa, a Roman Catholic church in the largely Polish Hawthorne area. "May the martyrs receive thee and mayest thou have rest everlasting with Lazarus, once a beggar."

The bishop stood before the chancel, his pious voice raised

with the volume required of an early twentieth-century orator, unaugmented by amplification. Flanked on each side by a total of twenty-one priests, Bishop Rhode stood illuminated by the light through the stained-glass windows and by hundreds of votive candles flickering in the airless church. Along the front of the nave were twenty-nine caskets, occupying the entire span of the chapel (including the first four rows of pews).

"Merciful father, bow down Thine ear in pity to Thy servants upon whom Thou has laid the heavy burden of sorrow," the Bishop went on, nodding at the grief-racked congregation. "Take away out of their hearts the spirit of rebellion and teach them to see Thy good and gracious purpose working in all the trials which Thou dost send upon them. Grant that they may not languish in fruitless and unraveling grief nor sorrow as those who have no hope."

Similar words were spoken at Mary Queen of Heaven on Twenty-fourth Street, at St. Dionysus on Twenty-ninth, and in many other churches, synagogues, and temples across Chicago. Clergymen understood that the ones who now needed God most were the survivors, the victims' families, the orphans, the bitter and disenfranchised. Many of those left behind found themselves in a crisis not only of life and death, but of faith. Story after story surfaced of widowers cursing God for the tragedy, widows rejecting the church, pain turning inward. The catastrophe had occurred with such abruptness that many of the survivors experienced mute dissociation: eyes were cried dry, hearts turned stony.

As the day wore on, the hardships continued to mount.

Cemeteries such as Bohemian National on Chicago's west side teemed with funeral processions. "Workers at the newly opened Section sixteen (of Bohemian National) were overwhelmed with 139 victims," wrote one historian, "more than any other cemetery."

"Back then it was all done by shovel," explained Gary

Neubeiser of Concordia Cemetery. "It would take two men four hours each to dig one grave—one man working at the foot end, and one working at the head end. The crew at that time was about sixty people. But those sixty people usually did two burials a day." The influx of *Eastland* victims caused awkward delays, bottlenecks, and maddening confusion.

For the Sindelar burial alone, a hundred cars and carriages jammed the narrow pathways.

Stonecutters labored overtime to meet the demand for grave markers. Tombstones reflected both the suddenness of the disaster, and the inextricable connection many survivors felt to the fate of the ship itself. Stone after stone was etched with a rendering of the vessel, and photographs of victims, their earnest faces full of life and hope, were arrayed around carvings of the ship.

Throughout the day mourners stood in clusters across the rain-swept burial grounds as beloved spouses, sons, and daughters were laid to rest. Small coffins were a common sight, flowers laid on graves with trembling hands. "The disaster wiped out twenty-two whole families," Hilton writes. "In the largest single class of deaths, 262 couples lost a total of 290 children."

The disaster also orphaned many children. A total of nineteen families lost both parents, leaving the children in the care of relatives and neighbors. A majority of the victims, 56 percent, were female. Many of these women were young, single workers at the Western Electric plant. The staff of one of the "twine" rooms, where women sat at long benches, winding cotton jackets around telephone cable, was entirely wiped out.

For many families, the black pall that hung over the city on that endless Wednesday afternoon meant only the beginning of a long period of misery.

THE WOUNDED CITY marshaled its resources as best it could, although relief was often insufficient. Only two years earlier,

Western Electric had instituted a new insurance plan, which included death benefits to families of employees with more than five years of company service. This amounted to six months' salary to survivors of employees with more than five years, and one year's salary to families of those with more than ten years. Out of the 600-plus employees who had perished on the *Eastland*, however, only 121 exceeded five years of service. Western Electric historians Stephen Adams and Orville Butler observed: "The magnitude of the disaster forced the company to improvise, allocating an additional 100,000 dollars for relief."

Given such tremendous loss, as well as a stoic rank and file that preferred to suffer in silence than ask for financial assistance, the company pooled its resources. Funds from the Employee Benevolent Association were added to the additional 100,000, bringing the total relief funds to 181,390 dollars. The company also offered its medical, nursing, and welfare staffs free of charge to survivors and families of victims. More than 200 people were inoculated at the plant for typhoid, and a reported 75,806 dollars went for funeral expenses.

"It was incredible what Western Electric did during this tragedy," recalls Cicero historian Georgiana Becker. "They didn't ask the people if they wanted help, they just stepped in and gave them help."

Other relief funds proved to be oversubscribed. The mayor's committee had targeted 200,000 dollars but found it difficult to collect all the money in the short amount of time earmarked for the project. Even the influence of Chicago's most prominent philanthropist, Julius Rosenwald of Sears, Roebuck & Company, was ineffective at loosening such an amount from the recalcitrant upper class. It took another two weeks for the committee to reach its goals, though ultimately it exceeded its targeted amount, raising more than 350,000 dollars.

The Red Cross concentrated on short-term relief. Faced with

more than 900 families with deaths or injuries, the organization adopted a practical policy: "Give prompt relief; ask questions later." After providing indigent families with funds for burial costs, the Red Cross concentrated on longer-term relief. A basic scale was established: 200 dollars to survivors for each adult lost, and 150 for every child. For those children orphaned by the disaster, the organization provided an income stream of twelve dollars per month until the age of sixteen. Widows received an additional 500 dollars for their widowhood. The total amount allocated through the Red Cross came to 379,415 dollars but the bureaucratic paperwork required in many cases slowed the distribution process to a crawl. Although survivors needed help immediately, the final payout of Red Cross funds was not completed until 1918.

No SINGLE EVENT would capture the misery and grief of those days more powerfully than a funeral that occurred one week after the capsizing. On Saturday, July 31, the largest of all the *Eastland*-related funeral services occurred in front of the Skola Vojta Napratek, a school on Homan Avenue, just north of West Twenty-Sixth. It was, as one newspaper noted, "a memorial service so representative in character as to take rank with the most noteworthy burials ever held in Chicago." Over 5,000 people attended the ceremony, including Mayor Thompson, who had recently returned from San Francisco.

"The ranks of vehicles made a procession a mile and a half long," wrote the *Tribune*. "The building was draped with huge streamers of black-and-white crepe, crossed in front of the Homan Avenue entrance to form a background for four coffins. Around the caskets were banked huge masses of floral offerings, elaborate and costly enough to have befitted the funeral of a great statesman. Boys and girls from all parts of the city were present."

The ceremony included a series of speakers, many of whom addressed the throngs in Bohemian (now called Czech). "Chicago wants not revenge but justice," boomed Julius Smietanka, a local dignitary. "This city will rise up in her might, and demand that this sacrifice of life be not in vain!"

Mayor Thompson spoke next. "My presence here is on behalf of the people of Chicago," he bellowed in his trademark stentorian tone. "I am here to emphasize the grief and indignation of this great city. The hearts of all Chicagoans go out in grief to the sufferers of this calamity."

As the occupants of the speaker's platform all stood up in solemn tableau, 200 boy scouts in uniform marched to the front of the dais. The scouts were joined by 430 other schoolboys, most of them from Bohemian schools in the area, all standing at somber attention, their faces turned toward the coffins. One of the scouts stepped out of rank and raised a bugle to his lips. As the quavering, childish rendition of taps echoed across the mourners, a low din of sobs nearly drowned the music.

The coffins, nestled at the front of the rostrum in a riot of flowers, sat gleaming in the sun. Inside one of them lay the body of James Novotny, thirty-three years old at the time of his death, a former cabinetmaker at Western Electric. Inside the others lay Novotny's wife, Agnes, and his daughter, Maimi, nine years old at the time of the capsizing. The fourth coffin contained the object of the most adoration and sorrow.

Unlike the victims of the *Lusitania* or *Titanic*, the occupant of the fourth coffin had been neither famous nor rich, neither a scion of old money nor the captain of any industry, neither an Astor nor an unsinkable Molly Brown. All Willie Novotny had been was an ordinary seven-year-old with big ears—the boy an entire nation of newspaper readers had come to know as "Little Feller."

CHAPTER NINETEEN

To Avenge the Dead

FOR TWO AND A HALF WEEKS, while state prosecutors and federal judges picked over the bones of the disaster in other parts of the city, the sun baked down on the *Eastland*'s exposed hull, water staining her bulwark, herring gulls defecating on her steel. By the time the salvage team arrived to begin the business of towing the wreck, the very presence of the ship had become an affront to the city.

"The hulk was a ghastly sight," wrote Hilton. "The white of its hull had become a sickly gray, on the port side from the mud in the river, and on the starboard side from the ashes spread to provide the survivors friction while they made their escapes. Windows were broken in the pilot house, and the hurricane deck was a shambles." Experts realized that to right the ship and haul it away would be one of the greatest challenges in maritime history.

Captain Alexander Cunning of the Great Lakes Towing Company won the job. Cunning commandeered the *Favorite*, a 181-foot specialized salvage vessel based in St. Ignace, Michigan, equipped with wrecking beams, hydraulic jacks, steam pumps and a small sawmill. The process of moving the *Eastland* required a crew of thirty-two men working fourteen-hour days over two weeks. It was tedious, dangerous work, much of it done at night under the glare of tungsten-nitrogen lamps, and the city watched with sickened fascination.

Divers sealed all the portholes and jagged openings below the water line, and pumps were installed inside the *Eastland*. Tens of thousands of gallons of water were extracted from the wreck in preparation for the raising. Wrecking crews removed the smokestacks, masts, and lifeboats in order to facilitate easier navigation. Then they positioned a massive pontoon barge, a hundred feet long, capable of displacing 1,200 tons of water, next to the hulk. The divers placed one-inch steel cables under the ship, the forward cable attached to the *Favorite*, and the aft attached to the pontoon barge. By August 11, the wreck had been completely emptied of water, and was ready to be raised.

The raising proved more difficult than Cunning anticipated. Mired in about two feet of mud, the *Eastland* leaked profusely. In addition, the coal in the ship's bunkers had shifted. After two days Cunning and his crew could get the ship up to only about 73 degrees, and it still wouldn't float. Cranes groaned, steam sputtered, and smoke billowed over the riverfront for another full day before the ship stood upright at last on August 14, floating for the first time since its capsizing. Harbormaster Adam Weckler suspended traffic on the river during the last few hours of the raising in anticipation of finding human remains beneath the wreck. Divers found no additional bodies.

THE CRIMINAL PROCEEDINGS seemed doomed from the start: too many inquiries in progress simultaneously, as well as a morass of conflicting agendas, made justice exceedingly elusive. At one time, seven separate inquiries probed the incident, many of them at odds with each other. These included official inquests by Illinois State's Attorney Maclay Hoyne, Cook County Coroner Peter Hoffman, United States District Attorney Charles F. Clyne, U.S.

Secretary of Commerce William C. Redfield, Supervising Inspector of the U.S. Steamboat Inspection Service George Uhler, the Harbors and Wharves Committee of the Chicago City Council, and the Illinois Public Utilities Commission.

Much of the legal fireworks in the days following the disaster came from Hoffman's group. This stemmed partly from Hoffman's righteous rage, built up during his agonizing tour of duty at the Armory building, and partly from the fact that Hoffman's jury was headed by the fiery Dr. William A. Evans of the *Tribune*'s health desk, whose every proclamation was promptly published in the pages of the widely read paper—Evans had drawn a bead on Captain Pedersen.

"If a captain stands by and sees his boat go over slowly while tied to the dock, and gives no command looking to the safety of the passengers," Evans announced in smoke-filled Room 811 of the Cook County courthouse, "then clearly he is not a man of decision and judgement."

Grilling a financial officer of the St. Joseph—Chicago Steamship Company, Hoffman posed this question with fire in his eyes: "As secretary of your corporation since this terrible loss of life, the turning over of the *Eastland*, have you made any investigation tending to place the blame for this tremendous loss of life, sadness and sorrow?"

Answer: "No sir, I have not."

Hoffman's angry sigh is practically audible in the grain of the printed transcripts.

At another point in the coroner's proceedings, Assistant State's Attorney M. F. Sullivan, a bear of a man with unruly gray hair, stared down the *Eastland*'s assistant engineer, Peter Erickson, who was giving somewhat smug answers regarding the malfunctioning ballast tanks. Sullivan had reached the end of his tolerance for the snickers and muttering heard among the sailors present.

"Well, how long could [the ballast tanks] trim her in?" Sullivan angrily asked Erickson.

Erickson said he did not know.

"You don't know?" Sullivan marveled.

"No."

"It is all Greek to you, eh?"

The assistant engineer seemed confused. "What do you mean by that?"

After a moment, Sullivan tried to continue: "What is your judgement as a sailor on it?"

The sound of sniggering laughter.

"Cut out that laughing business!" Sullivan boomed. "This is no small affair!"

Sullivan's rage and frustration were an early indication that legal stalemates would plague the proceedings. The convoluted chain of command on a Great Lakes steamer, the wide array of supervisory personnel, the continual shrugging off of responsibility, and the labyrinth of bureaucratic apparatus required to operate a ship such as the *Eastland*, all contributed to the growing legal quagmire.

WITH THE WRECK NOW RAISED, the *Eastland* once again became the sole property of the St. Joseph–Chicago Steamship Company. For three days, the ruined ship sat at the accident site. Martin Flatow, the company's local agent, sent out a call for freelance sailors to commandeer the wreck back up the north branch of the river to its dry dock. But something strange had happened, the first of many odd occurences in the ship's post-disaster life.

No one would serve on the *Eastland*.

In an era when seances, ghost stories, and magic were popular among sailors, always a superstitious lot, the ship had taken on a foreboding aura. The dark mood of Chicago in the aftermath of the disaster did not help matters. Every day Chicagoans awoke to grim headlines of convoluted inquiries and suffering communities. Regardless of the reasons given, nobody wanted to ride on the death ship. After wiping out so many families, the *Eastland* had become an orphan itself.

There are no records of who agreed eventually to commandeer the ruined vessel up the north branch. On August 17 Flatow convinced the crews of the *Kenosha* and *Indiana* to tow it, but nobody knows who rode on the thing.

In front of somber onlookers, tugs slowly towed the *Eastland* westward, through the open Wells Street Bridge, then up the north branch of the Chicago River.

The *Eastland* docked at a defunct shipbuilding yard on Goose Island. The previous week, William Hull had arranged to berth the wreck at dry dock number 2, and on that humid Tuesday in August, the vessel reached its temporary resting place amid the clutter of timbers and weather-beaten docks. Nobody knew at that time how long the giant iron carcass would remain there. Rumors had been circulating that Hull planned to repair the ship for eventual service out of another city, but it was too early to confirm this.

For weeks the wreck sat in its place, clearly visible through the trees from passing trains and streetcars, haunting the city. As Hilton writes with characteristic understatement: "The hulk provided an ideal visual reminder of the catastrophe while the efforts commenced to resolve the legal problems it had engendered."

THE JUDICIAL CIRCUS continued throughout the summer, as the victims' families continued to grieve. Most inquiries centered on the question of the *Eastland*'s seaworthiness. Citizens became concerned that government prosecutors were about to whitewash the proceedings, thus protecting their inspectors from conviction. Chicagoans had seen the adjudication of past catastrophes (such as the Great Fire) become mired in political infighting, but these had essentially been local inquests. The *Eastland* disaster was a national, if not global, matter. Maritime law was at stake, as well as the entire system of naval inspection. Letters were sent to President Wilson by concerned citizens groups. Redfield was under siege. Hoyne intensified his game of legal cat and mouse with the Feds.

Judge Kenesaw Mountain Landis became the bane of Hoyne's efforts. At one point, Landis issued an injunction against persons subpoenaed to appear before the federal grand jury, forbidding them to testify in any other hearing. Basically this shut out Hoyne and Hoffman from conducting parallel inquests. Hoyne grew desperate. He sent private investigators to St. Joseph, Michigan, to rifle through the steamship company's books. He searched everywhere he could think of for proof of improper collaboration between Federal Inspector Robert Reid and officials of the company. The fact that Reid's daughter was married to Joseph Erickson, the *Eastland*'s chief engineer, screamed conflict of interest to Hoyne, but no evidence of impropriety ever surfaced.

"The whole thing hinges on the water ballast," surmised William Nichols of the Federal Steamboat Inspection Service. "Who was in direct charge of ballast tanks—the captain? No. The operation of the tanks would be up to the chief engineer."

Testimony mounted against Erickson. Government officials demonized the plain-spoken, gangly Norwegian. Was he the logical "fall guy" for an inept inspection system? Was Erickson doomed to be the "goat" Pedersen had ranted about in the hours after the capsizing? Day after day, the coroner's jury bored into this soft spot. Walter Greenebaum, the transportation agent for the Chicago–Michigan City route, the man who had contracted the *Eastland* for Western Electric, made a key accusation when asked about the cause of the disaster:

Q: Is it your opinion if the boat had carried proper ballast it would be impossible for the boat to be turned over onto its side?

A: I cannot figure out how the boat, if she had been filled with water, could have turned over.

Q: And that is under the control of the captain and the engineer?

A: Yes, sir.

Q: Under whose control is it directly?

A: Chief engineer.

Later, officials questioned the assistant harbormaster, Joseph Lynn, about the inordinate amount of time that the engineering department had spent attempting to right the ship. Erickson's perceived malfeasance was further solidified in the minds of jurors and citizens alike:

Q: Do you think he was trying for 17 minutes to right the vessel?

A: I didn't say that.

Q: Testimony has been introduced here to that affect [sic].

A: I am not positive as to that. In fact, I am doubtful as to whether the engineer exercised good judgement in not so informing the other members of the crew. An engineer, as soon as he loses his bearing, should notify the first officer or second officer, who are deck officers, who would be very apt to give the first notification [to the passengers].

Q: As to this lapse of time, what do you say about that?

A: If [the chief engineer] has made a statement himself

that he was 17 minutes trying to get water ballast into that boat and was unable to get it in, there is negligence on his part in not notifying everyone in the crew of that boat, and notifying the passengers, and doing all that possibly could be done to get them off the boat.

HOYNE REFUSED to pin criminal responsibility on a few "little fellows." He saw company greed as the culprit behind the disaster, and was determined to prove the existence of a conspiracy among the ship's owners and the government. "You may depend upon the fact that this investigation will reveal collusion between private interests and government officials that will astonish the country," he told the *Tribune* during the proceedings. "I am after the men higher up, and I am going to get them." When asked about Chief Engineer Ericksen and the ballast issue, Hoyne scoffed: "The term 'water ballast' is absurd. This boat had no ballast, and by not having it, the officials violated the law."

Witness after witness supported Hoyne's theories. A marine architect named Devereux York testified that many safety principles were violated on the *Eastland* "in the interests of cheapness." Harbormaster Adam Weckler told Hoffman's jury that he believed the ballast tanks were dangerously low for economic reasons. "I don't think the *Eastland* should have been allowed to carry more than 1,200 passengers," Weckler said under oath. A shipbuilder named William Wood testified that the lines of the *Eastland*'s hull were of a "very unstable shape," and went on to add: "There seems to have been much incompetent inspection."

A portrait emerged of a ship designed primarily for speed and efficiency, built to get cargo from one side of the lake to the other as quickly as possible, with passenger safety of secondary importance—especially in light of the seesawing caps on maximum allowed capacity. Hoyne's crusade, however, was short-lived. With Landis's order of July 31 essentially ending testimony at rival inquiries, the urgency went out of local inquests. The Chicago City Council never had a chance to start an inquiry; and Pedersen and Erickson, shielded by lawyers, were hardly heard from. "The effect of Landis's order," Hilton writes in the early 1990s, after gathering as much data on the criminal proceedings as possible, "was to limit the historical documentation of the disaster seriously. The only thorough examination took place in the federal criminal trial, the transcript of which is an unpublished source so obscure that it lay unknown even to the archivists who held it."

Redfield's public hearings concentrated on the men who counted passengers boarding the *Eastland* before the capsizing, interviewing nearly 100 witnesses and lasting for three weeks. Chicagoans tracked the proceedings closely. Newspaper headlines reflected the city's nagging doubt that anything remotely like justice would ever prevail. EASTLAND DEAD MAY NOT BE AVENGED, proclaimed one paper, ALL INQUIRIES SLOWED UP; U.S. OFFICIALS DODGE BLAME BEFORE REDFIELD. Citizens groups sent protests. Many Chicagoans resented the fact that the government "was investigating itself."

On September 22, the federal grand jury handed down ten separate indictments. The official charges were "conspiracy to defraud the federal government by preventing the execution of marine laws, and for criminal carelessness." The jury indicted Captain Pedersen, Chief Engineer Erickson, Steamship Inspector Reid, Boiler Inspector Charles Eckliff, William Hull (co-owner of the *Eastland*), George Arnold (co-owner of the *Eastland*), Walter Greenebaum (transportation agent), Walter Steele (treasurer, St.Joseph–Chicago), the St.Joseph–Chicago Steamship Company, and the Indiana Transportation Company. The charges carried a possible prison term, two years for conspiracy and ten years for criminal carelessness, or a 10,000 dollar fine, or both.

Thus began the official criminal proceedings of the *Eastland*

218

disaster. They would drag on for years, yield very few convictions, and prove to be the only criminal action ever brought forth in the aftermath of this tremendous tragedy.

FOILING THE EFFORTS of Hoyne and Hoffman was not the last of Judge Kenesaw Mountain Landis's defiant acts.

On August 17, two Chicago aldermen, Robert Buck and Ellis Geiger, announced that they would seek a court order to take possession of the *Eastland*'s battered hulk. Chicagoans had grown weary of its presence, which tormented many, and the aldermen wanted to provide a positive gesture to salve the wounded town. They planned to seize the hulk as a "deadly weapon," have it scrapped, and then distribute the proceeds to the families of victims.

Landis had other ideas.

Upon hearing of the aldermen's plan, the judge immediately issued an order releasing the wreck to its owner, and five days later, issued an injunction against suits or legal actions of any nature against the steamship itself. This would ensure that all efforts at recovery or damages be made, as Hilton writes, "within the framework that Landis was establishing." The owner, by liquidating all its assets, requested that the ship be put under the control of a trustee. Landis appointed Captain Denis Sullivan as trustee for the *Eastland*, and three months later, Sullivan sold the wreck at auction.

According to historical records, only two bidders showed up at the macabre auction held on a cold December morning. One of them was an attorney from Boston, who represented an East Coast steamship company. The other was Captain Edward A. Evers of the Illinois Naval Reserve. Evers won the auction with a bid of 46,000 dollars, taking possession of the hulk on December 28. Reporters caught up with the captain, and asked for a statement.

"The boat will make a fine training ship for the reserve," Evers proclaimed. "There is nothing radically wrong with the hull. We could remove the two upper decks, put proper ballast in the hold, and provide watertight bulkheads and the *Eastland* hoodoo would be broken. It's a question of feasibility—not sentiment."

The captain walked away, leaving the reporters to stare in silence.

CHAPTER TWENTY

Sins and Omissions

THE OLD MAN sat in the rear of the Pullman car, reading a copy of the *Tribune*, his fedora tilted down over his craggy face as the streetcar clattered through the canyons of steam and marble. He wore a dapper black woolen suit, with a vest and a watch fob. But there was a rumpled aspect to the man that, upon closer viewing, became apparent in the sweat-spotted felt of his hat and the wrinkled tie knotted loosely around his wattled neck. The only indication that the man was anything other than an aging accountant or actuary was the glint of passion in those eyes buried in the shadow of that fedora.

Here were eyes so sharp and intelligent they were almost predatory; and when the old man spoke—often in courtrooms, often at the top of his gravelly, tenor voice—those eyes were fixed upon their victims with withering fury.

In ten years this man would serve as legal counsel for a young Tennessee high school teacher named John Scopes in one of the most celebrated trials of the twentieth century. Known as the "Scopes Monkey Trial," the circus-like proceedings centered around the young instructor's unforgivable infraction of introducing the concept of evolution to a 1925 biology class. The old lawyer would be unable to get the teacher acquitted, but the eloquence with which the case was presented against the State of Tennessee would become legendary in the annals of jurisprudence, as would the old man himself.

Chances are, though, very few people on that streetcar, on an early October morning in 1915, knew that Clarence Darrow sat among them. Darrow was quietly making his way out of town, to the District Court Building in Grand Rapids, where he would resume his defense of Chief Engineer Joseph Erickson, who was facing the wrath of a grieving Chicago.

The case had sunk into a legal quagmire. Each of the ten defendants had his own lawyer, and each defense team, it seemed, had its own version of why and how the disaster happened. Darrow's defense, based on the theory that the ship had been resting on some underwater obstruction, became a sore point for the city, since it implied partial responsibility of city agencies for the capsizing.

Darrow had difficulty proving his theory, though he went as far as hiring one of the hardhat divers who had worked on the recovery crew, William Deneau, to go back into the river and cut off the tops of two pilings near the accident site. The theory was subsequently disproved by naval architects who showed that the capsizing happened nowhere near the two pilings in question.

Other theories abounded. Some proposed that the shift in passengers to the port side caused the ship to tip over, a notion that gained wide acceptance among laymen, and seemed, for unknown reasons, to persist for years. To the contrary, all indications suggest that the passengers were distributed evenly at the time of the capsizing. Others blamed the premature movement of a tug, a tow line, or a cleat getting caught on the *Eastland* and pulling it over. Some claimed that the ballast intake was clogged. Also discussed was the interference of rubble from a demolished building in the area, strewn across the river bottom.

None of these theories stood up to scrutiny, but they served to confuse and complicate the proceedings.

Experts examined the wreck. A professor from the University of Michigan concluded that the ship was intrinsically unsafe as an excursion vessel. But the findings did little to convince Judge Clarence Sessions, who was presiding over the federal case, that there was a conspiracy among the defendants to defraud the government (as was laid forth in the indictments). On February 18, 1916, Sessions delivered his decision: Not guilty on all counts.

"It is difficult to find fault in Sessions's decision," writes Hilton.

At that point, there was no evidence of a criminal conspiracy, and nobody even remotely suspected the *Titanic* incident as the indirect cause of the *Eastland* disaster. But as Hilton methodically proved in his definitive book on the disaster, *Eastland: Legacy of the Titanic*, the true reason the ship went over was a dangerously low metacentric height (or stability profile) due in part to a glut of lifeboats on the uppermost deck.

As Hilton concludes of the federal court's exoneration of the defendants: "They were all behaving as they habitually did, oblivious to the fact that a worldwide movement for increasing boat and raft capacity relative to passenger capacity would affect their ship . . . and in the process produce a catastrophe."

CIVIL LITIGATION dragged on. With a final tally of 844 wrongful deaths, the process was understandably slow and acrimonious. Still, no one in their wildest dreams would have imagined it would take twenty years to conclude the final law suit.

Landis assigned Judge Lewis F. Mason as commissioner of the estates of the deceased, and action was taken to limit liability. Maritime law limited the payout to the value of the *Eastland*'s hull—46,000 dollars—but the law also stipulated that creditors be paid first.

"They had to pay the company that raised the *Eastland* from the Chicago River," recalls historian Ted Wachholz, "which approximately was 35,000 dollars. And they had to pay the coal company, the concession companies. All these other creditors had to be paid prior to the victims' families. The owners of the ship—the company itself—never really paid them a dime."

Two key players in the civil actions passed away before definitive judgments could be made regarding their guilt or innocence.

Steamboat inspector Robert Reid, the man at the center of swirling conflict-of-interest questions, died of natural causes in 1922.

Chief Engineer Joseph Erickson enlisted in the military immediately after the federal proceedings, and served in World War I as a lieutenant in the Army Transport Service. While serving in Europe he developed a heart condition and returned home on medical leave to Grand Haven, Michigan. "He expected to return to his military service," Hilton wrote, "but his physicians were pessimistic." Erickson died at home of valvular heart disease on April 3, 1919, only five days after his thirty-seventh birthday.

The morass of litigation continued for nine more years, until all petitions were put before Judge Mason for a final ruling. On November 20, 1933, Mason concluded: "At the time of the disaster, the steamer *Eastland* was seaworthy in every respect, properly equipped and manned and fit for the carriage of passengers if properly handled."

Joseph Erickson, the coarse, stoic Norwegian and hapless chief engineer—the only crewman who willingly went down with his ship and risked his life to shut down the boilers in order to prevent an explosion—became the only person to be convicted of criminal negligence in association with the disaster. Erickson was blamed posthumously for the accident, a decision upheld in August 1935, essentially putting the *Eastland* affair to rest almost precisely twenty years after it happened.

"Blaming Erickson was attractive," writes Hilton, "because both parties to the trial had alleged that his behavior had been negligent, and he was not alive to explain and defend his actions."

The true history of the disaster was doomed to be buried alongside the victims.

Maritime law was hardly affected by the accident. The excursion industry carried on as before. Many of the survivors, as well as their direct descendants and relatives, went to their graves without saying another word about the incident. For decades, anniversaries of the disaster were rarely, if ever, observed by anyone.

For most of the twentieth century, in fact, the waterfront at Clark Street bore no marker. The city simply went about its business of becoming a great Midwestern metropolis, as though nothing ever happened.

River traffic continued to wax and wane, day in and day out, the backwash of history rippling out into Lake Michigan where it dispersed and vanished without a trace.

*

Epilogue:
The Smell of Violets

Injustice, swift, erect, and unconfined,
Sweeps the wide earth, and tramples
o'er mankind.

—Homer, *Iliad*

*

CAPTAIN HARRY PEDERSEN never again commanded a ship, but he lived a long, lonely post-disaster life. After the tragedy, he retired to his family farm in the small lakeside village of Millburg, Michigan, a patchwork of fields and orchards just east of Benton Harbor.

There Pedersen lived quietly with his wife until his death twenty-four years later at the age of seventy-nine. For income he worked the sparse farmland and consulted occasionally for compass manufacturers. One can't resist imagining the ruddy old man sitting on his dilapidated porch late into the long Michigan evenings, ruminating on the bad decisions, the hubris, and the lies. Hilton believes that Pedersen perjured himself at least once in the final round of civil trials when he stated that he believed the *Eastland* capsized because it was resting on an obstruction on the river bottom—testimony that directly contradicted statements made by the captain to Clyne and Hoyne in the criminal proceedings.

Pedersen died of kidney failure on July 25, 1939, one day after the twenty-fourth anniversary of the disaster, at Cook County Hospital in Chicago. He was buried next to his wife in a tiny cemetery in Millburg.

"His final lie was at least locally successful," writes Hilton. "The St. Joseph Herald-Press stated in his obituary that the cause of the disaster was the *Eastland*'s resting on a hidden spile."

Today the captain's tombstone stands—small, plain, overgrown with weeds, and void of any maritime symbols or signs of his one-time metier as a master of steamships.

* * *

THE DESTINIES over the years, of other crewmembers and principal players in the *Eastland* affair were wide and varied.

First mate Del Fisher became a policeman in St. Joseph, Michigan, and died in the mid-1930s. Assistant engineer Fred Snow returned to work for the Pere Marquette Railway ferry system. On December 16, 1929, while walking from the ferry terminal to his home in Ludington, Michigan, he collapsed on the sidewalk and died suddenly.

Walter Greenebaum sold his firm, the Indiana Transportation Company, and became a ship broker. After World War I he moved to Michigan City and became the secretary of the town's chamber of commerce. He died in 1960 at the age of eighty-one, one of Michigan City's most revered local figures.

The *Eastland*'s owner, William Hull, left the ship business and went into banking. He became a director of finance for the Union Bank of St. Joseph, and was always reluctant to travel for fear of further prosecution. He died of heart failure in St. Joseph in 1933.

As noted earlier, Judge Kenesaw Mountain Landis became high commissioner of baseball four years after the *Eastland* disaster. The "stern-visaged, shaggy-haired dictator" ruled the national pastime with the same iron-handed techniques he used on the bench. He repeatedly infuriated owners and players, inventing free-agency in 1940 and routinely handing out fines. He served as commissioner until the day he died of a massive heart attack, on November 25, 1944, at St. Luke's Hospital in Chicago.

Maclay Hoyne went on to become a legendary figure in the annals of Chicago history. Throughout the teens he fought organized crime and vice with the iron fist and unorthodox techniques of a folk hero. In 1916, he staged an infamous raid on the mayor's office in search of evidence of corruption. He made enemies everywhere, from merchant groups to power companies, from milk combines to associations of coal dealers—whoever or whatever he thought was gouging the public. "Even the people who hated him," wrote one reporter, "had to admit he was high class . . . no ordinary reformer." For the last nineteen years of his life, Hoyne ran a busy private law practice. He died in 1939 at the age of sixty-six. "What a fighter!" proclaimed one obituary. "What a man!"

Coroner Peter Hoffman gained his own brand of notoriety in the years that followed. He remained coroner until 1922, at which time he was elected Cook County Sheriff. During Hoffman's tenure as sheriff, a major scandal rocked Prohibition-era Chicago, involving two infamous gangsters, Terry Druggan and Frankie Lake. While incarcerated at the county jail, Druggan and Lake were caught spreading mob money among guards and administrators to obtain special privileges. Because of the scandal, Hoffman received a thirty-day jail sentence for contempt of court, thus becoming the only county sheriff in the history of Chicago to serve time while in office. Hoffman's hard-edged manner became such a joke among Chicago insiders that newspaperman Ben Hecht spoofed the sheriff in his 1929 hit play *The Front Page*.

After leaving office, Hoffman served with the park district until his retirement in 1932. He died in 1948. The *Eastland* incident is not mentioned in any of Hoffman's obituaries on file in Chicago's Harold Washington Library Center or in the Chicago Historical Society.

IT SEEMED AS THOUGH a layer of denial—or at least one of repression—had formed over the city's memory of the disaster. So little import had been placed on this tragedy—to this day, the greatest disaster in terms of loss of life in the city's history—that even the death ship itself was disguised and paraded before the people like a felon living under an alias.

Chicago's captains of industry participated wholeheartedly

in this conspiracy of silence. Old-money families, their names including Field, Armour, McCormick, and Reynolds, contributed funds through personal notes to the consortium established to convert the *Eastland* into a training vessel for the Navy. Renovators tore away the boat's superstructure above the promenade deck, opened the cabin and 'tween decks, and replaced the flooring with teak. They riveted over the gangways and lower portholes, and constructed a new bridge and deck house. Quarters for 244 crewmen and twenty-one officers were installed, as well as the accoutrements of a gun boat, including four large-caliber guns, two forward and two aft.

They renamed the boat the USS *Wilmette*, and put it into active service in 1919. The only trouble was, by the time the ship was launched, World War I was over.

The government immediately designated the boat a training vessel as originally intended. One of its early missions took it on a gunnery exercise in which it sank a German U-boat in Lake Michigan. The submarine had been impounded at Harwich, England, at the end of the war, and had been shipped to America under the terms of the Treaty of Versailles, which mandated that the U-boat had to be destroyed by July 1, 1921. On June 7, the *Wilmette* steamed about thirty miles north of Chicago, located the sub, and opened fire. The U-boat sank in less than a minute.

For the next twenty-plus years, the *Wilmette* spent its summers plying the waters of the Great Lakes, loaded with young sailors, most of whom were oblivious to its dark history. On August 1, 1943, in one of her most celebrated excursions, the *Wilmette* carried President Franklin Roosevelt on a summer cruise across McGregor and Whitefish bays. Harry Hopkins, the architect of the New Deal, was also on board, and the men dined in style, talking war strategy and sleeping in lavishly appointed officers' berths, completely ignorant of the boat's tragic past.

Toward the end of the Second World War, the Navy decommissioned the *Wilmette*, and it ended up as part of a series of lake-front exhibitions of military and naval equipment. Thousands of Chicagoans boarded the boat and inspected her cabins, guns, and boiler rooms. A sign greeted visitors with no mention of the *Eastland*. The obliteration of the tragedy was complete.

In 1946 the *Wilmette* was sold for scrap.

"On November 1st," Hilton writes, "she was slowly towed up the Chicago River past the point at which she had capsized. She was towed to the wharf of William J. Howard on the South Branch near 16th Street, where her superstructure and machinery were removed. The hull was then towed to the Inland Steel Company's plant at East Chicago, Indiana, where what had been the *Eastland* was finally cut up early in 1947."

ONE OF THE MANY "near-miss" stories back in 1915 concerned a man named Walter Lucas and his sixteen-year-old niece, Eleanor. A bookkeeper at Western Electric, Walter had planned to attend the July 24th company picnic with Eleanor, but early that morning, Walter was delayed when he cut himself shaving, and got blood on his collar. The time it took him to change his collar (collars were removable in those days) caused him to miss boarding the first ship.

Walter and Eleanor arrived at the Clark Street bridge in time to see the *Eastland* flop over into the river. Walter merely considered himself lucky, but the girl was scarred by what she saw.

"My grandmother, Eleanor Pycz, never talked of what she saw happen on the river that day," remembered Ralph Harmon. "She didn't sleep well for quite some time, and even later in life she had nightmares."

Harmon grew up in the Chicago area, somewhat haunted by the *Eastland* disaster and his family's connection to it. "I was too young to remember my grandmother talking about it," he recalled, "but I remember my sister said that she did not like to discuss it, and looked visibly shaken when the subject was brought up."

Harmon landed a job with a large manufacturing company in Wauconda, Illinois, and in 1991 met Christine Bartell, whom he married three years later. Ralph and Christine shared their life stories but the subject of Chicago's worst disaster never came up until one evening when Christine showed her husband a family heirloom. It was in pristine condition, about the size of a plum, its gold housing ornately monogrammed and engraved, and its gleaming surface was burnished from years of loving touch. The turnip watch still kept time.

Josephine Sindelar's pocket watch had been passed down through four generations of Sindelar women. Christine Harmon was Josephine's great-great-grand-niece, and had kept the memory of the Sindelars and the disaster alive mostly because of the family connection, but also because of the watch. The watch represented the stubborn resilience of oral history. It is the reason for books such as this one. And it also connects Ralph and Christine in a bond beyond matrimony.

"When I heard Christine's story about the watch," Ralph explained, "I said that my grandmother probably saw her relatives perish. I was amazed that we had this common link. Not many people seemed to ever have heard of the *Eastland*, yet here was a connection that had ended in death for her family and life for mine.

"Whenever I see the watch, or hold it," Harmon reflected, "I feel a great sadness. I prefer not to hold it, but I hope my daughter feels differently when she is passed the watch . . . when Christine feels the time is right."

THE HAWTHORNE WORKS never had another annual picnic cruise.

* * *

OTTO MUCHNA continued for much of his life serving the Lawndale community as one of its most trusted undertakers. He moved to a new chapel on Twenty-Seventh Street in 1917, and his business flourished. The new facility featured massive stained-glass windows and eight interior archways on which a well-known artist named Hamous painted a series of murals depicting "The Story of Life"—infancy, childhood, adulthood, marriage, parenthood, work, old age, and death. Otto modernized as the century progressed, motorizing his hearses and putting in air conditioning and state-of-the-art "restorative" equipment.

Jerry Muchna, Otto's middle son—the same boy who was sailing wooden boats on the day of the disaster—followed in his father's footsteps, graduating from Warsham College of Mortuary Science in 1938 and entering the family business shortly thereafter, working alongside his dad at the Twenty-Seventh Street chapel. Jerry ultimately became the president of the Chicago Funeral Directors Association.

Otto Muchna developed cancer of the larynx in 1935, and slowed down considerably. Surgery stole his voice, and he took a backseat to his son Jerry, who managed the funeral home for the remainder of Otto's life. Otto died peacefully in his bedroom above the chapel in 1958.

Jerry Muchna passed away in 2000.

Jerry's son, Roy, still lives in the Chicago area, and keeps a piece of stained glass salvaged from his grandpa's chapel hanging in his living room.

IN THE YEARS immediately following the disaster, the Illinois National Guard established a new armory on Madison Street, and the old 2nd Regiment Armory at Washington and Curtis—the place where entire families were laid in rows on the floor like so much cordwood—was turned into a storage garage for the U.S. Postal Service.

The space was big enough for 112 delivery trucks, and its central location was ideal for the citywide distribution of mail. Very little information exists in Chicago historical archives on the building during this middle period. We do know that some time in the 1920's the U.S. Government sold the building, and throughout the middle part of the century the facility served, at one time or another, as a horse stable, bowling alley, and film studio.

In 1989, Chicago talk show queen Oprah Winfrey purchased the building for her burgeoning film and TV production company—Harpo Productions. The space was completely renovated by the prestigious architectural design firm Nagle, Hartray & Associates, and the old Victorian lines and gothic stone turrets were demolished and sandblasted away in favor of the stylish Art Deco Revival so popular in the late '80s.

Today the facility is a massive, state-of-the-art media production center, complete with soundstages, editing suites and administrative facilities. Oprah's Emmy-winning talk show is produced there, as well as such television miniseries events as *The Women of Brewster Place*. But beneath the modern stucco facade and ornate glass-block windows still lay the original beams and joists of the temporary morgue—timbers marinated in horrible memories and unbearable grief. After hours, security guards have reported unexplained phenomena.

"It is no accident that unusual activity flared up at Harpo Studios just after Oprah opened the complex in 1989," writes Richard Crowe, an expert in the paranormal. "The structural and extensive cosmetic changes may have caused the stirring up of dormant ghosts. Very often ghostly activity begins after some psychical change to property, as if the long dead tenants object or are riled."

Night-shift workers at Harpo have witnessed activity ranging from doors opening and closing by themselves to the sounds of children laughing and playing. Others have noticed the odors of antique perfumes hanging in pockets in the corridors. Some have witnessed the appearance of a ghostly woman dressed in the style of the early 1900s. Known to insiders as the "Gray Lady," the apparition wears a flowing dress and fancy hat, and has been captured on security cameras wandering the halls.

"The gray-shadowy figure doesn't exactly walk," writes Crowe, "but floats."

Even Oprah herself has admitted the possibility of such phenomena. On a 1996 Halloween edition of her talk show, she mentioned the history of her own studios, and confessed that she preferred not to be there after hours. Other members of her staff have come forward over the years, providing more specific detail.

Robin Hocott, who has been a security guard at Harpo for three years, reported hearing loud crashing sounds after hours, but searches revealed nothing out of the ordinary. The situation intensified. One evening Hocott's phone rang; it was a producer working late in another part of the building. The sounds of laughter from an empty hallway had terrified the producer so severely that she had locked herself in her office.

What has rattled Hocott most has been the phantom perfume. "It was a strong odor of violets," Hocott recalled. "Like a cologne your grandmother would wear." The scent is always accompanied by the sound of sobbing.

THE DISASTER changed Reggie Bowles.

Bowles's descendants paint a picture of a man who lived a complex life, full of contradictions and inner turmoil. Although many of the details of Bowles's life are either apocryphal or disputed by family members, there are things we know for certain.

In the months after the accident, Bowles contracted typhoid from ingesting so much dirty water. Eventually he recovered and closed the doors of his repair business in order to travel and widen his horizons. Stories vary regarding his whereabouts during World War I. Some believe he went to Canada. Others maintain he went overseas and served in the British Naval Transport Service. We do know he enlisted in the National Guard in McAllen, Texas, and suffered a series of illnesses and injuries.

After World War I Bowles began a series of restless endeavors. He was a car salesman in Montana and Wyoming; he worked at a detective agency; he flew biplanes in stunt shows, booking himself as 'Daredevil Rex'; he ran a series of repair garages, and was a self-styled inventor.

By 1929, Bowles had married four times and had fathered several children, some of them out of wedlock. He served in World War II, rising to the rank of lieutenant colonel. In middle age, he exhibited behavioral symptoms that today might be diagnosed as bipolar disorder, and likely contributed to his troubled relationships with many family members. "He left a trail of heartbreak and a wake of human debris," explained one descendant.

Bowles seemed happiest in his waning years, playing solitaire with his fourth wife, listening to opera, and cooking elaborate meals. If asked about the *Eastland*, he was quick to pull out old, yellowed, crumbling articles, and revel in the glory of being the "Human Frog," the youngest hero of that terrible day.

Reggie died on April 28, 1990. "He was no saint," recalled his grandson David Bowles, "but he was a true American character."

THE RIVERFRONT near the Clark Street bridge evolved over time with the changing fortunes of the city.

For years the expansion to the south of Chicago's central business district had been prevented by the barrier of the river bend. In 1928, construction started to straighten the river and allow access to railroads and through streets. Classical balustrades lined the waterfront, and Wacker Drive, carved out of the banks of the main channel, obliterated the old produce markets. The town grew exponentially, and nobody seemed to have time to commemorate something as sad and delicate as the *Eastland* disaster.

The twentieth century brought equal amounts of growth and tumult to Chicago. In 1933, the town hosted one of the greatest world's fairs of all time, the Century of Progress, along the shores of Lake Michigan between Twelfth and Thirty-Ninth Streets. Thirty-nine million visitors came to the fair to see new technologies and glimpse into the future. During the war years, Chicago helped usher in the atomic age by being the site of the first controlled nuclear reaction, achieved underneath the football field at the University of Chicago. In the 1950s, the city virtually invented modern machine politics with the election of Richard J. Daley. And through it all, hardly a single ceremony took place to honor the victims of the *Eastland*. No plaques, no statues, no citywide memorial. The disaster had been relegated to obscurity. The *Eastland* became an occasional subject for old-timers bellied up to a neighborhood bar or sitting on a porch swing, the facts of the accident lost or scrambled across the passing decades.

Was this withering of attention because the *Eastland* lacked renowned or wealthy passengers? Was it the fact that most victims were immigrant factory workers—Hungarians, Poles, and Czechs from lower-class neighborhoods, without fame or fortune or political pedigree? Or was it due to the prosaic nature of the accident itself: a steamship suddenly flipping over at its berth in front of thousands of onlookers, crushing or drowning hundreds of men, women and children in what was essentially a freak accident?

On its fiftieth anniversary in 1965, as the town endured riots and the tumult of clashing cultures, the disaster was given a few column inches of remembrance in a few newspapers, but still no plaque or marker.

By the late 1980s, the memory of the *Eastland* disaster had become so dim that most Chicagoans simply shrugged with ignorance if asked about it. Maybe a senior citizen or two might perk up, eyes glinting with recognition, but for the most part, the disaster had been lost to the dusty shelves of obscurity.

Occasionally, a student might stumble upon a citation of the tragedy in some musty text and be intrigued enough to write a report. This is exactly what happened in 1987, when a student at the Illinois Mathematics and Science Academy in Aurora, Illinois, happening upon an article about the *Eastland*, discussed it with his teacher as a subject for study. Before long the disaster became a research project for honors students whom the academy had been established by the state to instruct. Two of the participating teachers, William Stepien and Bernard Hollister, took the project a step further. "Partly with their contributions, and with the cooperation of the Illinois State Historical Society and the Chicago Maritime Society, a large aluminum plaque was struck giving a short but accurate account of the event," writes Hilton. "The text raised the questions of the ship's seaworthiness and of the adequacy of the federal inspection, but did nothing to perpetuate the casual explanations of the disaster."

The plaque was unveiled at the edge of the river, and dedicated in a short ceremony, on June 4, 1989. Professor Ted Káramanski of Loyola University spoke of the disaster's importance in the context of Chicago's developing social fabric, and Frank French of AT&T spoke of Western Electric's relief efforts. The modest ceremony sparked a new interest among Chicagoans in the event, and provided the riverfront with a sorely needed, permanent commemoration of the event.

Records vary, but the best estimate is that several dozen survivors of the capsizing were still alive on that mild summer day in 1989 when the plaque was dedicated. Among them was 88-year-old Borghild Aanstad, better known as Bobbie.

* * *

BOBBIE AANSTAD'S family survived the lean years after the disaster, and went on to live long, productive lives in spite of the occasional nightmare.

Uncle Olaf received a medal of honor from the coroner for saving dozens of passengers from certain death that July morning. The medal, a silver star embossed with a rendering of the capsized ship and the words "For Valued Services Rendered— *Eastland* Disaster 1915," occupied a place of honor in Olaf Ness's life.

Ness married and left Chicago for the West Coast, settling in northern California where he established a cattle ranch and raised his own family. He died in the mid-1960s.

Marianne continued to work as a cleaning lady, raising her two daughters in a time when a single working mother was rare. She remarried in 1919—to a foreman of a silk factory named Victor Jensen, and became a naturalized citizen in 1942. Marianne rarely spoke of the disaster, and led a quiet life in Chicago until her death on June 6, 1966.

If Marianne Aanstad rarely spoke of the capsizing, Solveig Aanstad hardly ever mentioned it.

Solveig went about her life quietly, marrying a man named Arthur Swanson and raising a family in the Chicago suburbs. But she never completely resolved the tremendous emotional weight that pressed upon her in the aftermath of the *Eastland*. She died on June 23, 1989.

Only Bobbie seemed to heal from the trauma of that day in 1915. She grew up strong and independent, and would readily talk about the *Eastland* whenever anybody expressed interest. Photographs of her in the decade following the disaster show a free spirit, eyes glinting with life. Many pictures taken at the beaches of Lake Michigan show Bobbie clowning with friends, soaking up the sun and enjoying the water.

"She never stopped loving the water," recalled Bobbie's daughter-in-law, Jean Decker.

Bobbie worked as a switchboard operator throughout the war years in order to help with family expenses. In 1922, she married a dapper young businessman named Leonard Decker, and after the couple had a child, Leonard, Jr., they settled into a comfortable existence on Chicago's northwest side. The diminutive, bright-eyed Norwegian woman took to motherhood well, and continued to recount freely her experiences on the *Eastland* if the subject came up.

Bobbie lost her husband in the late 1950s, and found work subsequently as a clerk at Marshall Field's on State Street. Grandchildren—two girls—came along and Bobbie became "Nana" to the little ones. The Decker family recalls fondly the life force that burned warmly within Bobbie in her latter years.

"She was a girl's girl," Jean Decker remembers with a smile, "always game to go out to lunch or shopping or swimming. She had this darling, petite figure, and she used to dive right off the pier and swim from pier to pier, doing the breast stroke so she wouldn't get her hair too wet. I'll always remember that white cap—we could always see it bobbing out there as she swam from pier to pier."

When Bobbie was in her early seventies, her life changed yet again when she received an invitation from an old friend to visit Arizona on a brief vacation. Bobbie was delighted to rekindle an old friendship, and agreed to meet the man, who had recently lost his own spouse, at a hotel in Tucson.

The man was Ernie Carlson, the young neighborhood boy who had taught Bobbie to swim, the same rascal that Bobbie had thought about so often during those terrible hours trapped in the sunken hold of the *Eastland*.

"I sat behind the door of that lobby," Carlson recalled years later with a grin. "And I figured if I saw this big tough gal walk in, I was going to run the other way. But I'm sitting there, and then Bobbie walks in. This little perky gal, just as cute as she can be! I said, 'Bobbie?' And she goes: 'Errrrnnnnnnie!'"

The spark between Bobbie and Ernie was undeniable, and the two married within the year. Carlson lived for twelve more years, the couple enjoying a peaceful existence in California.

Borghild Amelia Aanstad, better known as Bobbie, passed away on August 2, 1991, at the age of ninety. Her death reduced the number of living *Eastland* survivors to fewer than two dozen. At the time of this writing, there are four documented living survivors.

Their stories—as well as the stories of those who have passed away—live on. They must live on.

Notes

THIS BOOK would not exist without the generosity of scholars, histo-rians, descendants, and survivors—many of whom are quoted in these pages. Of the many sources consulted, however, I am most indebted to the Eastland Disaster Historical Society (EDHS), P.O. Box 2013, Arlington Heights, IL 60006; (877) 865-6295.

This amazing organization was cofounded by Ted Wachholz and Bobbie Aanstad's two granddaughters, Barbara and Susan Decker, who remember growing up hearing their "Nana" tell stories of the "big boat turning over in the river." The sisters' fascination was passed on to Ted, Barbara's husband, who joined the two women in the late 1990s to start EDHS. Much of what is known about this tragedy has been passed down through oral histories, and it is part of this organization's charge to collect these personal accounts. (These can be read on-line at www.EastlandDisaster.org.)

During the course of my research, these folks treated me like a member of their family. They opened their extensive files to me, they took me to cemeteries and museum exhibits, and they either found or cleared practically every photo in the gallery that precedes this sec-tion. But what I found most interesting about Ted, Barb, and Susan was their commitment. They are completely dedicated to preserving the memory of this important event in American history. Although family connection obviously is a huge part of that commitment, what truly motivated the EDHS was the dearth of public awareness.

"A few years back, right after Nana died," Ted Wachholz recalls, "we decided to buy the new book that had just come out on the *Eastland* for Barb's mom for Mother's Day. We went to two or three bookstores—a mom and pop place, a big franchise place—and all we got were blank stares. And we thought, 'This is bizarre.' In the middle of Chicago, maybe six blocks from where the disaster occurred only seventy-some years earlier, and nobody had ever heard of it?! That really inspired us to see if we couldn't do something about this situation."

My other principal source, which I mined at virtually every turn, is the book Wachholz mentions above, *Eastland: Legacy of the Titanic* by George Hilton, published in 1995 (the same year that Alderman Ed Burke of the Chicago's Fourteenth Ward managed to drum up enough interest to hold a commemoration of the *Eastland*'s eightieth anniversary). This book is one of the most amazing feats of scholarship I have ever encountered.

Hilton documented practically every rivet on that ship, found practically every blueprint, every court transcript, every shred of literary evidence, and built a case for what happened on that gray July day with the aplomb of a legal demigod. After reading Hilton's book—the only other full-length work to date on the disaster—I decided that no one would ever delve deeper into *what* happened that day, and *why* it happened. However, I realized that my book could give readers an inkling of what it was *like* to be there that day, and to be a passenger on that ship. I figured my book could be a decent companion to Hilton's.

As of this writing, Hilton resides in a retirement home on the East Coast, his eyesight failing. Hilton is a true mensch, an inspiration to me as a writer, who encouraged me throughout all phases of this project and, when asked for permission to use large chunks of his book, replied in his trademark baritone growl: "Just give me footnote glory." Consider it done, George, and thanks.

Other particularly helpful sources include *Chicago by Gaslight:*

A History of Chicago's Netherworld 1880–1920 by Richard Lindberg. An atmospheric glimpse into that alien planet known as Chicago, this book would make one hell of a movie. I used it extensively for background on crime and crime-fighters of the era. *Manufacturing the Future: A History of Western Electric* by Stephen Adams and Orville Butler was invaluable for background on the Hawthorne works and its parent company, as well as on the passengers themselves. Finally the *Chicago Tribune* provided me with an endless gold mine of information and eyewitness accounts of the disaster. It is impossible to overstate the importance of this great newspaper to the history of Chicago.

In creating the individual chapter notes that follow I endeavored to make things as simple as possible. Much of the dialogue throughout the book is extrapolated from as least two sources. To paraphrase the words of the great popular history writer Erik Larson, I reconstructed some of these scenes in the manner of a defense attorney creating a summation. I wasn't there, of course, but I believe I can make educated speculations backed up by historical record and oral histories.

The three most frequently sited sources—Hilton's book, the Eastland Disaster Historical Society, and the *Chicago Tribune*—are abbreviated as HIL, EDHS, and TRIB, respectively. Also abbreviated are the Chicago Historical Society (CHS) and the *New York Times* (NYT). All other sources are fully sited here and/or in the bibliography.

PART I: Low Sky at Dawn

CHAPTER ONE: A Jungle of Iron And Smoke

3. **Borghild Aanstad**   Much of what is reported in this opening scene is a reconstruction from taped interviews (held 5/20/03), with Jean and Barbara.
   She was a petite   Decker family (photographic evidence); also Decker interview (5/20/03).
4. **Western Electric**   EDHS, various oral histories.

5. **The Scandinavians brew**   Decker interview (5/20/03).
   "Don't get excited"   TRIB, 7/24/15.
6. **A hacker's fare**   Urdang, *The Timetables of American History*, 289;
   also TRIB, 8/2/15, 2.
   Since the turn of the century   Young, *Chicago Transit: An Illustrated
   History*, 75.
7. **They carried baskets**   TRIB, 7/30/15.
8. **Airplanes**   Urdang, *Timetables*, 289.
   Mary Pickford   TRIB, 7/24/15.
   And D. W. Griffith's   Finler, *The Movie Director's Story*, 48.
   The Crescent   Dale, *The World of Jazz*, 29, 30.
   There wasn't a brothel   Lindberg, *Chicago by Gaslight*, 127.
9. **The popular marchlike rhythms**   Schwartz, "What Is Stride Piano"
   ("Irwin's Website": members.aol.com/midimusic/strdtxt.html).
   File clerks   EDHS, various oral histories.
10. **The Sindelars**   Christine Harmon interview, May 29th, 2003. (Christine Harmon, a great-great-grand-niece of George Sindelar, has kept
    alive the oral history of this family and their tragic story. Much of what
    is speculated here comes from Harmon's generous retelling of her
    family mythology. Harmon, incidentally, is the current owner of the
    magnificent, fabled turnip watch.)
    Most likely the Sindelars   Young, *Chicago Transit*, 74.
    The interior of the 2700   Moffat, *The "L" - Chicago's Rapid Transit,
    1892–1947*, 112.
11. **Chances are**   Harmon, private collection (photographic evidence).
    No ordinary timepiece   Ibid.
12. **The Sindelar family**   Moffat, *The "L"*, 112–116.

CHAPTER TWO: Weird Dreams and Strange Presentiments

13. **This region**   Kay, Cicero, *The First Suburb West*, 7.
    That same year   Adams, Butler, *Manufacturing the Future*, 22–30.
14. **"I read whatever "**   Ibid., 22, 23.
    In 1872   Ibid., 30.
    ". . . the company's plants"   Ibid, 81.
15. **In 1886, a riot**   Chicago Municipal Reference Library, *Historical
    Information about Chicago*, 6.

75,000 calls Western Electric Company, Annual Report, *Hawthorne: Its Life and People*, 3.

"How could the Western" Adams, Butler, *Manufacturing the Future*, page 80.

"We have been having" Ibid, 82.

By 1915 Western Electric Company, Annual Report, *Hawthorne: Its Life and People*, 5.

16. **A tremendous din** Muchna, private journals.

    "This is Clark Street!" Bruce Moffat interview, 6/13/03. (If it has to do with mass transit in Chicago, Bruce Moffat is your man. This veteran of the Chicago Transit Authority literally wrote the book on Chicago surface line history. His book *The "L"—The Development of Chicago's Rapid Transit System* is a definitive text on the subject.)

    Borghild Aanstad slipped Decker interview (5/20/03).

17. **Nineteenth-century tunnels** Knox, Belcher, *Chicago's Loop*, 46.

    funneling into the mouth CHS, various photographs.

18. **The smokestacks of the *Theodore Roosevelt*** HIL, 88–90 (map), also CHS (photographic evidence).

    a languid procession Ibid., (timeline) 94–95.

    A narrow walkway Ibid., (photographic evidence) 91.

19. **But this boat!** Decker interview (5/20/03); also The Keewatin Museum, Douglas, Michigan (For the impressions of approaching and boarding the *Eastland*, which I am attributing to Borghild Aanstad, I have extrapolated from family remembrances as well as a personal visit on 5/31/03 to an almost identical ship currently in dry dock in Douglas. Curators Cindy and Bob Zimmerman are as gracious as they are knowledgeable. As are the Wachholz and Decker families.)

    Five stories HIL, 91.

    "It does not care" Dreiser, *Sister Carrie*, xiv.

    A single city block Lindberg, *Chicago by Gaslight*, 128.

    "A man can't hold" Ibid., 123.

20. **"Only two out of 68"** Ibid., 114.

    Activists such as Duis, *Challenging Chicago*, 254.

    In 1915 spiritualism Jay, *Learned Pigs and Fireproof Women*, 166–171.

    Conan Doyle Sir Arthur Conan Doyle Web site, www.siracd.com/life_spirit.shtml.

21. Two years earlier   The *American Experience* Web site, www.PBS.org/wgbh/amex/houdini.
    While standing   TRIB, 7/27/15, 7.
    "Here's our key"   Ibid., 7.
22. "They were married"   Ibid.
    Three weeks earlier   Ibid., 7/26/15, 12.
    "Josie told my mother"   Ibid., 7/27/15, 7; also EDHS, passenger accounts, Markowski.

CHAPTER THREE: The Darkening Sky

23. In 1803   Karamanski and Tank, *Maritime Chicago*, 9–11.
    "Those who waded"   Ibid., 14.
    Mules dragged   Ibid., 15.
24. Theodore Dreiser called   Ibid., 17.
    Fueled by   McBrien, *Skyline Chicago: Part 1, Chicago's Riverfront* (Documentary film).
    In 1890, an epidemic   Ibid.
25. "There used to be"   Karamanski, Tank, *Maritime Chicago*, 33.
    The sound   Ibid., 26.
    Accidents   Ibid., 47.
    The Sindelars arrived   Harmon interview, 5/29/03.
26. The ship bore   HIL (photographic evidence)
    "When I started down"   Transcript of testimony, Coroner's inquest, 3.
27. The capacity of the Eastland   HIL, 50, 76.
    nearing 1,700   Ibid., 98.
28. He had purchased   TRIB, 7/25/15, 8.
    One can imagine   CHS (photographic evidence).
    The muffled jangle   Transcript of testimony, Coroner's inquest, 90.
    Playful shouts   HIL, 109; also EDHS, various oral histories.
29. Bowling, checkers   Hawthorne Club, Constitution and Bylaws, 1915.
    Founded in 1911   Western Electric, Interdepartmental memorandum, 10/7/11.
    A total of 3500   *Western Electric News,* August 1912.
30. "Had the weather"   Ibid.
    "The excursionists"   Ibid.
    Picknickers enjoyed   Ibid., August 1913.
    Earlier that year   TRIB, 7/26/15, 5.

31. **"Wow! Whoop 'er up"** Ibid., 7/25/15, 8.
    Readers of the Jubilator Ibid.
    "I was working" Ibid., 3.
32. **"They forced them"** Ibid., 7/27/15, 10.
33. **As the passenger count** HIL, 98.
    A heavily jowled man Ibid., 99.
    What he saw Transcript of testimony, Coroner's inquest, 36–37.
34. **Weckler couldn't take** Ibid., 37.
    A paunchy, HIL 173 (photographic evidence); also page 68.
    "Put in your ballast" Transcript of testimony, Coroner's inquest, 37.
35. **He had been a master** HIL, 68.

CHAPTER FOUR: Too Many People on This Boat

36. **In the early days** HIL, 15–17.
    The high keening TRIB (various advertisements).
37. **The most popular routes** HIL, 16–17.
    The new ship Ibid., 19–21
    Four decks Ibid., 21–22.
38. **The *Eastland* was launched** Ibid., 29.
39. **"I don't like the feel"** *Daily Herald*, 7/22/85
40. **Born in 1878** Decker, taped interview (5/20/03)
41. **"Got to steady her"** HIL, 100.
    Situated in the bottom The Keewatin Museum, Douglas, Michigan (notes from comparable engine room).
42. **A Chadburn telegraph** HIL, 34.
    More obscure messages Transcript of testimony, Coroner's inquest, 133.
    At seven-sixteen HIL, 100–101.
    He'd certainly logged Ibid., 73.
43. **At the other end** Transcript of testimony, Coroner's inquest, 90.
44. **Olaf, sitting** Decker, taped interview (5/20/03). (Although this positioning is speculative, the Decker and Wachholz families have helped with the extrapolations through eyewitness accounts related by Borghild Aanstad and by the specifics of the cabin deck, as well as the "sky" being visible after the capsizing.)
    Moments later *Daily Herald*, 7/22/85.

45. **In July**   HIL, 37–72.
    "The owners and inspectors"   TRIB, 7/25/15, 8.
    In the summer of 1904   HIL, 48–49.
46. **In the aftermath**   Ibid., 50–51.
    The summer of 1906   Ibid., 55–59.
47. **"Many women and children"**   TRIB, 7/25/15, 8.
    The remaining staterooms   HIL, 58.

CHAPTER FIVE: Sladkey's Leap

49. **On her maiden voyage**   HIL 1–13.
50. **At precisely seven-seventeen**   Harmon, taped interview 5/29/03.
51. **Candy sellers**   NYT, 7/25/15, 2.
    Chicago was a beer-drinking town   Lindberg, 128.
    Ed Bartlett and Le Roy Bennet   TRIB, 7/27/15, 1.
52. **"You are aware"**   TRIB, 7/26/15, 2.
    The *Eastland*'s was slashed   HIL, 50.
    "Mr. Hull"   Ibid., 76.
53. **"She was not very profitable"**   Transcript of testimony, Coroner's inquest, 78–79.
    Years of spilled drinks   HIL, 71–72.
    2500 life preservers   Ibid., 77.
    "Boys, I believe we're getting her!"   Ibid., 102.
54. **"Cap!"**   Ibid. (Most of what is on this page is from HIL, including the actions of O'Meara, Pedersen, Erickson, et al.)
55. **A few feet away**   Transcript of testimony, Coroner's inquest, 140. (An educated speculation based on the testimony and musings of William Redfield, U.S. Secretary of Commerce.)
    Bobbie Aanstad perched   Various taped interviews; Decker, Harmon, Muchna, and Warnes. (The "final" positions of the principal figures are based on best guesses extrapolated from oral histories and the physical nature of the boat after capsizing.)
    On the dock   HIL, 88–89; also Transcript of testimony, Coroner's inquest, 10.
56. **One picnicker reached**   HIL, 103.
    But the boat was starting   Ibid.
57. **The boat looked overloaded**   Transcript of testimony, Coroner's inquest, 40.

It was Charles   HIL, 104.
"No lines!"   Transcript of testimony, Coroner's inquest, 42.

58. **Later, during testimony**   Ibid., 37.
"Stop the engines!"   HIL, 104.

59. **The massive crash**   Transcript of testimony, Coroner's inquest, 3.
Charlie Silvernail   HIL, 105.

CHAPTER SIX: The Water Is Coming In

60. **On the other side**   TRIB, 7/25/15, 12.
Many of the picnickers   www.parlorsongs.com (mp3 recording); also "Songs About Ireland and the Irish" (Ibid.)

61. **"The water is coming in!"**   HIL, 105.
Fred Snow acted   Ibid.
At exactly seven-twenty-five   Ibid., 107.

62. **The 500 or so**   Ibid.
Motion picture   Katz, 1067.

63. **"The crowd had so encroached"**   HIL, 108.
The number 4 and 5 tanks   Ibid., 53.
Joseph Lynn   Transcript of testimony, Coroner's inquest, 52.

64. **The valve**   HIL, 32–33.

65. **Snow heard**   Ibid., 107.
"Folks! Please move"   Ibid., 109.
"I began to get"   Transcript of testimony, Coroner's inquest, 54.

66. **"Get off!"**   TRIB, 7/25/15, 12.
A slight pause   HIL, 108.
One of the picnickers   EDHS, oral histories.
"I was really of the opinion"   Transcript of testimony, Coroner's inquest, 55.

CHAPTER SEVEN: On the Death Stairs

68. **According to Chief Engineer**   HIL, 108.
On the main deck   TRIB, 7/25/15, 3.

69. **"There was a sudden hush"**   NYT, 7/25/15, 3.
The piano plowed   EDHS, oral transcript.
"The panic was now universal"   HIL, 109.

70. **Clinging to a davit**   NYT, 7/25/15, 1.

71. "They jammed them" Ibid.
"FOR GOD'S SAKE" HIL, 109.
"There was a roar" Transcript of testimony, Coroner's inquest, 54.
72. "A woman with a child" NYT, 7/25/15, 1.
The cabin deck Decker, taped interview, 5/20/03.
72. "People were falling" TRIB, 8/3/91.
73. Bobbie's chair *Daily Herald*, 7/22/85.
A policeman, John Lescher TRIB, 7/27/15, 4.
74. "They were a very close-knit" Harmon, taped interview, 5/29/03.
In that single horrible Transcript of testimony, Coroner's inquest,
127–128.
75. Pedersen timed Ibid., 35–36.
"The boat just turned" TRIB, 7/27/15, 4.
Standing on the opposite Ibid., 7/25/15, 3.

PART II: Into Eternity

CHAPTER EIGHT: Down and Down

79. Policemen ran HIL, 113.
"Most of them" NYT, 7/25/15, 1.
80. "From my place" Ibid., 7/25/15, 3.
"They caught hold" TRIB, 7/25/15, 3.
"Miss Koren fell in" Ibid.
81. "One passenger" Ibid.
"I went down and down" Ibid.
One eyewitness Ibid., 7/26/15, 5.
"Never, to my dying" NYT, 7/25/15, 2.
82. Bobbie Aanstad dog-paddled Decker, taped interview, 5/20/03; also
Daily Herald, 7/22/85, 7/25/90
A slice of soggy bread My speculations based on oral histories and
literary evidence of the Aanstads' position on the sunken ship.
"I can see my mother" TRIB, 8/3/91.
83. Luckily, Bobbie Decker, taped interview, 5/20/03.
Currently the Aanstads See "soggy bread" note above; also literary
evidence based on Hilton/Polemis sketches.
A narrow wedge Decker interview, 5/20/03; also *Daily Herald*,
7/22/85.

84. **"By the end of the day"** *Daily Herald*, 7/22/85.
    It was a small wooden   HIL, 115.
    Most of the crates   Ibid.
85. **"One employee said"**   Ibid.
    "The surface of the river"   NYT, 7/25/15, 2.
    "I couldn't stand"   TRIB, 7/25/15, 3.
    "God, the screaming"   Ibid.
86. **"I started to throw"**   Ibid.
    The closest emergency craft   HIL, 88–89.
    A passer-by, John Parotto   Ibid., 114–115.
    "The Captain"   Ibid.
    Nurse Helen Repa   Ibid., 114.
87. **"One of the excursion boats"**   The dialogue here is my own recon-
    struction, drawn from Hilton and *Western Electric News*, August
    1915, 19.
    One of the first   HIL, 114; also CHS, photographic evidence.
88. **Repa pushed**   Ibid.; also CHS, photographic evidence.
    "I shall never"   Ibid.
89. **Forty miles**   NYT, 7/25/15, 1.
    Mostly women   Ibid., 2.
    "I saw strong men"   Ibid.
    Many of the riverfront businesses   Ken Little, taped interview,
    6/21/03. (A retired thirty-five-year veteran of the Chicago Fire Depart-
    ment, Little is a one-of-a-kind treasure-trove of information. He is
    also an author and the curator of the Chicago Fire Museum.)
90. **The closest firehouse**   HIL, 113.
    "I saw at least"   TRIB, 7/27/15, 10.
91. **"We had five"**   Ibid.

CHAPTER NINE: Daredevil Rex and the Human Frog

92. **"A big boat's gone"**   David Bowles, Alice Warnes, taped interviews,
    5/4/03; also "Human Frog," *Ft. Dodge Daily Chronicle*, EDHS
    archives. (Much of what is written here of Charles "Reggie" Bowles
    comes from the memories and oral histories shared by Reggie's daugh-
    ter, Alice Warnes, and grandson, David Bowles. Dialogue here is my
    speculation informed by three sources.)

93. **"I'm burning"** TRIB, 7/25/15, 3. (According to the historical record, Fire Chief Patrick Egan was among the first firefighters on the scene, and he related this story of saving a burning man pinned to the inner wall. It is highly probable, considering where Bobbie Aanstad was trapped, that she heard this occurring.)

94. **The only things** *Daily Herald*, 7/22/85; also Decker interview, 5/20/03.
"All I wanted" *Daily Herald*, 7/22/85.

95. **Somebody was trying** TRIB, 7/25/15, 3.
Tearing down the rutted David Bowles, Alice Warnes, taped interviews, 5/4/03. (Nobody knows how Reggie Bowles got from his garage to the scene, but I strongly believe it was via motorbike. The wrench has been mentioned in numerous accounts.)

96. **This was not a happy home** Ibid.

97. **A few minutes** HIL, 118.
"Dunham's tugs" Ibid.

98. **Fireman hurried** Little, taped interview, 6/21/03.
He wore between knots Literary evidence of the location of Bowles's garage in relation to the accident site.
In all the excitement David Bowles, Alice Warnes, taped interviews, 5/4/03.

99. **A beefy patrolman** CHS (photographic evidence).
"Lemme through!" My speculation based on Warnes/Bowles interviews, as well as "Human Frog," *Ft. Dodge Daily Chronicle*, EDHS archives.

100. **In the moments before** HIL, 111.
It wasn't even TRIB, 7/25/15, 3.
He saw a traffic cop Ibid.
"We pulled three women" Ibid.

101. **"We got one young girl's"** Ibid.
"Here!—HERE!" Ibid., 2; also Pietrzak, "All in a Summer's Day" (EDHS collection).

102. **"I could have killed"** NYT, 7/25/15, 3.
A group of firemen Ibid.
"Drown him!" Ibid., 2.

103. **In post-disaster hearings** HIL, 111.
A sturdy, barrel-chested Lindberg, 31, 113 (also photographic evidence).
"Clubs, bricks" Ibid., 31.

104. **Schuettler whistled** NYT, 7/25/15, 2. (The next page and a half of dialogue and description are my speculations drawn from both the *Times* articles as well as oral histories such as Pietrzak from the EDHS collection.)
"**I told him to go**" TRIB, 7/25/15, 2.

CHAPTER TEN: In the Grasp of Death

105. **Reggie Bowles burst** My speculation based on Warnes/Bowles interviews (5/4/03); also "Human Frog," *Ft. Dodge Daily Chronicle*, EDHS archives; also Karaminski/Tank, 28–31.
106. **The Reid-Murdoch building** HIL, 124; also photographic evidence courtesy of CHS.
"**Reggie had no relationship**" Warnes/Bowles interviews (5/4/03).
"**He learned to swim**" "Chronology of Reggie Bowles's life," Warnes family collection.
107. **Thomas A. Carter** HIL, 114.
The strychnine acted NYT, 7/25/15, 2; also Jon Austin interview (5/25/03).
Carter would feel HIL, 114.
If a person showed signs TRIB, 7/25/15, 2; also motion picture evidence from *The Eastland Disaster*, produced by Harvey Moshman and Chuck Coppola, © 2001 by Window to the World Communications Inc.
108. "**A score of machines**" TRIB, 7/25/15, 2.
"**The spectacles were harrowing**" NYT, 7/25/15, 1.
"**Much of the women's work**" Adams/Butler, 94.
109. **But 1915** Lindberg, 143.
A year earlier *Western Electric News*, August 1913, 12.
"**In the crisis**" TRIB, 7/25/15, 3.
"**I did not lose**" Ibid., 9.
"**I saw a mother**" Ibid.
110. "**I saw the woman's arm**" Ibid., 2.
For several agonizing minutes Ibid.
111. "**My husband I and the children**" Ibid.
"**As the child floated**" TRIB, 7/26/15, 1.
"**Women and children**" Ibid., 7/25/15, 3.
112. "**I saw two women**" Ibid.
He broke through Decker, taped interview, 5/20/03; also *Daily Herald* articles, 7/22/85, 7/25/90.

113. **Now Bobbie straddled**   *Daily Herald,* 7/22/85 (EDHS archives).
"Olaf!—OLAF!"   Decker, taped interview, 5/20/03.
A terrible swishing   *Daily Herald,* 7/22/85 (EDHS archives).
The wreckage had shifted   Ibid.; also Decker taped interview, 5/20/03.
(This is an educated guess based on oral history; after the wreckage
had careened, Marianne and her daughter had to have something on
which to rest.)

114. **Born on July 28**   Decker taped interview, 5/20/03.

115. **Such hardships**   My interpretation drawn from family interviews as
well as literary evidence. The local public record is plentiful with stories of Borghild's spirit and strength of character.
The *Eastland's* exposed hull   CHS; photographic evidence.
Struggling against the effects   NYT, 7/25/15, 3.

116. **Along the south dock**   EDHS archives; photographic evidence.
But deaths outpaced   TRIB, 7/25/15, 2.
The city coroner's head physician   Ibid.

117. **On December 30, 1903**   Chicago Municipal Reference Library, His-
torical Information About Chicago, 9.
"As a consequence"   HIL, 112, 122.
"The bridges creaked"   NYT, 7/25/15, 3.

118. **Even an unemployed man**   Ibid., 7/26/15, 1.
These men in dark   HIL, 123.

119. **O'Hearn found an opening**   Ibid.
"Jesus, Mary, Joseph"   Ball, *The Catholic Book of the Dead,* page
205. (My speculation on the words spoken by the clergy is situational.
Hilton put it this way: *"The Chicago Daily Journal,* ignoring that the
priestly function applies also to the dead, made a valid point—albeit in
offensive terminology—that the disaster, by producing few lingering
deaths, limited what the priests could accomplish among the living:
'There was little work for them. The result of the *Eastland's* somer-
sault could be phrased in two words—living or dead.'")

CHAPTER ELEVEN: Too Harrowing for Any Viewer

120. **The throat closes up**   Hocutt, *Emergency Medicine,* 119.
Without oxygen   Madda, *Outdoor Emergency Medicine,* 182.

121. **When the face**   *Funk and Wagnalls New Encyclopedia,* Vol. 8, p. 350.
A terrible sort of assembly   HIL, 124–125.

Hypothermic individuals   Auerbach, *Medicine for the Outdoors*, 30.
122. **"Policemen's hands began"**   TRIB, 7/25/15, 2.
    Ghostly white canvas   CHS, photographic evidence.
123. **Begun in 1847**   Wendt, TRIB, 1–50.
    On the morning   Ibid., 418, 497.
    The paper's staff   TRIB, 7/27/15, 7.
124. **"The load of wire work"**   Ibid., 7/26/15, 4.
    A motion picture crew   Ibid., 7/28/15, 3.
    Otto Muchna puffed   Roy Muchna, taped interview, 5/29/03. (Thanks to the generosity and enthusiasm of Otto Muchna's grandson, Roy, I've been able to reconstruct a vivid portrait of this complex gentleman. But family memories do not always come easily: "There's a reason I don't know as much about my grandfather as I would have liked," Roy explains. "In 1935, when I was just a young kid, my grandpa developed cancer of the larynx, and was taken to Mayo's by his daughter Mae, where he had his larynx removed. So from '35 on, he spoke with a whisper. It was an effort for him to tell stories of his past—of which there were plenty, I'm sure.")
125. **"They weren't morbid"**   Ibid.
    A rangy, olive-skinned man   EDHS archives, photographic evidence; also Roy Muchna, taped interview, 5/29/03.
126. **This was a watershed**   John N. Austin, Director, Museum of Funeral Customs, Springfield, Illinois, taped interview, 5/22/03. (Austin is a fountain of knowledge on this subject, and was profuse with his generosity to this author. Austin's organization is operated under the auspices of the Illinois Funeral Directors Association, and anyone visiting the Springfield area would be well advised to give this museum a look.)
    Otto's sister-in-law   Roy Muchna, taped interview, 5/29/03.
    "There's been a boating"   The interchange here is speculative, based on Muchna family accounts, as well as EDHS archival accounts. (The oddly sanguine phrase "boating accident" was used repeatedly by victims and their families, in letters and postcards. One would never refer to the *Titanic* or *Lusitania* events as such, but somehow the *Eastland* disaster had always been tagged, rightly or wrongly, as somehow more prosaic, more in the nature of a fluke, even by its victims.)
127. **Normally rock steady**   Jerry Muchna, unpublished journals; also Austin, taped interview, 5/22/03.

128. **"She's at Iroquois"**   My speculation with Roy Muchna's help; also EDHS archives.
129. **"The virtually instantaneous"**   HIL, 120.
130. **E. K. Plamondon stood**   TRIB, 7/25/15, 12 (Although the background is documented, the scene in front of the Reid-Murdoch Building is my embellishment; the record only suggests such a reunion.)
Seven of them   Ibid.
131. **"Rays of gold dust"**   Ibid., 2.

PART III: City of Constant Sorrow

CHAPTER TWELVE: That Final Parting Embrace

135. **"I am the only man"**   EDHS archives, Loeb personal account.
One of these divers   EDHS archives, photographic evidence.
One of the first   Ibid.; also, personal accounts by Johnsen, et al.
136. **In 1915**   "Diving," *Funk and Wagnalls New Encyclopedia*, Vol. 8, p. 251.
137. **Walter noticed**   Ibid.; archives, photographic evidence.
He signaled his dad   My speculation based on *Times* coverage. (Walter Johnsen serves here as a sort of composite figure. He was, according to historic records, among the first to go under.)
Cigarettes, jewelry, bread   Conjecture on my part based on various personal accounts.
Closed portholes   HIL, 111.
138. **He entered through**   NYT, 7/25/15, 2. (Historical records do not indicate precisely where the first divers entered the hull; photographic evidence suggests that they probably went into the water closer to the bow, which, following the coverage of the *New York Times*, is how I arrived at this reconstruction.)
The first body   Ibid.
139. **"It was strange"**   Ibid., 1.
"Sometimes they had to"   Ibid., 3.
Falling debris tore   CHS, Fujita photo album, photographic evidence.
"I wondered dully"   NYT, 7/25/15, 3.
140. **"Has it ever been"**   Ibid.
With varying degrees of success   CHS archives, photographic evidence. (Photographs reveal heartbreaking expressions on most of the recovery workers. One of these men, Leonard Olson, was depicted

carrying a lifeless toddler in a famous Fujita photograph that was conveyed around the world and became an iconic symbol of the tragedy [see photo insert].)

Pedersen sat bolt upright   HIL, 126–127; also TRIB, 7/25/15, 2.

141. Twenty policemen   TRIB, 7/25/15, 10.

142. "Mothers fell"   NYT, 7/25/15, 2.

"Nearly every room"   TRIB, 7/25/15, 10.

"Speed was important"   Austin interview, 5/22/03.

143. They affixed tags   TRIB, 7/25/15, 10.

Of the two men   Marquis, Albert, *The Book of Chicagoans*, "Maclay Hoyne."

144. Hoyne had been roused   TRIB, 7/25/15, 10.

At fifty-two, Hoffman   "Notable Men of Chicago," pamphlet c. 1908, pg. 159.

Unlike medical examiners   Wingate, Anne, *Scene of the Crime*, 13.

A stout, round-faced man   *The Public Safety Commission of Chicago and Cook County*, Annual Handbook, 6/25/17, 6.

145. Hoyne suggested   NYT, 7/25/15, 3.

146. Then he named   TRIB, 7/25/15, 10.

"As each man"   Ibid.

Minutes later   NYT, 7/25/15, 3.

At that point, one of the deputy   Ken Little, taped interview, 6/21/03.

CHAPTER THIRTEEN: Somebody Made a Big Mistake

147. The little boy materialized   TRIB, 7/27/15, 5.

148. The bodies of Josephine   Harmon, taped interview, 5/29/03.

Although the whiskey burned   "Human Frog," *Ft. Dodge Daily Chronicle*, EDHS archives.

Reggie emerged   Warnes/Bowles interviews, 5/4/03.

149. Dressed in a black   *Ft. Dodge Daily Chronicle*, EDHS archives.

"Steamboat *Eastland* sunk"   TRIB, 7/25/15, 9.

150. Published death tolls   My observations of various headlines and telegrams.

Organizers had planned   NYT, 7/25/15, 3.

Governor Dunne found   TRIB, 7/25/15, 1.

"I am shocked"   NYT, 7/25/15, 3.

Thompson had once   HIL, 129.

"Tears ran freely"   TRIB, 7/26/15, 7.

151. He arranged a command   HIL, 129.
An advance party   Ibid., 128.
Mary Clark—a lovely   NYT, 7/27/15, 1.
Hearing the news   TRIB, 7/25/15, 7.
152. "In the heart"   Ibid., 7/26/15, 11.
In Vienna   Ibid., 7/30/15, 4.
Lloyd's of London   Ibid., 7/26/15, 2.
153. "We in San Francisco"   Ibid., 7/26/15, 7.
Other U.S. news organizations   Ibid., 7/27/15, 8. (Extracts were all published in the *Tribune* three days after the event.)
Otto Muchna wiped   Roy Muchna, taped interview, 5/29/03.
154. Otto had already made   Jerry Muchna, unpublished journals.
The young Western Electric   EDHS archives, Juranek personal account.
155. A large glass bell jar   Austin, taped interview, 5/22/03
"They've identified another"   My reconstruction based on Roy Muchna interview, 5/29/03.
156. The carriage itself   Literary evidence, Otto Muchna business card.
Now the boy   Jerry Muchna, unpublished journals.
157. The 2nd Regiment Armory   Photographic and literary evidence, city maps, c. 1916 (CHS).
158. Directly across   Ibid.
A narrow balcony-walkway   Ibid.
"They were laid"   HIL, 124–125.

CHAPTER FOURTEEN: Sackcloth and Ashes

159. The hours crawled   *Daily Herald*, 7/22/85 (EDHS archives).
"He was up"   TRIB, 7/27/15, 5.
160. "At times it was"   NYT, 7/25/15, 2.
Perched on   Decker interview, 5/20/03; also *Daily Herald*, 7/22/85.
161. Hypothermia occurs   Handal, *The American Red Cross First Aid and Safety Handbook*, 117–120.
At that moment, in her imagination   Decker interview, 5/20/03.
"Everything oozed moisture"   NYT, 7/25/15, 2.
162. "It was reported"   Ibid.
"Had there been no water"   TRIB, 7/25/15, 11.
"The few that were"   NYT, 7/25/15, 2.
163. "Because of the turbid"   Ibid., 7/27/15, 1.
"I recognized"   TRIB, 7/25/15, 11.

"Many of the bodies"   NYT, 7/25/15, 3.

"If I could find"   Ibid.

164. Then one of the divers   Ibid., 7/26/15, 2.

"Four were women"   TRIB, 7/27/15, 5.

165. One of the divers   Ibid., 1.

And when Harry Halvorsen   CHS, photographic evidence.

On top of a nearby   HIL, 129.

166. He had witnessed terrible   TRIB, 7/26/15, 4.

Reggie's fingers   *Ft. Dodge Daily Chronicle*, EDHS archives.

167. Then a shade   TRIB, 7/27/15, 5.

"I'm puttin' you"   *Ft. Dodge Daily Chronicle*, EDHS archives.

168. "Sir, just let"   Ibid.

Max Hyman, a local   TRIB, 7/25/15, 12.

Mandel Brothers   Ibid., 11.

169. By late afternoon   HIL, 124.

"A crowd of willing"   Ibid., 127.

Many of their dispatches   Ibid.

CHAPTER FIFTEEN: The Rustle of His Spectral Robe

170. Bobbie Aanstad heard   *Daily Herald*, 7/25/90, EDHS archives.

The Aanstads had been   Ibid., 7/22/85, EDHS archives. (In her *Daily Herald* interview, Bobbie places the time of rescue at "about six p.m.")

171. Solveig went first   Ibid. (In order for Solveig to be separated from her family, she would have had to have been the first one rescued; my speculation that there was a weary disagreement as to who would come out next is based on this deduction.)

172. As she emerged   Ibid.

"There were so many"   Ibid.

"In the name of God!"   TRIB, 7/25/15, 1.

173. For a while   HIL, 125–126.

"Listen carefully please!"   My reconstruction based on facts presented in HIL, 125–126.

174. Among the gathering   TRIB, 7/26/15, 3.

Bodies lined the floor   CHS, EPHS, photographic evidence.

"On he went"   TRIB, 7/26/15, 3.

175. "His wish fulfilled."   Ibid.

"Face after face"   NYT, 7/26/15, 1.

As each body   HIL, 126.

176. "Tears were in every" TRIB, 7/26/15, 3.
"Four policemen" NYT, 7/26/15, 1.
"There are lines" Ibid.
177. "I'm so busy trying" TRIB, 7/26/15, 3.
"The first thing" Ibid., 2.
"The sight of" NYT, 2.
178. "I know that at least" Ibid. (Italics added for dramatic emphasis.)
"On the floor" Ibid.
He was number 396 HIL, 133.
179. Otto Muchna worked alongside Roy Muchna, taped interview, 5/29/03
The undertakers had access Austin, taped interview, 5/22/03.
180. "In the name of decency" NYT, 7/25/15, 3.
On the floor CHS, photographic evidence.
They were a peculiar" TRIB, 7/27/15, 6.
"I will arrest" NYT, 7/25/15
181. Some time later Hoffman TRIB, 7/25/15, 10. (The time of day this comment was made is unclear; I have positioned it here in the interest of clarity and narrative flow.)

CHAPTER SIXTEEN: An Unearthly Glow

182. "The old *Eastland*" TRIB, 7/25/15, 1.
A few feet off CHS, photographic evidence.
Workers had strung TRIB, 7/25/15, 1.
183. "Strings of electric bulbs" NYT, 7/25/15, 2.
"As we sank" TRIB, 7/28/15, 1,5.
184. Countless items shimmered Ibid., 7/27/15, 4.
"One large house" NYT, 7/25/15, 2.
"For blocks" Ibid.
"All night long" TRIB, 7/26/15, 5.
185. "In the communities" Ibid.
In the end, Josephine Harmon, taped interview, 5/29/03.
186. Barrels, axes CHS, photographic evidence.
More police arrived TRIB, 7/27/15, 1.
At city hall Ibid., 7/25/15, 11.
187. "We must show" Ibid.
Margaret Condon HIL, 132–133.
188. Hoyne grilled TRIB, 7/27/15, 1.

"I'll tell you"   Ibid. (This reconstruction of a conversation that took place between Hoyne and Pedersen, although never cited verbatim, was referenced in numerous contemporary articles and citations.)

CHAPTER SEVENTEEN: Coffins in Every Mirror

189. The owner   HIL, 143.
On Sunday   TRIB, 7/27/15, 1.
190. "The United States inspection"   Ibid., 7/26/15, 1.
U.S. Secretary of Commerce   HIL, 157.
191. "Quite often"   TRIB, 1/26/44 (CHS archives).
More than 300   Ibid., 7/26/15, 1.
192. "A light load"   NYT, 7/26/15, 2.
"Instead of the usual"   Ibid.
Major-league baseball   HIL, 128.
193. "In every church"   TRIB, 7/26/15, 5.
"Six of our congregation"   Ibid., 9.
"A coffin in every"   Ibid., 7/28/15, 4.
"On each house"   Libby Hruby interview; The Eastland Disaster, Moshman and Coppola.
"Kolin Avenue"   TRIB, 7/27/15, 1.
194. "Persons who fell"   Ibid., 7/25/15, 11.
"A new breed"   Ibid., 7/27/15, 2.
195. Loan sharks   Ibid., 7/29/15, 7.
"It was extortion"   Ibid., 8/1/15, 2.
One of these men   Ibid., 7/29/15, 1.
"Let me alone"   Ibid.
196. "Through the daylight"   Ibid., 7/26/15, 5.
"Those who stood"   Ibid.
Around the same time   Ibid., 9.
197. BLAME U.S. OFFICIALS   Ibid., 1.
"On one bench"   Kay, 36.
198. "Only in a few"   TRIB, 7/27/15, 5.
"Four special policemen"   Ibid.
Rumors circulated   Ibid., 7/28/15, 4.
199. "The situation took on"   Ibid., 7/27/15, 7.
Several local cemeteries   Ibid., 7/25/15, 11.
His name was De Witt   Ibid., 7/27/15, 4.
In life, Number 396   Ibid., 7/30/15, 5; also photographic evidence.

200. **"That's him!"** Ibid. (Identification of Willie Novotny's body actually happened on Thursday, July 29, 1915, but I've placed it here for dramatic emphasis, as part of the preparation for the coming day of mourning.)
201. **The package contained** Ibid.

CHAPTER EIGHTEEN: Black Wednesday

202. **So many funeral processions** TRIB, 7/28/15, 5.
  "It was too much" Jerry Muchna, unpublished journals.
203. **Marshall Field allowed** Kay, 34.
  "The bell towers" *The Eastland Disaster*, Moshman and Coppola.
  Photographs survive EDHS archives.
  The previous day TRIB, 7/28/15, 1.
204. **One thing is known** David Bowles, Alice Warnes, taped interviews, 5/4/03.
  "She observed the grief" Decker, taped interview, 5/20/03.
  "The towers" TRIB, 7/28/15, 5.
  "May the angels" Ibid., 7/29/15, 2.
205. **Flanked on each side** Ibid.
  Similar words Ibid.
  "Workers at the newly opened" *The Eastland Disaster*, Moshman and Coppola.
  "Back then" Ibid.
206. **"In the largest"** HIL, 139.
  A majority Ibid.
207. **This amounted** Adams/Butler, 91–92.
  "It was incredible what Western" *The Eastland Disaster*, Moshman and Coppola.
  Faced with more than 900 HIL, 143.
208. **It was, as one newspaper** TRIB, 8/1/15, 3.
  "The ranks of vehicles" Ibid.
209. **"Chicago wants"** Ibid.
  "My presence here" Ibid.
  Inside one EDHS.

CHAPTER NINETEEN: To Avenge the Dead

210. **"The hulk was"** HIL, 154.
  Cunning commandeered Ibid., 144.

211. **Mired in about two** Ibid., 150.
     These included official Ibid., 154.
212. **"If a captain"** Ibid., 155.
     "As secretary" Transcript of testimony, Coroner's inquest, 71.
     At another point HIL, 173; also, photographic evidence.
213. **"Cut out that laughing"** Transcript of testimony, Coroner's inquest, 125.
     With the wreck now raised HIL, 151.
     No one would serve *Chicago Daily News*, 8/17/15.
214. **In front of somber** HIL, 151–154
215. **At one point, Landis** Ibid., 158.
     "The whole thing hinges" TRIB, 7/26/15, 2.
216. **Q: Is it your opinion** Transcript of testimony, Coroner's inquest, 33–34.
     Q: Do you think Ibid., 125.
217. **"You may depend"** TRIB, 7/27/15, 2.
     A marine architect Ibid.
     Harbormaster Adam Weckler Transcript of testimony, Coroner's inquest, 64.
     "I don't think the *Eastland*" TRIB, 7/28/15, 2.
     A shipbuilder named William Ibid.
218. **"The effect of Landis's"** HIL, 158.
     The official charges Ibid., 159.
219. **On August 17** Ibid., 163.
     Upon hearing Ibid.
220. **"The boat will make"** Ibid.

CHAPTER TWENTY: Sins and Omissions

221. **The old man sat** Ibid., 168; also CHS, photographic evidence.
     Known as the "Scopes Monkey Trial" *Funk & Wagnalls New Encyclopedia*, Vol. 23, p. 224.
222. **Darrow's defense** HIL, 168.
     To the contrary Ibid., 171–172.
223. **A professor** Ibid., 175–180.
     "They were all behaving" Ibid., 179–180.
224. **"They had to pay the company"** *The Eastland Disaster*, Moshman and Coppola.
     "He expected to return" HIL, 181.

225. **"Blaming Erickson"**   Ibid., 195.
     Maritime law   HIL, 165.

EPILOGUE: The Smell of Violets

229. **Captain Harry Pedersen never**   HIL, 233.
     Pedersen died   Ibid.
     "His final lie"   Ibid.
     Today the captain's tombstone   My observation.
230. **First Mate Del Fisher became**   HIL, 231–235
     As noted earlier   *Chicago Daily News*, 11/30/44.
     Maclay Hoyne went on   Marquis, *The Book of Chicagoans*.
231. **Coroner Peter Hoffman**   TRIB, August 1979, page unknown.
232. **Old-money families**   HIL, 207–208.
     One of its early   Ibid., 220.
     On August 1, 1943   Ibid., 226.
233. **A sign greeted**   Ibid., 227.
     "On November 1st"   Ibid., 229.
     One of the many "near-miss"   Harmon (unpublished remembrance).
234. **The Hawthorne works never had**   EDHS archives.
235. **The new facility**   Jerry Muchna, unpublished journals.
     In the years   CHS, literary evidence.
236. **In 1989**   Crowe, 27–30.
     "It is no accident"   Ibid.
237. **On a 1996 Halloween**   Ibid.
     "It was a strong odor"   Ibid.
     In the months after   Bowles, Warnes, taped interviews, 5/4/03.
238. **"He left a trail"**   Ibid.
239. **In 1933, the town**   Chicago Municipal Reference Library, *Historical Information About Chicago*, 13.
240. **This is exactly what happened**   HIL, 234.
     "Partly with their contributions"   Ibid.
241. **Bobbie Aanstad's family**   Decker, taped interview, 5/20/03.
242. **"She never stopped"**   Ibid.
     "I sat behind"   Ibid.

Sources

Adams, Stephen, and Orville Butler, *Manufacturing the Future: A History of Western Electric*, New York: Cambridge University Press, 1999.

Algren, Nelson, *Chicago: City on the Make*, Chicago: University of Chicago Press, 1951.

Auerbach, Paul S., *Medicine for the Outdoors*, New York: The Lyons Press, 1999.

Central Electric Railfan's Association, *Chicago's Rapid Transit, 1892–1947*, Chicago: CERA Publications, 1973.

Chicago Historical Society, Books and Periodicals Collection, "Notable Men of Chicago," pamphlet c. 1908.

Crowe, Richard T., *Chicago's Street Guide to the Supernatural*, Oak Park, IL: Carolando Press, 2000.

Dreiser, Theodore, *Sister Carrie*, New York: Signet Classics, 1961.

Duis, Perry R., *Challenging Chicago, Coping with Everyday Life, 1837–1920*, Chicago: University of Illinois Press, 1998.

Fujita, Jun, Chicago Historical Society Archives, Personal Photo Album, c. 1946.

Heise, Kenan, and Mark Frazel, *Hands on Chicago*, Chicago: Bonus Books, 1987.

Hilton, George W., *Eastland: Legacy of the Titanic*, Stanford, CA: Stanford University Press, 1995.

Chicago Municipal Reference Library, "Historical Information About Chicago," pamphlet.

Handal, Kathleen A., *The American Red Cross First Aid and Safety Handbook*, Boston: Little Brown and Company, 1992.

Hocutt, John E., *Emergency Medicine*, New York: Arco Publishing, 1982.

Jay, Ricky, *Learned Pigs and Fireproof Women*, New York: Warner Books, 1986.

Karamanski, Theodore J., and Deane Tank, *Maritime Chicago*, Chicago: Arcadia Publishing, 2000.

Kay, Betty Carlson, *Cicero, the First Suburb West*, Chicago: Arcadia Publishing, 2000.

Knox, Janice A. and Heather Olivia Belcher, *Chicago's Loop*, Chicago: Arcadia Publishing, 2002.

Lindberg, Richard C., *Chicago by Gaslight: A History of Chicago's Netherworld (1880–1920)*, Chicago: Academy Chicago, 1996.

Lindberg, Richard C., *Ethnic Chicago*, Lincolnwood, IL: Contemporary Books, 1997.

Lindberg, Richard C., *Quotable Chicago*, Chicago: Wild Onion Books, 1996.

Lindberg, Richard C., *To Serve and Collect: Chicago Politics and Police Corruption*, Carbondale, IL: Southern Illinois University Press, 1998.

Madda, Frank C., *Outdoor Emergency Medicine*, Chicago: Contemporary Books, 1982.

Marquis, Albert, *The Book of Chicagoans*, Chicago: City of Chicago Publications, 1917.

Mayer, Harold M. and Richard C. Wade, *Chicago: Growth of a Metropolis*, Chicago: University of Chicago Press, 1969.

Sandburg, Carl, *Chicago Poems*, New York: Henry Holt, 1916.

Swanson, Stevenson, editor, *Chicago Days*, Lincolnwood, IL: Contemporary Books, 1997.

Wendt, Lloyd, *The Chicago Tribune: The Rise of a Great American Newspaper*, Chicago: Rand McNally, 1979.

Wingate, Anne, *Scene of the Crime*, Cincinnati: Writer's Digest Books, 1992.

Young, David M., *Chicago Transit*, Dekalb, IL: Northern Illinois University, 1998.

Acknowledgments

FIRST AND FOREMOST, I wish to thank the families of survivors for their generosity. These include Jean Decker, Barb Wachholz, and Susan Decker for insights into the experiences of Bobbie Aanstad; Alice Warnes and David Bowles for the sections on Reggie Bowles; Roy Muchna for background on his grandfather, Otto; and Ralph and Christine Harmon for information and impressions on the Sindelar family.

Other individuals who were indispensable were Jon Austin, Georgiana Becker, Bruce Moffat, Ed Eckert, Arnold Bas, Piriya Vongkasemsiri, Jim Rodgers, Ken Little, Noah Lukeman, Bob and Cindy Zimmerman, Michaela Hamilton, Peter Miller, and the staff of the Chicago Historical Society. I also wish to thank my long-suffering wife, Jeanne Bonansinga, for encouraging me every step of the way, as well as my two boys, Joey and Bill-Will, for tolerating an absent daddy during the long months of gestation on this work (I love you, my Buddy-Cats). A special thank you to Andrew Iver Johnsen for setting the record straight in the paperback edition regarding his grandfather's heroic recovery efforts.

Index

Aanstad, Akim, 114–15
Aanstad, Borghild "Bobbie"
  background of, 114–15
  boarding *Eastland*, 16–19
  capsizing of *Eastland*, 61, 63, 69,
    72–73
  funerals and, 204
  onboard *Eastland*, 39–41, 44
  post-disaster life, 240–43
  preparations for picnic, 3–5
  rescue of, 170–72
  in the water, 82–84, 93–95, 112–15,
    159–61
Aanstad, Marianne
  background of, 40–41, 114–15
  boarding *Eastland*, 16–19
  capsizing of *Eastland*, 61, 69
  onboard *Eastland*, 39–41, 44
  post-disaster life, 241
  preparations for picnic, 4–5
  rescue of, 170–72
  in the water, 82–84, 93–95, 112–15,
    160
Aanstad, Olaf Ness
  boarding *Eastland*, 16–19
  capsizing of *Eastland*, 61, 69, 73
  funerals and, 204
  onboard *Eastland*, 40–41, 44
  post-disaster life, 241
  preparations for picnic, 4–5
  rescue efforts of, 83–84, 94–95,
    112–15
  rescue of, 170–72

Aanstad, Solveig
  capsizing of *Eastland*, 61, 69
  funerals and, 204
  onboard *Eastland*, 40–41
  post-disaster life, 241
  preparations for picnic, 4–5
  rescue of, 170–72
  in the water, 112–15
Abbott, Grace, 20
Adams, Stephen, 109, 207, 247
Adams Express Company, 168
Albright, H. F., 196
Alice Stafford, 98
Allen, Henry, 146
Altman, Mrs., 21–22
Ambulance baskets, 143
Ambulances, 87–88, 94, 98, 107
American Red Cross, 108, 116–17,
    169, 177, 186, 207–8
American Waltham, 11, 185–86
Armory, 146, 155–58, 172–81,
    199–201, 235–37
Army Corps of Engineers, U.S., 24–25
Arnold, George, 218
Ashtabula, 43
Austin, Jon, 142–43

Babcock, Harlan, 81–82, 85
Balfour, Arthur, 20
Ballast, 26, 34, 63–66, 212–13, 215–17
Ballast technology, 41–42
Bartell, Christine, 234
Bartlett, Ed, 165

Barton, Enos, 14, 15
Baseball, 126, 191, 192
Baubles, Frank, 31–32
Bear Trap Dam, 89
Beck, Edward "Scotty," 123–24
Becker, Georgiana, 207
Beifeld, Eugene, 146
Bell, Alexander Graham, 14
Bell divers. See Divers
Belsan, James, 80
Bennett, LeRoy, 165
Benton Harbor, 37, 151–52
Birth of a Nation, The (movie), 8,
    62–63
"Black Wednesday," 202–4
Bloomer Girls, 126
Bode, William, 146
Bohemian National Cemetery, 205–6
Bordellos, 19
Boston News Bureau, 14
Bowles, Berwyn, 92–93, 95–97,
    98–100
Bowles, Charles "Reggie"
    background of, 96–97
    funerals and, 203–4
    post-disaster life, 237–38
    rescue efforts of, 105–8, 148–49,
        165–68
    responds to emergency, 92–93,
        95–97, 98–100
Bowles, David, 106
Boyle, Peter, 118
Bradfield's Orchestra, 43, 66, 68
Braitch, Frederic, 178
Braitch, John, 178
Braitch, Mary, 178
Braitch, Rose, 178
Brandt, Otto, 178
Buck, Robert, 219
Buckley, John, 163
Burials, 199, 202–9
Burke, Ed, 246
Burroughs, Mrs. J. B., 22
Butler, Orville, 109, 207, 247

Cabin deck, 38, 40, 43–44, 61, 72–73
Cabs (hacks), 6
Capacity of Eastland, 27, 33–34, 46
Carlson, Ernie, 83, 114, 161, 242–43
Carson Pirie Scott & Company, 168

Carter, Thomas A., 107
Carter H. Harrison, 98
Case, Charles, 141
Cech, William, 200
Cemeteries, 199, 205–6
Cervak, Anna, 126
Cervak, John, 126
Chaplin, Charlie, 8
Chicago by Gaslight (Lindberg), 246–47
Chicago Daily News, 123
Chicago Daily Tribune, 5, 31, 32, 45,
    108, 109, 122, 123–24, 131, 142,
    146, 150, 182, 198, 212, 217, 247
Chicago Harbor #4, 98
Chicago Health Department, 107, 194
Chicago Herald, 81–82
Chicago Maritime Society, 240
Chicago Police Department, 20, 90–91,
    98, 99–100, 103–4, 107, 121–22,
    141, 195
Chicago River, 24–25, 192, 238–39
Chicago Steamship Company, 189,
    212–14, 218
Chicago Surface Line, 10–11
Chicken coops, 84–85
Child care, 38, 177
Chivalry, 111–12
Cholera, 24
Christening of Eastland, 39
Churches, 204–6
Cicero, Illinois, 13, 14, 15, 16, 184–85,
    192–99
Cicero Police Department, 195
Civil litigation, 223–25
Clark, Mary, 151
Clark Street Bridge, 17, 18, 33, 108,
    117–18, 192
Clausen, Salomon Martinius, 40–41
Cleveland Plain Dealer, 47–48
Clothing, 7, 11, 80–81
Clyne, Charles F., 211–13, 214–20
Coast Guard, U.S., 64, 94
Coe, A. D., 90–91
Coffins (caskets), 179–80, 193
Coliseum, the, 145, 146
Colosimo, Big Jim, 19–20
Commerce, 98
Commonwealth Edison, 182–83
Concordia Cemetery, 206
Condon, Margaret, 187

Coroners, 116–17, 141, 142–46, 158, 164, 172–81, 199–201
Cougel Brothers, 84–85
Cox, Henry, 5
Creiger, De Witt C., 199
Crime, 19–20, 163–64, 194–95
Criminal conspiracy, 221–23
Criminal proceedings, 211–13, 214–25
Crowe, Richard, 236, 237
Cunning, Alexander, 210–11
Customs Department, U.S., 27
C.W. Watson, 43

Daley, Richard J., 239
Dance floor, 63
Darrow, Clarence, 221–23
Daughters of the American Revolution (DAR), 96
Davis, Samuel, 175
Dawn of Tomorrow (movie), 8
Deadlights, 137–38
"Death stairs," 69–70, 74
Death toll, 150
Decker, Barbara, 245
Decker, Jean, 204, 242
Decker, Leonard, 242
Decker, Susan, 245
Decomposition of bodies, 177
Deneau, William "Frenchy," 183, 222
Department stores, 6, 168
Divers, 135–38, 147–48, 159–60, 182–83, 186, 191, 197, 210–11
Diving reflex, 121
D.J. Swenie, 98
Dog paddling, 83, 93–94, 114, 161
Dolezal, Regina, 203
Douglas Park, 6–7
Doyle, Arthur Conan, 20
Dreiser, Theodore, 19, 24
Drowning, 120–21
Druggan, Terry, 231
Dunham Towing and Wrecking Company, 97–98, 189–90
Dunkley-Williams Transportation Company, 36–37
Dunne, Edward F., 150
Durand, David, 85–86

Eastland Navigation Company, 47
Eckliff, Charles, 218

EDHS, 245–46
Edison, Thomas, 8
Elbert, John, 129–30
Embalming, 126, 142–43, 153–57
Emergency response, 90–91, 97–98, 116–17, 121–22
Emergency vehicles, 87–88, 90, 94
Employee Benevolent Association, 207
Employees' clubs, 29–31
Engine room, 41–42, 61, 63, 65, 163
Epidemics, 194
Erickson, Joseph
    background of, 42–43
    capsizing of Eastland, 41–42, 61, 63, 64, 68
    cooling down the boilers, 162
    court proceedings and, 187–88, 215, 217, 218, 222
    post-disaster life, 224
Erickson, Peter, 41–42, 212–13
Erie Railroad, 98
Evans, William, 108, 145, 146, 212
Evers, Edward A., 219–20
Extortion, 195

Favorite, 210–11
Federal Steamboat Inspection Service, 215
Ferry service, 37
Field, Marshall, 20
Financial assistance, 207
Fire department, 90, 98, 116
Fisher, Del
    capsizing of Eastland, 65, 74
    court proceedings and, 187–88
    Pedersen and, 140–41
    post-disaster life, 230
Fitzsimmons, Father, 118–19
Flatow, Martin, 71, 213–14
Formaldehyde, 155
Fort Dearborn, 23–24
Fort Dodge Daily Chronicle, 108
Freemasons, 74
Fundraising, 187
Funerals, 199, 202–9
Funkhouser, Major, 149, 167–68

Gangways, 27–28, 37–38, 71
Garfield Park, 6–7
Gee, Daniel, 32

Geiger, Ellis, 219
Gender roles, 108–9, 111–12
George W. Gardner, 45
Glinka, Helen, 22
Goose Island, 214
Graeme Stewart, 86, 105, 140–41
Gravediggers, 202–3, 205–6
Gray, Elisha, 13–14
"Gray Lady," 237
Great Fire of 1871 (Chicago), 6–7, 14,
    17, 24
Great Fire of 1906 (San Francisco),
    153
Great Lakes Towing Company, 210–11
Greenebaum, Walter, 215–17, 230
Griffith, D. W., 8
Guenther, Willie, 66, 69
Gunderson, Charles, 135, 164–65
Gunderson & Son Submarine Divers,
    135

Halvorsen, Harry, 137–38, 147–48,
    159–60, 165
Hamilton, Frank, 45
Harmon, Christine, 74, 234
Harmon, Ralph, 233–34
Harpo Productions, 236–37
Harrison, Carter, 20
Hart Schaffner and Marx, 114–15
Hawthorne Club, 29–31
Hawthorne Works, 15, 234
    death toll and, 184–85, 197–98,
        204
    information bureau at, 187, 196
    women at, 108–11, 126
Haymarket Square riots (1886), 15,
    103
Head count, 27, 33
Hecht, Ben, 231
Heideman, Lillian, 81
Henrotin Hospital, 116
Henry, W. F., 32
Heterson, Mr. (foreman), 32
H.F. Watson Company, 85–86
Hilton, George, *Eastland: Legacy of
    the Titanic*, 63, 69, 85, 86, 98,
    117, 129, 192, 206, 210, 214,
    218, 219, 223, 224, 225, 229,
    233, 240, 246

Hoffman, Peter, 143–46
    background of, 144–45
    coronary duties of, 172–73, 175,
        176–77
    criminal investigation and, 189–90
    criminal proceedings and, 211–13,
        214–20
    morbid curiosity of onlookers and,
        180–81
    post-disaster life, 231
Hollister, Bernard, 240
Holy Name Cathedral, 119
Homer, 227
Hoover, Dickerson, Jr., 153
Hopkins, Harry, 232
Hospitals, 116–17
Houdini, Cecelia, 21
Houdini, Harry, 21
Houger, C. W., 15
Howard, William J., 233
Hoyne, Maclay, 143–46
    background of, 143–44
    criminal investigation and, 187–88,
        189–90
    criminal proceedings and, 211–13,
        215–16
    post-disaster life, 230–31
Hoyne, O'Conner and Hoyne, 143
Hubbard, F. G., 90–91
Hull, William, 151–52, 214, 218, 230
Humboldt Park, 6–7
Hungary, 152
Hurricane deck, 38, 62, 65, 80
Hyde Park, 6–7
Hyman, Max, 168
Hypothermia, 120–21, 148, 161,
    170–71

Identification, 116–17, 141–43, 145,
    158, 172–81, 199–201
Illich, Frankie, 156
Illinois Mathematics and Science
    Academy, 240
Illinois National Guard, 150, 235. *See
    also* Second Regimental Illinois
    National Guard Armory
Illinois Naval Reserve, 219–20, 232
Illinois Public Utilities Commission,
    212

Illlinois State Historical Society, 240
Immigrants, 6–7, 9–10, 19, 20, 125, 152
"I'm On My Way to Dear Old Dublin Bay," 60–61
Indiana, 97–98, 214
Indiana Transportation Company, 218
Inland Steel Company, 233
Inquiries, 211–13, 214–20
Intake valves, 64
Investigation, 189–91
Iroquois Memorial Hospital, 117, 128, 154
Iroquois Theatre, 117

Jackson Park, 6–7
Jahnke, Louise, 21–22
Jahnke, Paul, 21–22
James, M. R., 8
James, William, 20
Javanco, Mike, 66
Jazz, 8–9
Jenks, Sidney, 39
Jenks Ship Building Company, 37–39
Jim Crow laws, 8
Job-seekers, 198
Johnsen, Iver, 135–38, 148, 165
Johnsen, Walter, 136–38, 165
Joplin, Scott, 9
July Jubilator, 31
J. W. Taylor, 104

Karamanski, Ted, 240
Kay, Betty Carlson, 197–98
Kearney, William P., 85
Kelly, Thomas, 119
Kenosha, 19, 65–66, 214
Keogh, J. S., 146
Kista, J. H., 104
Korn, Miss, 80
Krohn, Gretchen, 139–40
Ku Klux Klan, 8

Lake, Frankie, 231
Landis, Kenesaw Mountain, 191, 215, 217–18, 219, 223
  post-disaster life, 230
Laryngospasm, 120

League for the Protection of Immigrants, 20
Lescher, John, 73
Lifeboats, 46, 89
Life preservers, 85, 86, 94, 112–13
Life saving devices, 84–85
Life Saving Devices Company, 107
Lincoln, Abraham, 123
Lindberg, Richard, 246–47
Lindbergh, Anne Morrow, 133
Little, M. K., 108
"Little Feller," 199–201, 209
Lloyd's of London, 152
Loan sharks, 195
Loop, the, 6, 10, 17
Lucas, Walter, 233
Lung motors, 107, 108
Lusitania, 7–8, 130
Lynn, Joseph, 63–64
Lyons, Patrick, 86

McCutcheon, John T., 197
McKenny, James, 13
McLaughlin Company, 146
Magnussen, Irene, 174–75
Magnussen, Robert, 174–75
Male passengers, 111–12
Maritime law, 215, 223, 225
Markowski, Josie, 22
Marquette Park, 6–7
Marshall Field & Company, 6, 168
Mary Queen of Heaven, 205
Mason, Lewis F., 223–24
Mass transit system (rail system), 6–7, 10–11, 13
Meagher, Thomas, 177
Media. See Newspapers
Medill, Joseph, 123
Merchant's Lighterage Company, 98
Michigan, Lake, 23, 24
Michigan City, Indiana, 29–30, 37
Michigan City Evening News, 30
Michigan Steamship Company, 36–37, 47
Miller, Harry, 70, 71, 72, 79–80, 139
Modoc whistle, 61
Moir, Henry, 146
Mongrieg, Chief, 195
Moore, R. J., 26

Moorhouse, William, 150–51, 186, 192, 196
Morbid curiosity, 180–81, 191–92
Morgues, 121–22, 141–43, 145, 154, 155–56, 163–64, 172–81, 199
Morrison Hotel, 146
Morse telegraph, 14
Morton, Jelly Roll, 9
Motion pictures (movies), 8, 62–63, 124
Mourning, 193–94, 202–6, 208–9
Muchna, Jerry, 156–57, 235
Muchna, Mary Juranek, 126–28, 155
Muchna, Otto, 124–28, 153–58, 179–81, 202–3
    background of, 125–26
    post-disaster life, 235
Muchna, Roy, 125, 235
Muranek, Jenny, 126–28, 154–55
Music, 8–9, 60–62, 63, 68, 69

Negligence, 197
Neubeiser, Gary, 205–6
New Orleans jazz, 8, 9
Newspapers, 122–24, 150, 153. See also specific newspapers
New York Times, 72, 80, 108, 111, 118, 142, 153, 163, 176, 184
Nichols, William, 215
Novotny, Agnes, 209
Novotny, James, 209
Novotny, Maimi, 209
Novotny, Willie, 200–201, 209

Occult, 21–22
O'Connor, John J., 116, 169, 186
O'Hearn, Father, 119
Old Irving Park, 92
O'Meara, Captain, 65–67, 71
Oram, J. C., 123–24
Oram Printing, 123–24
Order of the Eastern Star, 74
Orphaned children, 206
Overland Limited, 150–51
Oxweld Acetylene, 101

Parotto, John, 86
Passenger count, 27, 33

Passenger distribution, 222–23
Pedersen, Harry, 34–35
    capsizing of Eastland, 62, 63, 71
    criminal proceedings and, 187–88, 212, 215, 218
    post-disaster life, 229
    on prow of Eastland, 75, 100–104
    Schuettler and, 103–4, 140–41
Penfield, Frederic C., 152
Pereue, Frances, 39
Pereue, John, 45
Petoskey, 118
Pickford, Mary, 8
Plamondon, Ambrose, 130
Plamondon, E. K., 130
Plamondon, W. J., 130
Poland, 152
Police, 20, 90–91, 98, 99–100, 103–4, 107, 121–22, 141, 195
Pollution, 24
Porter, Augustus, 13
Portholes, 137–38
Postal Service, U. S., 235–36
Potowatami tribe, 13, 24
Press. See Newspapers
Priests, 118–19
Promenade deck, 38, 43, 63, 66, 71
Prostitution, 19
Psaris, Mike, 72, 75
Public hearings, 190–91, 211–13, 214–20
Public transportation. See Streetcars
Pugh, James, 187
Pullman, George, 20
Pycz, Eleanor, 233

Racine, 97–98, 105
Record keeping, 177, 191
Recovery efforts, 135–50, 159–60, 164–65, 182–84, 191–92
Red Cross, 108, 116–17, 169, 177, 186, 207–8
Redfield, William, 150, 190–91, 212, 218
Reid, Robert, 43, 215, 218, 224
Reid-Murdoch building, 106, 121, 128, 142, 146, 164, 169
Relief efforts, 186–87, 206–8

Relief funds, 207–8
Repa, Helen, 86–88
Resources, 245–47
Rhode, Paul, 204–5
Rita McDonald, 97–98
Roda, Frank, 195
Rolph, William, 152–53
Roosevelt, Franklin, 232
Roosevelt, Theodore, 191
Rosary, 119
Rosenwald, Julius, 207

St. Dionysus Church, 205
St. Joseph, Michigan, 151–52
St. Joseph—Chicago Steamship
    Company, 189, 212–14, 218
St. Joseph Herald-Press, 229
St. Louis Globe Democrat, 153
St. Luke's Hospital, 130
Salak, John, 195
Salvage operations, 189–90, 210–11,
    213–14
Sandburg, Carl, 1, 25
Saunders, George A., Sr., 165
Schad, Charles, 80
Schlemmer, Mrs. John, 109
Schuettler, Herman, 103–4, 140–41,
    145, 187
Scopes, John, 221–22
Sears, Roebuck & Company, 207
Seasickness, 45
Second Regimental Illinois National
    Guard Armory, 146, 155–58,
    172–81, 199–201, 235–37
Segregation, 8
Sessions, Clarence, 223
Settlers, 23–24
Shenandoah Garage, 155–56
Siebe, Augustus, 136
Silvernail, Charlie, 41
Sindelar, Adella, 12, 27, 185–86
Sindelar, Albert, 12, 27, 185–86, 197
Sindelar, George, 185–86
    boarding *Eastland*, 25–29
    capsizing of *Eastland*, 61, 62, 70, 74
    preparations for picnic, 10–12
Sindelar, George, Jr., 12, 27, 148,
    185–86

Sindelar, Josephine, 185–86, 234
    boarding *Eastland*, 25–29
    capsizing of *Eastland*, 61, 62, 64, 70,
        74, 147–48
    preparations for picnic, 10–12
    retrieval of body, 197
Sindelar, Sylvia, 12, 27, 185–86
Sindelar, William, 12, 27, 64, 70,
    147–48, 185–86
Skola Vojta Napratek, 208–9
Slave culture, 9
Smietanka, Julius, 209
Smoking room, 38
Snow, Fred, 41, 61, 65, 230
Sources, 245–47, 269–70
Souvenir hunters, 163
Spiritualism, 20–21
Springer, Thomas, 116–17, 121, 122,
    145–46, 175
Stability problems, 41–46, 63–66
Stand-by order, 62, 63
Steele, Walter, 218
Steel hulls, 25
Stepien, William, 240
Streetcars, 6, 10–11
Strychnine, 107
Suffrage, 109
Sullivan, Denis, 219
Sullivan, Michael F., 145, 212–13
Swigert, Fred, 164

Telegraphy, 13–14, 42
Telephone, 14–15, 187
Thayer, H. B., 196
Theft (pilfering), 163–64, 194–95
Theodore Roosevelt, 18, 60, 105, 121,
    192
Thompson, William, 144, 150–51,
    186–87, 208, 209
Ticket prices, 27–28
Ticket sales, 31–32
Titanic, 8, 18–19, 81–82, 130,
    223
Tombstones, 206
Trade, 23–24, 25, 36–37
Turnip watch, 11, 62, 185–86, 203,
    234
Typhoid, 194, 204, 207

Uhler, George, 212
Undertakers, 124–28, 142–43, 153–58, 179–81, 199, 202–3

Wachholz, Ted, 224, 245–46
Wakes, 193–94
Warkman, T. C., 152
Washington Park, 30
Water ballast, 26, 34, 41–42, 63–66, 212–13, 215–17
Watson, Thomas, 14
Waukegan, 97–98
Weather forecast, 5
Weckler, Adam, 33–35, 64, 211, 217
Weiss, Peter, 77
Wells, H. G., 8
Western Electric Manufacturing Company, 11, 14–15, 151–52, 196, 197–98. *See also* Hawthorne Works death toll and, 175–76, 184–85, 197–98, 204

Hawthorne Club, 29–31
insurance plan, 206–8
picnic, 4–8, 9–10, 16–19, 29–32, 126, 234
women at, 108–11, 126
Widows, 208
Wilmette, 232–33
Wilson, Woodrow, 8, 149–50, 215
Winfrey, Oprah, 236–37
Wood, William, 217
Work (movie), 8
Work day, 4, 15
World's Columbian Exposition (1893), 7
World Series (1919), 191
World War I, 7–8, 152, 224, 238
World War II, 232–33, 238
Wrecking crews, 211

York, Devereux, 217